# MARIE'S VOICE

27-12-90

Dear Wolfhound Press,

The enclosed story is about someone very special with whom I spent the last seventeen years of my life. She cannot speak — I am her voice. Having been kicked out of school at fifteen I make no claims at being a writer, I simply felt it was my duty to speak up for someone who could not speak up for herself.

I do hope you find the story interesting. I am enclosing a cheque for £5 to cover return postage.

Yours sincerely,

*Michelle Daly*

# MARIE'S VOICE

## Michelle Daly

WOLFHOUND PRESS

First published 1992 by
WOLFHOUND PRESS
68 Mountjoy Square,
Dublin 1.

**Acknowledgements**
The author wishes to extend special thanks to the *Sunday People* newspaper, Pete
Reynolds of the *Lincolnshire Echo*, Paddy Greally, Brothers of Charity, Galway, Finbarr
Kilgannon, Áras Attracta, Swinford, and Eamonn Hannon of the Western Health
Board.


Photographs reproduced by kind permission of the *Sunday People* (pages 97, 98 *bottom
left*, 99, 100 *top* and *bottom left*, 101, 103, 104), *Woman's Own* (page 100 *bottom right*) and
the *Lincolnshire Echo* (page 102 *bottom*)


British Library Cataloguing in Publication Data
Daly, Michelle
    Marie's Voice
    I. Title
    362.4
    ISBN 0 86327 340 8

Cover design: Jan de Fouw
Typesetting: Wolfhound Press
Printed in the Republic of Ireland by Colour Books, Ltd

# 1
~

I T WAS April 10th 1970, just two weeks before my seventeenth birthday, when I arrived at the Nazareth House children's home in Bristol.

Feeling tired and a little apprehensive I lifted my heavy blue suitcase off the ground where the taxi driver had just deposited it and made my way towards the main entrance. I had heard so much about this former monastery from one of the nuns in my previous job. Up until three years ago she had been in charge of the nursery here and it had been one of her favourite places. Birds chirped noisily in the background as if to spread the news that a stranger had arrived. Pressing the bell I waited nervously on the step.

The door was opened by a small, rather timid looking nun, dressed entirely in black. Shaking my hand warmly, she showed me into the parlour while she went off to find someone to take charge of me.

'It's just as I imagined,' I thought as I looked out of the window at the landscape. Outside, a solitary nun stooped to pull the odd weed scattered here and there. The grounds were enormous. The convent not only housed the nuns, but also provided residential quarters for child-care and domestic staff.

The minutes ticked slowly by. The convent seemed so quiet I thought all the nuns must have been in chapel. Then I heard the unmistakable swish of a long gown together with the familiar sound of soft leather shoes on wooden floors. I looked towards the door expectantly.

'Are you ready?' a little Irish nun asked me popping her head inside the room. Putting my bag over my shoulder, I picked up my case to follow her.

'You're a long way from Liverpool,' she said, opening a door which led onto a corridor, 'won't you get homesick?' We walked past the chapel and up a spiral staircase.

'Not really, Sister,' I told her as I tried to absorb the beauty of the architecture. 'My sister is at Art College here.'

We seemed to go up one staircase after another. The higher we climbed the heavier my suitcase became.

'You've got your own bathroom,' she smiled as we came to yet another flight of stairs. 'You're at the top of the house now.' She climbed the last one: 'Will you mind being on your own?' Turning the handle she opened the bedroom door.

I put down my case and strolled across the bedroom to stand by the window before replying. 'Oh no Sister, I'm one of seven children so it will be quite a change having some space around me.'

I was given an hour to unpack. I slowly folded my clothes away in an old-fashioned dressing table on top of which I placed a picture of my mother. Looking at her smiling face I was suddenly overwhelmed with guilt. She had been very worried because I was moving so far away from home. I hadn't told her that my sister Cathy was going away to India for the summer. She'd have been frantic.

When Sister Alfred returned we walked slowly towards the nursery. I could see the children playing outside in the garden. The sound of their laughter reached my ears. Putting a spring in my step I went forward to meet them.

I was aware of the traumatic world these children came from. A world, in most cases, where grown-ups had let them down badly. Yet, cocooned in the safety of the convent, they put their trust in anybody.

The gate into the nursery yard creaked, immediately attracting the children's attention. Struggling to get off their battered old toys these little tots came running over to greet us.

It was quite a large house with the children split into two age groups. The toddlers slept on the top floor, using the ground floor during the day. The nursery floor where I was to work was in between. Sister explained that she had overall responsibility for the children.

On the toddlers' floor I was introduced to Sister Rosina along with Janet and Christine, the two housemothers. Then together we went upstairs to the nursery. The two nursery nurses were in the middle of their coffee break. I followed Sister into the kitchen to meet them.

'This is Michelle. She's come to help us look after the babies.'

They both nodded with an air of indifference before continuing their own conversation.

We moved on to the bedrooms. The babies lay on their cots like tiny balls of fluff. They were from six days old to nine months with the exception of a little girl called Marie to whom I had just been introduced. She was just turned five.

'Marie is mentally handicapped,' I was informed. 'We've had her since she was six weeks old. We're waiting for a hospital bed for her,' Sister went on, 'and she's getting worse as she gets older. We can't cope with her for much longer.'

Marie had short cropped hair and the most beautiful blue eyes. She was very thin. I noticed a large lump on her forehead.

'What's the matter with her head, Sister?' It looked so sore I almost cringed.

'Poor little thing,' she answered as she looked down at Marie, 'she screams and screams — sometimes for hours on end — and bangs her head on the floor or on the side of her cot. 'Look!' she said, pointing to a rope around the pipe attaching itself to Marie's cot, 'this is to stop her from tipping herself over.'

I looked at Marie's face: her eyes were like glass. I thought how strange it was that we stood so close to her and she didn't reach out to be picked up — as though she were used to being looked at but not touched. Sister said that Marie should have been moved long ago, but the waiting list was so long they couldn't say when there would be a place for her. As we walked across the room I watched her sad little eyes follow me.

~

The following morning when I went on duty the two nurses greeted me as they were dashing about trying to get the babies fed before Sister went to chapel. One of them disappeared and returned carrying Marie on her hip.

'Will you feed Marie, please?' she asked me as she sat Marie in a high chair with the legs sawn off. She seemed too big for it but I suppose this prevented her from sliding out and going off.

'Will she take her food from me?' I asked, looking at Marie dubiously as she rocked in the chair. 'She doesn't really know me, does she?'

'Well, she'll just have to get used to you then, won't she?' came the curt reply. I was given a small plastic bowl into which Linda dropped a tablet.

'What's that for?' I enquired as I sat down preparing to feed Marie.

'It's Librium to calm her down. She has one three times a day: just stir it in with her food and she'll take it,' she instructed as she lifted one of the tiny babies out of its bouncing chair.

Stirring Marie's cereal I attempted to give her the first mouthful — no problem, but as I looked at the bowl to get some more she suddenly reached out and grabbed my hair with both hands. I flinched with pain as I told the little monkey to let go but she just seemed to tighten her grip and hurt all the more. The nurses finally came to my rescue; as one tickled Marie the other tried to undo her hands.

'I forgot to tell you to watch your hair,' Linda said. 'She does it all the time.' And with that bit of late advice I sat down to try again. This time Marie didn't get my hair because I didn't take my eyes from her, though I found this difficult at times because the lump on her forehead kept turning my stomach. I had not been so close to a handicapped child before; I didn't know how to react to her as she sat grinding her teeth in between mouthfuls of food.

'Is this all she has for breakfast?' I asked, scraping the last of the cereal out of the bowl. She still seemed hungry.

'She can't chew anything so she has cereal most of the time,' Linda replied as she patted her baby on the back trying to bring up its wind. Even though I felt Marie had not had sufficient to eat, she didn't look for any more; there was no expression on her face; even when I fed her she'd opened her mouth in a sort of methodical way.

After breakfast I was asked to take Marie into the bathroom to change her nappy and dress her (much to my horror). Within minutes of attempting this she'd pulled me down to the floor by my hair. I was shouting to Sister for help as Marie's hands firmly gripped my locks once again; she'd made a quick grab for me as I went to lift her onto the changing locker. This time Sister came running to my rescue, shouting at Marie as she tried to unclench her fists.

'You're a little devil; let go, you naughty girl!' she was saying as she finally freed me and sat Marie back up on the locker.

'You'll have to keep your eyes on her all the time, Michelle,' she said as I felt to make sure my hair was still there; 'or she'll grab you quickly when you're not watching.'

Marie sat like a floppy doll making no attempt to help Sister as her clothes were put on. 'Can't she walk?' I asked, because everybody seemed to carry her about.

'No,' she answered firmly; 'she's a spastic.' To elaborate she stood Marie up to demonstrate how she was able to hold onto things but Marie just plonked onto the floor refusing to impress me.

'Goodness me, look at the time,' Sister shrieked, 'and here am I standing here talking!' She hurried out of the bathroom leaving me standing there with Marie at my feet. I tried very hard to sound cross when I spoke.

'You're just naughty!' I said, stooping to lift her up. 'If you pull my hair again,' I threatened, 'I'm going to pull yours.' I managed to carry Marie back to the dining room for my next instructions.

The bottles were just being cleared away; the babies fed and lying on their cots contentedly. I stood in the doorway awaiting my orders.

'Can you put Marie in that room at the end?' Linda asked me. 'If you put her on the floor she'll play in there but make sure the veranda door is closed.' She disappeared into the kitchen.

I carried Marie towards the room she had indicated. Standing in the doorway I thought I must have misunderstood my instructions as I looked around the room.

'They can't mean in here,' I thought. I took Marie back to check.

'Did you mean that room at the end?' I asked; 'the one with all the prams stored along the walls?'

'Yes!' she almost hissed at me. 'Just put her on the floor, close the door and she'll play on her own.'

I laughed nervously. 'Do you mean for me to leave her in there on her own?'

Glaring at me she answered, 'Yes!'

I did as I was told and put Marie on the floor. She immediately crashed her head down onto it with such force that she knocked the top off her sore and a little trickle of blood ran down her forehead. I didn't know what to do. I tried consoling her but it just made her worse. To my relief Sister Alfred appeared in the doorway.

'Come on away, Michelle,' she said with a sense of urgency; 'she'll be all right in a while: she'll probably have a sleep on the floor.'

I bit my lips as I listened to Marie's screams in the background.

'Why do you put her in that room, Sister?'

'Because there are things to do, Michelle,' she replied, tying her apron over her habit. 'We have the floors to polish each morning and if Marie is allowed out she'll drag her feet all over them. Besides,' she added irritably, 'Mother Superior gets angry because she's always bringing visitors around and she likes the nursery to be spotless.'

'How long does she have to stay in there?' I asked, not quite believing my ears.

'She can come out for dinner,' she told me as if she were kindness itself! 'And don't look so worried,' she added, laughing as she handed me a tin of polish and told me to start the bedroom floors. But I wasn't worried — I was disgusted.

Marie did quieten down eventually, after what seemed like hours. Her screams had followed me from room to room as I spread the polish over the already polished floors. Everybody was obviously used to the noise she made because the staff laughed and chatted, going about their duties as though it was an everyday occurrence, which of course it was.

At lunch time when I saw Jackie wheeling the trolley full of bottles and dinners into the dining room I went along to fetch Marie. My eyes stung as I looked across the room at her; she was curled up in a ball fast asleep on the floor.

'Hello Marie,' I said gently. She immediately woke up and shuffled across the floor to me on her bottom. By the time she reached my feet she was giggling, arms outstretched for me to pick her up which I gladly did. Carrying her to the dining room I sat her in her little chair.

'We didn't want her yet,' Jackie moaned; 'we usually do her last.'

'Never mind,' I said cheerfully, trying to ignore her disapproval, 'she's here now so she can watch, can't she?' I began to feed one of the babies.

~

After a few days I was starting to get used to the routines and finding out a little about tiny babies. It was my first experience in looking after them. There was no time to learn things step by step; I was thrown in at the deep end and would sometimes have five or six babies to feed each meal time.

Because we worked such long hours we were allowed two hours off during the day, either in the morning or afternoon. Whoever was left on duty in the afternoon did the laundry which was on the toddlers' floor leaving the nursery floor unattended for an hour or two as all the children lay on their cots. At 3 o'clock the children were undressed, given their teas and put on their cots for the night. Marie was included in this routine.

I noticed that even though Marie had lived at the Home for five years she didn't appear to have any identity or possess anything personal. Instead of having pretty clothes hanging in the wardrobe, all she had was a pile of bitty tights and jumpers folded on a shelf in the bathroom.

~

I was growing concerned about Marie being put in a room on her own. I felt her panic like an electric shock each time I closed the door on her and her screams began. I could not prevent Marie from being isolated but whenever the opportunity arose, I would keep her with me. She would follow me on the floor as I did my chores. She was a funny little soul. I was surprised at how little trouble she really was as she sat by my feet watching me feed the babies. She didn't respond to very much and was quite happy sitting doing nothing; I felt there was just no need for her to be left alone in that room.

In the mornings when I went on duty all the babies were usually in the dining room. As I passed Marie's bedroom she would be sitting on her cot looking through the bars waiting for me to get her up. She would laugh excitedly when I approached her: I think she knew I was sticking up for her and her life had improved a little, though not much. Lifting her out of the cot I'd put her in her chair where she'd sit grinding her teeth waiting for the babies to be fed because she was always 'done' last.

I thought it was sad that the cleaning took priority over the children's needs. Gradually I was given a certain amount of freedom with Marie, though there were still times when I had to do something important and Sister Alfred told me to put Marie in the pram room. This used to make me so angry. I would unclench Marie's hands from around my neck with a lump in my throat, as she cried knowing she was going to be left alone. I soon found myself taking Marie with me on my two hours off each day to avoid her being shut up alone.

Sometimes I would take her out into the garden to see the toddlers. She would walk unsteadily holding onto my hand as they ran forward to welcome her. She did not respond very much to the children and seemed happier amongst adults. If it was raining I would sneak her into my room. On those days, I was glad to be at the top of the house because once there I was unlikely to be discovered; the problem was getting to it. Because Marie was such a noisy child people heard her before they saw her. I had to cover her mouth with my hand as I walked through the convent because the nuns were usually in chapel and children weren't allowed into our rooms.

I discovered not long after I met Marie that she had a fascination for mirrors — perhaps due to the fact that she spent long hours alone in the pram room where she could see herself in a long mirror on the wall. In my room she would sit on the floor and play for ages as she moved different parts of her body. It seemed as though without the mirror she didn't know they were there. Her little head would bob up and down; she would lean quite close to the glass and open her mouth trying to see inside. If I moved to another part of the room she would change positions on her bottom, shuffling about until she could see my reflection again in the mirror. Her only demand was to be close by.

She also loved me to sing nursery rhymes to her and would watch my mouth as she clapped, head turned to one side as though trying to work out where the sound was coming from. 'Baa Baa Black Sheep' was a favourite: she would repeat 'Baa Baa,' but that was as far as we got. I was rather pleased with this little attempt on her part and wondered how much potential she had. Sometimes I would pretend to cry and take her hand to stroke my hair: then I would put my hands over her face and she would moan as if she was crying, so that I could comfort her. She made me laugh. I could see little bits of her personality slowly emerging.

~

'Why was Marie never adopted?' I asked Sister Alfred one day as we sat feeding the babies.

'She was born two months premature,' she told me; 'and five minutes afterwards she stopped breathing and had to have mouth to mouth resuscitation: they think she may have suffered brain damage then.'

'Was she very small at birth?' I asked her as I looked across the room at Marie sitting in her little chair.

'Not really,' she answered pensively. 'She was 5lbs 8oz which is heavier than some of the healthy babies we've had in here.'

'Didn't anybody want to adopt her then?' I asked.

'People don't usually adopt handicapped children,' she replied.

I later learned that Marie had seen a paediatrician when she was three months old because she was bringing up her milk all the time: it was then suggested that she be put on semi-solids. After that she slowly started to gain weight. At the age of eleven months her development appeared very slow; she could only sit if she was propped up. On a further visit to the paediatrician it was discovered the fontenella had closed on Marie's head. Marie was eventually diagnosed as severely mentally retarded, with mild quadriplegia (spasticity of the four limbs) and microcephalus (small head). At the age of 2½ she was able to stand holding onto things, but was unable to walk. There was no speech at all except babbling baby noises.

I also discovered there had been a nurse who'd taken a great interest in Marie, but she had left a few years previously and had not been back to see her. Marie had obviously known better times.

~

Unfortunately Sister did not allow any of the toddlers onto our floor; she would shoo them away as soon as they put their noses around the door at the end of the corridor. She didn't want them spoiling her nursery floor. Had she encouraged the children it would have been of enormous benefit to Marie who was loved by all the toddlers and was looked on as the 'big baby' of the nursery.

We were so busy it was almost impossible to look after the babies properly, let alone Marie. My conscience had been bothering me for a while over the risks Sister took with the infants. I reluctantly followed her orders because she was in charge, but common sense told me what she was doing was wrong. Sometimes we had twelve babies to feed. If we were having visitors — perhaps a couple coming to see a baby for adoption — Sister would be all in a flap, going around the babies as they lay on their cots putting their bottles in their mouths propped up with teddies... The job she gave me while the babies lay sucking usually prevented me from watching them. After what seemed like an eternity she would collect the bottles. My job then was to lie the babies on the floor on their tummies where they brought up their own wind.

There were three bedrooms with five or six babies in each one. Had our visitors come early they'd have been quite shocked as they slowly passed each room to see five little infants lying in their own vomit, having brought back their bottles with stomachs full of wind.

Sister Alfred was obviously under a lot of pressure from her superior, whose idea of a children's home was a dolls' house with spotless babies lying on their cots. The only time Mother Superior saw the children was when she brought a visitor around. She looked on with pride as people remarked how beautiful our nursery was, but she never told them it was at the expense of the children.

~

Marie screeched for the slightest thing, especially if I went out of the room and she was sitting in her chair which prevented her from following me. When I returned she stopped. Undoubtedly she irritated the staff.

'I think she's better on her cot,' Linda said one day as she went to lift Marie out of her chair. I was in a difficult position: she was 'trained'. I wasn't but I didn't take my orders from her: I took them from Sister, who had never objected to the interest I'd taken in Marie as long as it hadn't affected my work. I gritted my teeth before replying.

'Marie is all right where she is,' I told her: 'she's got a right to be here just like all the other children. If you put her on her cot I'll only get her up again.'

I could tell by the way she banged about that I'd upset her. I really wasn't bothered. It was either she or Marie who was going to be upset so I finished what I had to say.

'It's hardly surprising that she screams after me if everybody else locks her up, is it?' I asked her, glad that I'd cleared the air.

~

One afternoon I was doing the laundry. I could hear Marie banging her head on the floor above as I stood folding piles of nappies and baby-gros. The nuns were in chapel; nobody else was about so I sneaked upstairs to the pram room. As I opened the door Marie was sitting behind it crying.

'Come on!' I said, picking her up: 'you'll get me shot.' I ran back down the stairs with her. She laughed; glad to be rescued. I sat her on the table in the empty laundry basket while I emptied the drier. For a bit of fun I put the hot nappies over her. She laughed again: she loved to get attention which was rare in those days. I turned my back on her to fill the washing machine and when I looked around again she was fast asleep, her little face still wet from crying.

# 2

I HAD BEEN at the convent for eight weeks when the nuns were moved around. Sister Michael was put in charge of the nursery and Sister Alfred was sent to Wales. I was amazed at the coincidence. At home in Liverpool, I had finished school the previous year thinking there wouldn't be any openings for me, career-wise, as my headmaster had handed me a reference which said 'Michelle thinks life is one big joke,' and so I drifted into office work undecided about my future.

One day one of the girls in the office told me about her sister who had just left a job in a children's home because the work was too hard and the pay too low. It was a convent, and the home was run by nuns.

'I'd love a job working with children,' I told her; 'but I haven't got any qualifications.'

'You don't need any!' she said to my surprise, 'and they're always looking for staff.'

The home was on the other side of the River Mersey which meant that because of the distance from my home I would have to live in.

Four weeks later, much to my parents' horror I started working there. I loved it! I worked with the toddlers never dreaming anything could be so rewarding as I tucked them into bed at night, knowing that each of the children had experienced tragedy at some time in their lives, yet they were happy noisy little souls.

I couldn't believe my luck to have found a job I enjoyed so much. It was there that I met Sister Michael, and worked for her. At first she didn't appear very friendly as she quietly gave me my instructions for the day until I slowly got used to things, yet I enjoyed working for her until I left for my new job at the Bristol convent.

I certainly hadn't expected to see Sister Michael again — and now I was working with her — and so far away from where we had first met! I wasn't looking forward to it, but any reservations I'd had soon disappeared after a few days as I got to know her and realised I had mistaken her shyness for unfriendliness. She had a very pale complexion, was very tall and wore gold rimmed specs. Her lovely Welsh accent almost sounded like she was singing when she spoke. I watched her discreetly and thought how different she was to Sister Alfred. She was so different in fact that the babies were never fed on their cots again and Marie was never put back in the pram room. Instead of crawling after me she was soon walking at my side. Allowed to wear her shoes all the time, she was encouraged to stay on her feet by the noise they made.

Marie still plonked on the floor and would panic if she was left alone for a minute, banging her head onto the ground, though not as frequently as she had done. The quality of Marie's life improved so much that I hoped Sister Michael was going to stay for a long time.

There were lots of subtle changes in our home, one of them being that we opened the door to the toddlers, which gave us enormous pleasure as different children would pop in to see us throughout the day. One of them was a little boy called Morgan who took a great interest in Marie. She didn't take the slightest bit of notice of him except to grab his hair if he got in the way of her reflection in the mirror. More often than not he managed to jump out of the way but just sometimes he wasn't quick enough.

'Oh Shelf,' he'd say, eyes full of unshed tears, 'why does she pull my hair? Doesn't she like me?'

He was desperate to be Marie's friend and refused to accept her rejection, but approached her each day to say hello.

~

Sister Michael let me take Marie out almost every day, even if it was only to collect prescriptions from the chemist. I would sit Marie up in the big old-fashioned baby's pram and off we'd go to the shops. She was walking much better by this time but was still unsteady on her feet and couldn't walk very far. Marie enjoyed our little trips and watched everything around her, still not responding to people except to screech if they approached her. I would leave the prescription in at the chemist's and while we were waiting for it I'd take Marie to the shop next door for our supply of chocolate. She wasn't very happy if I stood her beside me; she became very nervous and noisy. Returning home she would sit up contentedly in the safety of her pram, sucking her chocolate and smiling at me as it slowly dribbled out of her mouth.

Marie was much more alert than she had been when I met her. If I went on duty and didn't know where she was she would come running out from another room, recognising my voice, arms outstretched for me to pick her up. Lifting her to rest on my hip, she wasn't affectionate like other children; she didn't know how to hug me or give me a kiss. Instead she had a funny little habit of shaking her head as she looked away from me as though trying to hide. She was still in nappies and would screech loudly when she sat on the toilet, and hardly ever use it, mainly because we were not consistent enough with her. We just didn't have the time to take her as often as we should have done.

~

After Sister Michael had been at the nursery for a month I decided to go home for a few days. My visit was long overdue. My sister Maureen had just had a little girl — my first niece, Sara.

I wasn't worried about leaving Marie. I knew that when the staff were busy the worst that could happen was that she'd go on her cot.

I loved seeing my family again. They couldn't believe I could enjoy a job working under such appalling conditions.

'Don't eat that bread,' Maureen said to me one day, 'it's stale.'

'No it isn't,' I answered, 'it hasn't even got any mould on.' I was so used to picking the mould off the bread before I ate it because at the convent we had stale bread free from the bakeries. For months I had virtually lived on tinned baby food: I was very pale and thin.

When I eventually left, my sister Trish who was fifteen returned to the convent with me where she helped out for the rest of her school holidays. Trish worked with the toddlers. When the weather was nice she would take them to the pond at the back of the convent. Very soon Marie was included in the little party as Trish came to fetch her and take her with them.

At last we had a happy little home. Although we didn't stop for a minute I loved my job and found it so fulfilling, especially as I watched Marie becoming more confident each day. Sometimes when I was going off duty I'd plan to have a sleep. Shouting goodbye as I reached the landing door Marie would plonk herself in the middle of the big hall and look at me sadly.

'See you later!' I would say. She never moved. In the end I would take her with me.

~

One sunny afternoon my sister Cathy came strolling into the convent: at long last she was back from India. We sat in the kitchen wide-eyed as she told of the places she had visited and cringed in horror at her tales of crummy youth hostels and bed bugs. I laughed at the contrast in our lives. I'd probably made as many bottles and changed as many nappies as the miles Cathy had travelled across the earth. I was pleased she was back!

I remember that the following morning Sister Michael returned from chapel looking very troubled. I didn't approach her because I felt she wanted to be left alone. I'd seen her like this before on the odd occasion when I'd found her relaxing as she rocked one of the babies to sleep. Sometimes when I was changing a baby on the locker in the bathroom I'd glance out of the window to see her returning to the convent, walking slowly as though her legs pained her. At these times I always disappeared from view realising I'd caught her in an unguarded moment: by the time she reached the nursery she was her usual cheerful self. That morning, however, she informed us that the home was being closed down by the Home Office. There had been rumours about this and it was for this reason the Nursery Nurse Course I had intended doing had been stopped. Nobody had believed it would actually happen. The house had been condemned because it was so old.

'Where will everybody go?' I asked Sister sadly as Marie sat on my knee sucking a biscuit. 'What's going to happen to all the children?'

'That has to be decided yet, Michelle,' she told me quietly.

The social workers started buzzing in and out, getting children fostered or adopted or even placed in other children's homes. Nobody came to see Marie. I worried more and more about her future as I watched her growing happier and stronger each day. Quite a few of the children were going to the home in Wales with two of the staff: although their surroundings would be new they would still be with familiar faces... Still there was no mention of Marie.

There was a ray of hope one day when I discovered Marie's annual appointment with the paediatrician was due.

'Would you like to take her, Michelle?' Sister asked me.

'Oh yes, Sister, I'd love to,' I told her. 'Maybe if I tell the paediatrician how much Marie has improved she'll be able to go to a residential school,' I added enthusiastically.

'She might, Michelle, but don't build your hopes too high,' she told me kindly.

That afternoon I took Marie into the garden. Sitting on the grass watching the birds fly by I envied their independence, suddenly realising how vulnerable Marie was — so totally dependent on people that it frightened me. After seeing the way Sister Alfred treated her and then Sister Michael's kindness I knew the pendulum could sway either way depending on what people saw as they looked at her — some seeing Marie, others seeing nothing.

During the two weeks building up to Marie's appointment I was planning her debut with the doctor down to the finest detail.

'Which dress do you like, Sister?' I asked, hoping she could help me choose — as if one colour would make Marie look less handicapped than another. Sister listened to my constant talk about the big day without a flicker of impatience, though I must have driven her mad.

'Where are you going?' little Morgan asked as he listened to our conversation. He was such a friendly outgoing child, he missed nothing. He sat on the chair in the bathroom, a tall boy for his seven years looking at me from under his fringe and waiting for an answer.

'I'm taking Marie to see the doctor at the hospital,' I told him. He frowned. 'She's coming back,' I added quickly.

'Can I come with you?' he shouted, making my poor baby jump as she lay in the bath with my hand supporting her head.

'You'll have to ask Sister.' I knew she'd let him come along.

~

At long last our appointment day finally arrived. I had just finished combing Marie's hair as I waited nervously for the ambulance to arrive; it was already fifteen minutes late. Sister Michael appeared in the doorway.

'Don't worry, Michelle,' she said, fastening her apron; 'I've just phoned the hospital and they're sending a taxi for you.'

My stomach was in knots. I was so nervous knowing that Marie's future could be decided in the next hour, praying that she'd be able to go to a school when the doctor saw she was able to learn little things.

Shortly after we arrived at the hospital a nurse called Marie's name out. We followed her into a little room where I stripped Marie to her underclothes to be weighed. She immediately started to cry out at the sight of the weighing machine so I kept hold of her hands as I stood her on it. It seemed to ease her fear a little. She was frightened of so many things, so insecure in strange places.

Ten minutes later I was sitting opposite the paediatrician; next to her stood a young woman in a white coat. The doctor was a lot older than I'd expected. Sitting behind her desk there wasn't a flicker of warmth as her cold, clinical eyes looked over at me. My little friend sat quietly on my knee. There was an unnerving silence as the doctor continued to ignore us and write some notes in what I presume was Marie's file. I was very disappointed that she had not made a fuss of Marie. The sad, wilted little flower she had seen once a year seemed to me to have turned into a beautiful red rose who, with the right treatment and care, would continue to blossom. The minutes ticked slowly by and still she ignored us. Today, I would not put up with such intimidating treatment from anybody, but at the age of seventeen I had no experience of dealing with doctors on this level, and I was not equipped or articulate enough to deal with it. Eventually, she started to question me.

'Is she at school?' she asked as she started writing in a file.

'No,' I replied, but before I could explain why she went on to the next question.

'Does she have any kind of therapy?'

'No,' I answered, feeling very uncomfortable when I saw her giving her assistant knowing looks.

'What about her diet?' She put her pen down as if she was really getting interested: 'does she eat meat and fruit?'

I shifted uneasily in my chair: 'No,' I whispered, 'she can't chew properly.' Again she didn't give me the chance to explain. She suddenly started shouting at me: 'This child has been neglected!' Looking at her colleague she said, 'I think I'll keep her in for observation.'

I was bewildered. I thought I must have misunderstood until she asked her colleague to arrange a bed for Marie.

'What!' I said not believing my ears; 'just like that! You mean just take her along there and put her in a bed?'

'Wait outside,' she said dismissing me.

~

I sat outside the paediatrician's room wiping my eyes while Marie sat quietly on my knee. Sister was trying to get information from me about Marie's history. I shrugged my shoulders unable to get any words out. Besides, I didn't know anything about Marie's family.

'She'll think we don't want her any more,' I said keeping my arms protectively about Marie, wondering how I could prepare her for the distress she was obviously about to encounter. I realised once again how desperately alone in the world she was. A nurse came and sat next to me. She rested her hand gently on my shoulder.

'Would you like to bring her down to the ward?' she asked.

'Her name is Marie,' I quietly told the nurse. Carrying Marie, I followed the staff nurse along the corridor with poor little Morgan at my heels probably wondering what was going on.

'She hardly understands anything that's said to her,' I muttered as we walked along. 'She'll probably screech all the time.' I was trying to pull myself together and give them as much information about her as I could. I knew no matter how much I told them, nothing would alleviate the fear and isolation she would once again feel.

Sister in charge of the children's ward was waiting outside to greet us. 'Is this the little girl?' she asked cheerfully before opening the ward door for us to follow her.

'Her name is Marie,' I muttered. I handed her over. Never before in my life had I felt so helpless. I stood there sobbing like a child.

'Come in with her if you want,' Sister offered. I shook my head and walked away.

We walked the 2½ miles home. It never occurred to me to catch a bus. I don't even remember the journey as I walked along unaware that I still held Marie's clothes loosely in my hands without having bothered to fold them as I'd expected to put them back on her.

Arriving back at the home I sent Morgan into the nursery and walked over to my room. I remember sitting on my bed still stunned as I looked down at Marie's clothes.

~

'What's happened, Michelle?' Sister Michael said, rushing into my room. 'Morgan said they've taken Marie off you.'

Slowly I began to tell her what the doctor had done.

'Wait here,' she said, 'I'll go and see Mother Superior. I'll be back in a minute.'

'Of course,' I thought, wiping my eyes and jumping off the bed; 'she'll lend Sister Michael the car to fetch Marie back.' I stretched Marie's crumpled clothes out on the bed trying to get the creases out.

Before long I could hear Sister's heavy footsteps on the stairs. She didn't speak when she came into my room: she just looked at me sadly.

'What did she say?' I asked miserably. I could tell from her expression it hadn't been good.

'Mother said maybe they will find Marie somewhere else to live,' she answered quietly.

I was overwhelmed with pity for Marie. After 5½ years living at the home she was just another name to cross off the list. They were proving the doctor right by the very fact that they weren't representing her.

~

The home was unusually quiet without Marie. Her demands had been modest but she had always been there: it was a different nursery without her. I couldn't help glancing over at her cot as I passed the bedroom door; her face no longer looked for me through the bars, and as day turned to night I looked sadly at her little nightdress still folded on the bathroom shelf as I realised she was never coming back.

I started to strip Marie's cot.

'Don't upset yourself, Michelle,' Sister told me. She was such a kind and thoughtful person: I often wondered how she managed to work under a superior who seemed to test Sister Michael's faith constantly with her unChristian ways.

'I'm more angry than upset!' I snapped as I dragged the sheets from the bed. 'I feel so frustrated because I can't do anything: people have no right to treat Marie as they do. It shouldn't be allowed to go on.'

~

As I lay in bed that night I wondered how many other children there were like Marie, in the hands of nobody, with nobody responsible for them but heartless officials doing as they liked.

I remembered my school friend, Angela, who had lived in a foster home since she was a baby. Her schooldays during the week were spent with her widowed foster mother, and weekends were spent in a convent where her foster sister was a nun. Angela had a welfare officer but he very rarely visited her and she had nobody to talk to about her problems. We sat together in class, and as we became close friends, Angela told me of her unhappiness. I had never met anybody in care before and felt very sad at the lonely life she lived. Quite often after school I would get the bus into town with her: we'd go to the Children's Department at the Social Servces in an attempt to get things sorted out. Angela's welfare officer appeared not to care in the least about her, and would look up to heaven as he came out of his office and saw us sitting there waiting for him. 'Just go back and try once more, Angela,' he would say: 'just try once more.'

It seemed now that Angela's welfare officer had not been an isolated case: Marie too had lived in care, and nobody appeared to worry about her happiness. As I thought about it all, I didn't know which was worse; the fact that the doctor had just removed Marie from the home or the fact that she hadn't been represented by the nuns in her hour of need.

The following morning I rang the hospital and spoke to the staff nurse on Marie's ward.

'She's cried for most of the night,' she told me, 'and refuses to sit on her pot.'

'Can I visit her some time?' I asked half expecting her to say no. But as I was to learn later on, life is full of surprises.

'Just come in whenever you want,' she answered.

An hour later I was on my way to the hospital. Poor Sister Michael was on her own with all the babies. I insisted on staying for an hour to help her, despite her efforts to get rid of me. As soon as the babies were fed, winded and changed, I grabbed my coat and ran for the bus.

We lived in a very posh part of Bristol, just the other side of the Clifton Downs. The bus ride was a familiar one but I looked anxiously out of the window at every stop until we passed the University and approached St Michael's Hill. Jumping down at the approaching stop, I hurried on to the top of the steep hill. Arriving at the hospital I climbed the steps two at a time. My mind had gone blank and I couldn't remember which ward Marie was on. I stopped to look in the windows of the wards, scouring the little faces of the children until I saw her. She was sitting on the floor on her own.

'Hello!' I chirped walking into the ward. Marie started to laugh loudly when she realised who I was, and shuffled over to me on her bottom as I stooped down to pick her up. She looked so happy. I tickled her and she wriggled excitedly: 'Have you been a good girl?' I asked teasingly.

I found her cot with her name on it and sat on the chair at the side of it with Marie on my knee. We spent a long time watching the other children playing on the ward. Singing our nursery rhymes Marie gently took my hand for 'Round and Round the Garden', staring at my face as she dribbled in concentration. Perhaps in a way my visit brought a little understanding to her. Seeing a familiar face from her past seemed to help.

She started to cry when I left. I longed to walk out of the hospital with her and take her back to the home, but I knew Mother Superior would probably refuse her entry.

I waved to Marie from the ward door but she was already slipping into her old habits; banging her head on the bars of her cot, thinking I'd already gone. I slowly walked out of the hospital and down the steps towards the bus stop.

The next morning when I visited Marie she was sitting on her cot with blood down the front of her nightdress and on her face. The nurse said Marie had spent most of the night screaming and banging her head on the side of the cot. I was angry as I lifted Marie out, wondering once again what on earth she was doing in a hospital for sick children. I laughed to myself as I wondered whether Marie could be removed from the hospital because she was 'being neglected'.

When I took Marie to the bathroom to dress her she never took her eyes off me. I knew my visits were important to her: I was the only link from her past. She needed that contact every day at least until she found another home.

~

I liked the nurses on Marie's ward. Watching them go about their duties I marvelled that they managed to stay so pleasant when they were nursing children with cancer.

I visited Marie every day on my two hours off, either in the morning or afternoon. Leaving the ward one day, I forgot my bag. Rushing back to collect it I hesitated at the door as I looked at Marie through the glass. She was curled up in a ball on her cot, crying. I signalled to the nurse for my bag to avoid upsetting Marie any further. Running from the hospital I was glad of the pouring rain as it mingled with my tears. It wasn't the nurses' fault: hospitals are for sick children. Marie wasn't sick, but she just had nowhere else to go. Allowing her to stay up all day would have been like letting a twelve-month-old baby crawl around, with no sense of danger and needing to be watched constantly. The nurses were so busy it would have been impossible. I began to wonder whether Marie might be better off if I stopped visiting her, thinking at least she wouldn't get upset when I left.

When the opportunity arose I spoke to Sister Michael about it.

'Do you think I'm selfish going to see Marie every day, Sister?' I asked.

She looked puzzled. 'I don't understand what you mean, Michelle.'

I told her of my reservations.

'You mustn't look at it like that. Marie needs you: it's better to have a little love than no love at all.'

'Even if it hurts?' I asked her.

'It isn't always possible for children in care to be loved by other people, and whenever it is it should never be discouraged, even if parting comes after it. No matter how it seems to you now, Michelle, she can only benefit from it.'

And so I continued to visit my little friend.

Then one of life's surprises came about. Lo and behold, two weeks after Marie was admitted to the hospital I was allowed to bring her home on Sunday afternoons! On her first visit we all watched her through blurred eyes; she'd been missed so much and brought a kind of tranquillity onto our little floor. After the babies had been fed she followed me as usual as I laid them on their cots, and only then did she raise her arms for me to lift her up.

When I took Marie back to the hospital that evening we seemed to be waiting ages for the bus. I held her in my arms to protect her from the cold wind. Out of the blue, a car pulled up and a very kind couple offered us a lift — such timing! I was grateful to be dropped off at the entrance to the children's hospital.

That couple, like many other people, had been surprised when I told them I worked in a children's home. They always thought I looked too young to have such responsibility. Most of the parents on Marie's ward had thought I was one of the children from the home and hadn't realised I worked there.

Throughout my life, especially after I left home, most people I met thought I was from Ireland. I think that was one of the reasons most of the nuns took me under their wings. I felt a great affinity with Irish people. My grandmother, Annie Burke who died of consumption she'd caught in the Liverpool workhouse when my father was three years old, came from Castlebar in Co. Mayo. I often think Liverpudlians are more Irish than English anyway. Even though I did not learn about my grandmother until much later in life, I always felt very close to the Irish.

# 3
~

OUR LITTLE HOME was slowly emptying as children were found other homes and the babies from our floor went out for adoption. Instead of waiting for a new arrival to fill the cot, the bedding was stripped and the cots stayed bare.

Marie's final visit to the home was a few days before it closed down. It was a cold, sunny day. When I arrived at the hospital the nurse said Marie had a temperature and couldn't go out. Although I knew she was right I couldn't help feeling disappointed: I'd so much wanted Marie to see the other children who were left and most of all I wanted her to see Sister Michael without whom my visits to the hospital would not have been possible. She had made such a difference since taking over the nursery. Mother Superior had refused her permission to visit Marie so it was important that Marie went to see her.

Marie's temperature was taken on the hour and had gone down by the third attempt. By this time it was 3 p.m.

'Hurry up if you're going,' Sister said smiling. I threw Marie's coat on her and we ran for the bus. She was so excited as we rode through the city centre, and kept looking away from me, laughing in her characteristic way. As we reached our destination I put her little feet on the concrete. I always felt happy when we reached this spot: it meant we were going home. However that afternoon as we slowly walked up the drive to the convent I knew it would be for the last time. In a few days none of us would be living there.

The home looked poverty stricken. Most of the children had gone, leaving just a few babies on our floor. The furniture was stacked in the corners of each room — empty prams and cots with a forlorn looking teddy hanging here and there, sad for the child who'd left them behind.

Clinging onto my hand Marie walked across the landing towards the noisy kitchen.

'Hi everybody!' I shouted, bringing immediate cries of delight as they all came running out to greet Marie. Sister Michael scooped her up and gave her a big hug.

Marie loved the freedom of the nursery as she wandered from room to room. I found it relaxing compared to the hospital, where I had to watch her constantly in case she hurt another child. On this particular day, however, she never left my knee. She must have sensed things were different as she sat twiddling with the end of her dress.

'Have they sorted out anywhere for her yet, Michelle?' Sister Michael asked as she buttered the bread for sandwiches.

'Not yet, Sister,' I told her. 'At least nobody has said anything about it to me. They're such a nice bunch I'm sure they'd have let me know.'

'At least you will be in touch with her after we've all gone,' she said, knowing I'd arranged to live with Cathy for a while until Marie was settled somewhere. I would then decide what I was going to do. I had been offered jobs in different convents but I had not made any firm decisions about the future.

'I wish we could turn the clock back,' I whispered. 'Just to give us all a little more time together.' My throat felt like it had a tennis ball in it. Our ties were being severed and my little friend had no place to live.

When we were about to leave, Sister Michael gave me a bag of clothes and some soft toys for Marie to keep. I couldn't pretend any longer. I was sick of being brave.

'Don't get upset. She'll be all right, you'll see,' Sister assured me; 'things have a way of turning out.'

Everybody waved as we went out into the night. With Marie resting on my hip I headed towards the bus stop, her little possessions in two carrier bags, the remains of her $5^1/_2$ years at the home.

~

By the end of the week the home had closed down and everybody had gone. I lived only ten minutes away from the hospital, which enabled me to spend most of my time there, careful not to get under the nurses' feet. In all honesty, I think they were glad I took care of Marie — they had enough to do.

On some afternoons I took Marie home. She was always pleased to see Cathy whom she'd got to know quite well. One of the first things Marie did was to inspect herself in the mirror. She would sit smiling at herself as though she'd forgotten what she looked like and was pleased with what she saw. She had on a little name tag which had to be worn on the ward. This kept reminding me that she had to go back, like a library book with a stamp on it.

She was still unable to hold a cup, and I caught her attention from the mirror by putting a drink to her lips but she slowly moved her head back (still drinking) so she could see herself. As she stood up to admire herself I thought how small she was for her age, and because she was still unsteady on her feet she had a funny little stoop, exaggerated by the two nappies she wore, making her bottom stick out like a little duck.

On our return journey we always went through the back streets to avoid the noisy traffic on the main roads. Marie had spent so little time outside the convent that there was much she had to get used to. Recent IQ test results had been 20-25 which I now realise is dreadfully low, suggesting quite severe mental retardation. Her language was assessed as being that of an eight-month-old baby.

~

There was a young doctor at the hospital whom I'd got to know quite well. I asked her about the possibility of a residential school instead of a hospital for Marie, but I think the general feeling was that she was too severely mentally handicapped. I had one last try when this particular doctor came into the ward one day, and invited me to go along with herself and Marie to see the paediatrician.

'You must be joking,' I told her. 'She frightens me to death.'

She laughed and taking Marie's hand they both left the ward. A minute later I heard Marie scream and realised what a coward I'd been. She stood in the doorway. 'Can't do a thing with her,' she groaned.

Holding Marie's hands all three of us left the ward and went along to the doctor. Entering the room I couldn't blame Marie for screeching: it was full of medical students. I sat down and put Marie on my lap.

'This is the nurse to whom the child is very attached,' the paediatrician said, addressing the students. Turning to me she said; 'Now dear, is she able to do anything at all?'

'Oh yes!' I answered, grabbing the opportunity to demonstrate Marie's intelligence, 'she copies simple things.'

'Like what?'

'Sometimes I pretend to cry and she comforts me,' I said, hoping she wouldn't ask for any more examples because there weren't any.

'Do you think you could get her to show us?' she asked, to my horror. I was so embarrassed as I looked at the audience around the room — then looking at Marie I knew I had no choice. Lowering my head and covering my face with my hands I pretended to cry. Marie gently stroked my hair. The doctor then started to speak but Marie silenced her as she covered her own face with her hands and started to moan quite dramatically as she waited for me to comfort her. I was very pleased with Marie's performance, thinking it would have made a great difference to the doctor.

'Is she toilet trained?' she asked. Quite suddenly my leg felt hot. I looked down at the pool that was forming at my feet. Everybody was giggling quietly. The paediatrician grinned: 'Obviously not,' she said. I returned to the ward with the young doctor. I didn't know whether to laugh or cry. My last attempt had failed.

~

At the end of Marie's fifth week at the hospital I was changing her in the bathroom one evening when someone spoke from behind.

'Hello, are you Michelle?'

I turned around to see a middle-aged lady standing in the doorway. I nodded.

'I'm Marie's social worker,' she said to my astonishment and looking over at Marie she said, 'Hasn't she grown?'

'Well she would have, wouldn't she?' I said, surprised at her sudden appearance. 'Why didn't you visit Marie while I was at the convent?' I asked her, feeling the anger rising within me. 'I didn't even know she had a social worker.'

'I did visit the home,' she said apologetically, 'and Mother Superior always told me she was fine.'

I shook my head. 'But she wasn't fine and nobody bothered to help her,' I answered, wondering why she was making this sudden appearance. I then went on to tell her how angry I was that everybody had washed their hands of Marie.

'She's been taken from the home,' I told her, 'because she was neglected. She was then placed in a far worse situation. God,' I said angrily, 'people say don't get involved — it isn't fair on the child, I think it's unfair *not* to! She's in care,' I said, laughing sarcastically, 'but whose care?'

Marie started getting impatient. I lifted her off the locker and we all returned to the ward.

'I have some good news,' said the social worker. 'We've got Marie a bed in a hospital.' She smiled at me as though looking for some kind of approval. 'She goes on Monday and as you know her so well I wondered if you would like to go with her?'

'No, I *wouldn't* like to go with her,' I said rudely, 'and if I had my way Marie wouldn't be going either.'

Ignoring my rudeness she went on to tell me about the hospital and how Marie would attend the hospital school. With great reluctance I agreed to meet her on the ward the following Monday at 9 a.m.

I didn't go home that evening when I left the hospital: instead I walked around Bristol city centre looking in the shop windows. The lack of concern for Marie's welfare was beyond my comprehension: she seemed a burden to everybody, with a social worker who only appeared to sign exit and entry forms — no doubt to allow Marie's whereabouts to be recorded.

I dreaded Monday. I couldn't even explain to Marie what was happening; she was just being taken there and left. I would no longer be around to help her through her new experience. The hospital was thirty miles away. I didn't even think I'd be allowed to visit. She was being somersaulted back into loneliness.

In the short time Marie had spent in the children's hospital I'd got to know many of the parents and children. They'd seen me laugh, they'd seen me cry — they'd even seen me fall asleep in the bedside chair when I had rushed to the hospital straight from work. They had been very kind to me and had spurred me on when I was feeling despondent. They had even taken it in turns to keep an eye on Marie when I wasn't around so she wouldn't have to stay on her cot. Saying goodbye to them was very hard indeed.

~

It rained as we left the hospital. Marie laughed with excitement as she sat snugly on my knee. She kept taking my hand to play 'Round and Round the Garden' and laughed with pleasure when I tickled her.

'She's a sweet little thing, isn't she?' the social worker said; 'if only she didn't screech so much.' My blood started to boil.

'Maybe it's a good thing that she does screech,' I told her: 'at least she knows how to object to things.' I knew I was being very intolerant, yet I continued, 'When you think of the awful life she's had it's hardly surprising, is it?'

We didn't speak much after that; there didn't seem to be anything else to say. We travelled from Bristol along the A38, through Bridgewater and on to Taunton until we came to a sign for Bishop's Lydeard which was seven miles past Taunton. We finally approached the hospital gates and drove up the mile-long drive towards the buildings. It was just outside a small village and seemed very bleak and isolated. Very slowly we passed the rows of pre-fabricated wards and drove towards a big old mansion which stood in the centre of the grounds. Matron came out to meet us. After the formal introductions she walked on ahead with the social worker leaving me to follow, carrying Marie. We passed reception in the main hall and followed Matron into a room where a man was waiting with some forms to sign. Marie screeched.

'That's a good pair of lungs she's got,' Matron said cheerfully.

'Yes, she can be quite a noisy child,' the social worker commented as she smiled at me. I gave her a filthy look and turned away. At that moment I hated them all.

~

We were soon back in the car heading towards the ward. Rain danced on the windows: the windscreen wipers started the countdown.

Again, there was a member of staff to greet us as we reached Marie's ward. This time it was the sister in charge. I lifted Marie from the car.

'I'll wait here,' the social worker said.

I felt as though I had swallowed a tennis ball again. I had never been on a ward for the mentally handicapped before; I didn't know what to expect. Sister led the way, for us to follow.

The ward was full of very noisy children. Looking around the room in horror, my eyes rested on a child who had the largest head I had ever seen. Tears ran down my face as we made our way through the ward, stepping over children as they lay on the floor. We arrived at Sister's office. By this time Marie was becoming very noisy, making any conversation difficult to hear. I wanted to screech too: I had no control over the awful things that happened to her.

We could see the dormitory through the office window. Sister was pointing to where Marie was going to sleep: 'She'll be No 11,' she stated, trying to give me some idea where her cot was in the large dormitory. In my over-sensitive mood it was the straw that broke the camel's back. I handed Marie over to Sister and walked out of the office.

The social worker was sitting in her car reading the paper.

'Matron wants to see you,' she said as I sat in beside her. 'I'll take you there first, and then we can have some lunch.' We drove back to the mansion. I went in alone. I didn't have a clue what she wanted, and I wasn't even interested. My mind was full of Marie. Last time she'd been taken, this time I'd given her away: she was free to anybody that would have her because nobody wanted her — she was anybody's.

'Sit down,' Matron offered kindly when I walked into her office.

'Have you got a job to go to?' she asked. I couldn't speak. I just shrugged my shoulders.

'Would you like to work here?' she asked to my surprise. I looked at her, sitting behind her desk in her blue uniform, not quite believing what she had said. I finally managed to speak: 'You mean work here in the hospital?'

She nodded. 'Would you like to work with handicapped people?' she asked. It could have been a million pounds this kind lady was offering me, for I had never dreamt thirty minutes before when I was driven through those gloomy hospital gates that I would be returning.

'Take these forms home with you and think about it,' she told me. I didn't have to think about it — I'd already made up my mind.

Fifteen minutes later I was sitting in the dining room trying desperately to pull myself together. Relieved that the build-up of the past few months was over, and saddened that Marie would never be able to understand that I had no choice but to leave her.

'Eat up, Michelle,' the social worker said, trying to sound cheerful. My tears wouldn't stop. I sat with my head down and watched them dripping onto my dinner.

# 4
~

I SHOOK THE snow from my coat as I boarded the train for Taunton. I hadn't seen Marie for six weeks: it seemed like six years. I had spent Christmas at home with my family and New Year with Cathy in Bristol. It was now January 2nd 1971.

By late afternoon I was being driven through the hospital gates in a taxi and heading up the drive. Approaching the wards, I glanced quickly over to Marie's building before driving on to the mansion. I longed to go straight over to see her but I realised I would have to tread carefully now that I was one of the staff. I walked into the mansion and finding nobody on reception I put my case down by the desk and walked over to Matron's office, knocking gently on the door. It was almost dark outside. I assumed it was tea time on the wards but I hoped that Matron might suggest I visit Marie if I didn't stay too long. Some hope!

'Hello,' I said stupidly when she opened the door. I was not yet aware of the formalities.

'Good evening,' she said without a flicker of friendliness. 'Would you wait over there and I'll get someone to show you where your room is.' She closed the door again so I went and stood by my case. I looked at the room opposite with the door wide open revealing the long table we'd sat around when I'd first brought Marie.

When the nurse arrived I followed her through the door by reception into the big hall and up a flight of stairs into the nurses' home.

'Are you hungry?' she asked, opening the landing door. I shook my head and explained how my health conscious sister, Cathy, had filled me with her macrobiotic food. I followed her into my room putting my case on the bed while she quickly gave me lots of helpful information and advice before rushing back on duty. Thanking her, I gently closed the door and walked towards my bedroom window. Sitting on the ledge I looked out at the snow-covered wards still bright with decorations. My eyes rested on Marie's ward, too far to see anything: I longed for just a glimpse of her...

The next two hours were spent sitting in my room. At 7.30 when I heard the nurses coming off duty I went along to the staff sitting room.

Flopped in armchairs, looking exhausted, most of the nurses were there to greet me.

'Are you a new girl?' a nurse in the far corner asked.

'Yes,' I replied feeling a bit shy in a room full of strangers.

'Have you come to start your nurses' training?'

I shook my head. 'I'm a cadet nurse. I'm not old enough to do my training.'

'How old are you then?' she asked me, lighting a cigarette.

'Seventeen and a half,' I replied. Changing the subject, and longing to know, I asked if anybody worked on the children's ward.

'Which one?' a nurse in a pink dress asked me.

'I'm not sure,' I laughed nervously. 'Do you know a little girl called Marie?'

'She means the screamer,' said a nurse in a white coat. I bit my lip.

'Why do you call her that?'

'Because that's all she does,' she replied.

'Isn't she on the high grade ward?' the nurse in the pink dress asked. It sounded awful, so I asked them what they were talking about. Apparently there were two wards for each age group — low grade and high grade. That's the way it was in those days, when handicapped children were graded like vegetables.

'Why are you so interested in her anyway? Are you a relation?'

'No,' I replied, 'I used to look after her and I'm hoping that I can still visit and take her out.'

'If you've come to work here you'll not be allowed to visit her,' I was warned. 'The staff aren't allowed personal relationships with the patients.'

I finally made an excuse to return to my room where I sat on my bed, hoping what they had told me wasn't true. If it was, I'd have been better not taking the job.

I lay awake for most of the night and felt lonely for the first time since I'd left home. I lay there wondering what was in store for me and how Marie was coping with her new life on a 'high grade' ward.

~

Next morning I reported to Matron's office and was promptly collected again and taken to the laundry where I was given my white coat — then on to the sewing room where I collected my cape. Stepping outside in the cold morning air we walked across the paths carefully, trying not to slip in the snow. I appreciated my cape as I folded it around me to protect me from the cold.

I was put on the ward beside Marie's, separated by a small garden. It was still dark outside. The lights were on in Marie's ward but I was only able to glance over as Sister introduced me to some of the staff.

I smiled as I recognised some of the nurses from the previous evening. I was on the high grade ward for teenagers. When I was taken into the dormitory to be introduced I was grateful that the curtains were still closed, preventing me from looking over to Marie's ward and enabling me to concentrate on the job I had come to do.

Most of the patients were in the bathroom. Glancing along the dormitory I took in two rows of beds with little dressing tables between each one, with personal items placed on top — photographs and little ornaments. There was a unit which ran the length of the end wall where most of the patients kept their dresses and coats with little cubicles at the bottom for underclothes and nightwear. One by one, the patients returned from the bathroom. I was surprised at how friendly they were and how easily they accepted someone new to look after them. A young girl called Debra came and showed me a photo of her mum.

'What's your name, nurse?' she asked curiously.

'My name is Michelle.'

'We're not allowed to be called by our Christian names,' a nurse chipped in.

'Then my name is Nurse Shearon,' I replied.

We spent the next half hour folding nightclothes, straightening beds, brushing hair and generally being available if anybody needed help. I was finding it difficult to concentrate since they'd opened the curtains. Just a little peep at Marie would have been enough but I needed to see if she was all right.

'Are you coming to breakfast?' Jean asked me, handing me my cape. Following her out of the ward I knew I couldn't wait any longer.

'Actually I'm not very hungry,' I told Jean, hoping I didn't seem unfriendly. 'I'll come over to the dining room in ten minutes and have a cup of tea.' We parted to go in our different directions: she must have wondered where I was going.

Off I walked down the drive to the next turning. I was scared to go in when I reached the entrance. I hadn't seen Marie for so long. After being used to spending hours with her, this was going to be a snatched ten minutes, if I was allowed to see her at all. My watch said 8.15. I quickly walked through the entrance and into the day room, which was empty except for a cleaner mopping the floor. I glanced nervously down the ward to Sister's office: she saw me and came out.

'Hello, Sister,' I said cheerfully trying to ignore her deadpan expression. 'How is Marie?' My heart started thumping. I thought she would kick me off the ward for cheek with such an early social call.

'She's fine,' came the icy reply. She was the same ward sister I'd handed Marie over to when she'd been admitted.

'We weren't given all the facts about her when she came to us,' she went on, but I didn't understand what she meant. My legs felt like jelly as I stood there. Sister spoke again: 'Her mother has been to see her. We didn't know she lived so near.'

I didn't know what to say to her.

'I don't really know anything about Marie's history, Sister,' I said cautiously. I looked down the ward to see where the sudden noise was coming from: it was a porter. I cleared my throat.

'Can I go and see her, Sister? just for a minute?' My heart almost stopped as I waited for her to answer.

'She's in the bathroom,' she finally replied. Walking through the day room with me she pointed to a door where there was lots of noise coming from. In I went.

I shouted over to the nurse; 'I've come to see Marie.' All of the children were sitting on little pots on the floor. Then there was a sudden squeal to the side of me that I'd have recognised anywhere. My eyes rested on my little friend in the corner. She sat clapping her hands with excitement, laughing loudly as she looked at me.

'Hello Marie,' I said, crossing the bathroom and stooping down to look at her. Her hair had grown slightly and it bounced as she looked away from me and tried to hide. She wore an awful rust-coloured dress on top of which she had a pink cardigan with no buttons, but she looked well and seemed a bit chubbier.

'Did you think I'd forgotten you?' I whispered. Stroking her hair I lifted her fringe and saw the lump which told me of the hours she still spent banging her head. She laughed so loudly. Her little eyes watered as she studied my face. It must have been such a surprise to see me after such a long time.

'Doesn't she look happy?' the nurse shouted across the bathroom. She was busy washing one of the children's faces. 'Did you used to know her?'

'Yes,' I replied looking at Marie tenderly, 'I used to know her.'

I wanted to sit Marie on my knee but I couldn't because she was on her pot and besides it was almost time for school. I stayed crouched on the floor by her and she held onto my hand. The other children had shuffled over to us and were sitting around pulling at my cape; beckoning for attention. Somehow they didn't seem as grotesque as they had the first time I saw them.

I had to go. She was still sitting on her pot when I left her and she was crying.

As I walked out of the building there was a nurse in front of me. When I got nearer I saw that it was Sister. 'Shall I ask her?' I thought, and then suddenly ran to catch her up — I had to know one way or the other.

'Can I visit Marie again, Sister?'

'You can come between two and four Saturdays and Sundays,' she replied to my great relief.

'Thanks, Sister,' I said as I left her to run back to my ward before I was late. When I entered the day room the patients were sitting with their coats on.

'Are you coming to the disco tonight?' one of them asked.

'I don't know.' I was nonplussed.

'There's a staff Social Club and the patients have a disco down there every Monday night. You'll see tonight,' the nurse told me, 'because we take our patients.'

My first day went very slowly. After working in the convent and being so busy I felt quite bored at times, especially with the patients being at occupational therapy all day. I found it very difficult to try to look busy.

That evening when the girls arrived home it was chaos as they took their dresses out of the wardrobes and laid them on their beds. The disco didn't start until 7.30 and there was hours to go, but the nurses encouraged them and were carried along with the patients' excitement.

At 7.15 we were ready. Walking down the drive towards the Social Club I listened with great interest to the girls as they talked about their boyfriends and who they were going to dance with. The disco lights were low and some of the male patients started to cheer when the girls walked in. They giggled childishly and went off to mingle with the crowd. There was a bar in the corner where couples bought refreshments. Although I was starting to realise how 'normal' these handicapped people were, I wasn't too sure about the men: I was still a bit wary and felt out of my depth surrounded by so many handicapped people. Sitting quietly on a chair amongst the girls I watched some people dancing. The door opened occasionally and groups of people came in shouting greetings across the room to their friends who were waiting for them. It was all so different to what I had imagined. George Harrison's 'My Sweet Lord' was belting out in the background. It was almost a privilege to be there.

'Would you like to dance?' someone asked, breaking in on my thoughts.

'No thanks,' I replied feeling very guilty but not yet having the confidence to dance with a patient. Later on I had a dance with one of the male nurses — or so I thought! It wasn't until we were getting ready to return to the ward that I realised I'd danced with a patient and refused the nurse. Served me right!

~

'Why do they live here if there's hardly anything wrong with them?' I asked one of the nurses.

'Some of them have lived here all their lives,' she told them, 'and they're quite happy here.'

'Do you like working here?' I couldn't help noticing how kind she was to the patients, as though she really enjoyed her job. She nodded. Together with the patients we strolled up the moonlit drive towards the wards. There was something quite beautiful about these people, something that hit me with great force. Their naturalness and lack of pretence, their kindness to one another and their warmth and affection. It was overwhelming.

My eyes filled up when we passed my little friend's dormitory. The curtains were closed and she was probably asleep. I was very aware of our feet crunching in the snow and wondered if we'd wake her up.

'Are you from Liverpool?' the nurse asked me. I laughed and waited for another phony imitation of my Liverpool accent. 'You're a long way from home. What made you come this far?'

'It's a long story,' I answered and briefly told her about Marie and how I came to be at the hospital by accident more than anything. 'I only really came to see if she was all right.'

She groaned sympathetically. 'Have you met Sister Green yet? She's very strict with the nurses and I don't think she'll let you take your little girl out.'

'She said it's all right for me to visit,' I told her, feeling relieved as I reflected on the friendly warnings and sleepless night I'd had the previous evening...

That evening I lay in bed going over the day's events and for the first time in weeks, had a decent night's sleep.

The week dragged! When Saturday finally came around I wandered impatiently from room to room in the nurses' home as I waited for my two o'clock visiting time. With ten minutes to go I slowly made my way over to the ward. It was very unusual to see an off-duty nurse near the patients: it just was not allowed. Waving to some of the nurses through the ward windows, I must have been a curious figure indeed.

Marie and I were delighted to see each other. I lifted her off the floor and swung her around.

'You can take her into the dormitory if you like,' Sister Green kindly offered. Leaving the noisy day room I carried Marie to a chair at the side of her cot. We revelled in each other's company. It was as though we'd never been apart as we hummed our songs and walked up and down the ward making the most of what little time we had. There was a mirror at the end of the dormitory so I stood Marie in front of it. I knew on that day when I looked at her reflection in the mirror that I would always visit her wherever she was. We were friends for life.

I was very grateful to Sister Green for allowing us the privacy of the dormitory. I realised how easy it was to get the wrong impression of her. I liked her despite all I'd heard. I thought she was just a very direct person. During the afternoon she sent one of the nurses in with a cup of tea for me. She'd hardly spoken to me but in her own way she'd made me very welcome. I was forever grateful to her for that.

I visited Marie on the Sunday too, cementing our weekend routine. After a while, whenever I visited, Marie would be sitting watching the door. Peeping through the window of the day room I would see her sitting with her clean clothes on, waiting for me. As the weather became warmer I started taking her for walks around the hospital. It was on these walks we'd probably bump into Matron who always stopped to greet us. I had a rather strange set-up. Sometimes I could be sharing a dining table with Sister Green but neither of us mentioned Marie and we usually only greeted each other. Matron and I passed each other through the week with a formal, 'Good morning' or 'Good afternoon' but at weekends I was treated like a visitor. They were always friendly and kind.

There was a recreation hall opposite the mansion which visitors used at weekends and we were able to buy refreshments there. I used to take Marie there on a Sunday. By this time I had come to know quite a few of the patients so it was very interesting for me to be able to meet their families. It was through talking to those parents that I had a better understanding of why it wasn't always possible for patients to live at home. I had always thought they were in hospital because they had been rejected by their families but I learnt that there can be one hundred and one reasons. I began to realise how difficult it must be for parents when they visited their son or daughter, and could quite well see why many did not bother.

~

I liked my work on the wards although I missed the homeliness of the convent. I had been used to having one person in charge and working alongside her for most of the day, whereas on the ward there were two shifts with a different person in charge, and because of the different ideas they had it was sometimes rather confusing.

I am lucky in that I have always been a good mixer. I am also a very lazy person. If I like someone I love them; if I don't I find it very hard to make an effort and pretend. I think it's called not suffering fools gladly! I liked most of the nurses and made some good friends. Most of them accepted my relationship with Marie: some were a little resentful that I was allowed to take her out. I remember an incident in the nurses' sitting room when one of the staff said how unfair it was that I was allowed to take one of the patients out and she couldn't. On and on she went: 'You're not being very fair to her, are you? She must think you're her bloody mother.'

I tried to explain that I wasn't picked out for any special treatment, that I had looked after Marie before working at the hospital, but still she went on.

'What happens to her when you leave? She's so attached to you and you're just playing with her emotions.'

Although her attitude towards me seemed a little stronger than concern for Marie, I refused to justify my relationship any further because I didn't think I was accountable to her.

I told her: 'If you've got any qualms about my so-called "special treatment" then you are better taking them higher up, aren't you?' She didn't answer me. She just flung the magazine she'd been reading back on the table and walked out. She didn't bother me again and kept her resentment to herself, or just refrained from voicing it in my presence.

On the other hand, I didn't talk about Marie very much. I knew I was privileged and didn't want to rub salt in the wounds of other people but also I was very aware that the nurses were off duty, and I was afraid of becoming a bore.

One day I took the patients from my ward into the garden. I always stayed away from Marie's ward for fear of being a nuisance so I took the group of girls up to the top part away from Marie's day room. We were playing ball when one of the girls shouted.

'Somebody wants you, nurse.' When I turned around Sister Green was calling me to the window; she'd seen me out in the garden and fetched Marie for me to see. Running over to the day room I waved to Marie. Sister had stood her on the window ledge and her little face lit up when she saw me. This was a special treat for me. Sometimes when I took her back on a Sunday, I probably wouldn't see her until the following weekend when I was next off duty. I don't think Marie was aware that I was in the hospital all the time. There were odd occasions when I saw her going for a walk but I used to hide because I knew that if she saw me she would get upset, and it wasn't fair on her, so I would just follow her with my eyes until she was out of sight.

~

After I'd been at the hospital a couple of months I asked Sister Green if I could take Marie into Taunton to buy her some shoes.

'I don't see why not,' she answered, 'I'll have a word with Matron.'

The following week we were running down the hospital drive for the bus! We had a wonderful day. Lunch in a café: chips and ice cream! Sitting at a little table on our own, Marie behaved impeccably. When the meal was over, she kept herself occupied by looking down at people's shoes, attracted by the noise as they passed. She had hardly altered since I'd met her at the convent except that she was making an effort to feed herself a little. There was still no sign of any speech.

When I took her for shoes she screamed in the shop and went stiff with fear at the foot measurer but the poor woman persevered and Marie finally left the shop wearing a little pair of blue shoes.

Walking around the town, which was still strange to me, I discovered a little park full of rose gardens and little paths. Sitting on the bench I watched Marie stomp up and down making as much noise as her little feet could, never dreaming at the time that Marie's grandmother lived just around the corner.

Returning to the ward I gave Marie her tea, then it was time for me to go. She still cried after me. She plonked herself on the floor, and Sister would not allow any of the staff to comfort her as she sat crying hysterically, crashing her head into the ground. Perhaps she thought Marie would eventually stop it, but she never did. I just wished they would sit her on a chair so she wouldn't hurt herself so much. I knew she had to learn not to screech but we'd had such a wonderful day it seemed sad that it finished with her being upset. It was usually when I left her that I wondered whether I was doing her more harm than good. I was always glad of the nurses' company when I returned to the home and we'd make our plans for the evening. Some of them used to come out on Saturdays with Marie and I, and we'd take it in turns to give her a piggy back up the drive.

~

On occasions when I went to visit Marie and Sister Green was off duty it wasn't pleasant. Marie was always sitting on her cot in the dormitory crying. She had been put there so she wouldn't get dirty but she didn't understand. I would carry her off the ward hysterical, since she'd been so frightened to be left on her own. I used to get very angry. One of the nurses told me the person who'd requested Marie to be put on her cot liked neither Marie nor myself. She didn't agree with the freedom I was given with her and she thought Marie was a spiteful child because she pulled hair. I realised with some concern that she was using Marie to get at me.

It was at times like this I realised how vulnerable the patients were and how the quality of their day depended on who was running the ward. Even on my own ward, despite having a very kind and competent ward sister, something happened one day which shook my whole confidence in the establishment.

It was Sister's day off. An S.E.N. had been left in charge for the day with a student nurse. It was disco night. As usual the patients came running in from Occupational Therapy as though they had ten minutes to get ready instead of three hours. We laughed and encouraged them when they collected their dresses from the wardrobe. Denise, one of the patients, was walking over to her bed when the student nurse snatched her dress from her and threw it to the nurse in charge, who then childishly threw it back. Poor Denise started crying. The nurses continued throwing the dress and Denise's effort to recover it failed miserably. Screaming, she threw herself on the floor. Within minutes specks of blood appeared on her face as she flicked it with her nails. The nurses didn't like what they saw. They had carried the joke too far and it had backfired on them. One of the nurses got quite angry then and they both dragged her up off the floor instead of leaving her to calm down. She flung her glasses and smashed them as both nurses pushed and shoved her up the ward. Poor Denise was put to bed and of course her terrible behaviour was written in the diary but the nurses didn't add that they'd played a joke on somebody who wasn't emotionally mature enough to take it, and who had responded in the only way her mental age allowed her to. I was in such a dilemma! I wanted to report them but I knew I'd have to keep my mouth shut if I wanted to see Marie every weekend. I'd learnt that sometimes when a nurse complains about things she's seen as an upstart.

A few days later Sister was making out a list of patients to see the doctor.

'I don't know what to do about Denise,' she said, looking puzzled. 'It's not like her at all to behave like that.' She went on to say that her sedation might not be strong enough. Unable to contain my anger any longer I told her what had happened. I also added that if Denise was given more sedation because of the incident then I would report the two nurses. Sister knew something was wrong because she knew her patients well. Denise didn't see the doctor and her drugs weren't changed. I felt that the lack of concern by the medical staff about Denise's rebellious behaviour left an obvious question about the nurses' ability in looking after her and although it had been very upsetting for Denise, all the nurses had done was to draw attention to themselves. However, this ward was Marie's next stop: I'd seen too much to ignore it. I started to think of ways to get her out of the hospital but unless I was a relative it couldn't be done — or so I thought.

One evening something quite strange happened. I went home with one of the nurses and picked up the local paper to read as I sat idly waiting for her to make the coffee. I opened the obituary page and to this day I don't know what made me do it. I looked down the column to see if either of Marie's grandparents were in it. I was astonished to see Marie's grandfather had been buried that day. I felt quite shocked that I thought it was possible and it was there in black and white. The fact that Marie's grandparents' address was there made me wonder at the coincidence. I cut out the clipping and when I returned to my room at the nurses' home I put it away in my letter box. I remember sitting on my bed for a long while after wondering at the strange occurrence.

~

One day the thing I dreaded most happened; I was moved to the ward next to Marie's. This meant the same door was used for both wards on entering the building, but instead of going left onto Marie's ward I turned right into my own. This really did make things very difficult. Every morning the children from both wards travelled to school on the same bus: the problem was that a member of staff had to take the children to meet the bus outside. I avoided this whenever possible because Marie got very upset when she saw me and had to be pulled off me and put on the bus for school. It was useless. I knew it was a hopeless situation. I was trying to play the detached nurse and the loving mother at the same time. I couldn't do it. I began to think about leaving. My contract was coming up for renewal at the end of the month because I was almost eighteen and due to start my nurses' training which would have meant no more weekends off.

My mother must have been very disappointed though she never said anything. For the first time in my life I seemed to be doing something positive and sensible. My family knew about Marie but I don't think anybody realised how involved I was with her. To most people she was just a little girl I'd become fond of; to me she was like my own child. I now lived in a different world from that of my family, or so it seemed. We still kept in touch and wrote often. Leaving home so young and being so far away, I'd always had letters from them. They'd arrived in all shapes and sizes depending, of course, on who wrote them. I'd had pieces of toilet roll from Liz, full of news of Marathon the tortoise and Herbet the frog. I once received a letter from Maureen, written on a piece of Kleenex tissue. I remember the first letter I'd received from my mum at the hospital. A five pound note had dropped out of the envelope. 'Promise me you'll come home if you don't like it,' she'd said. 'Put this money away for your train fare in case you want to leave.' I knew I had caused her a lot of worry as I drifted further and further away. Following destiny's path — or so I thought. Still rebelling against my Catholic upbringing, I had closed the door on God.

My final month was full of turmoil. Had I done the right thing? Would I still be able to visit Marie? All these questions and many more played havoc with my sleep. And without realising it, my relationship with Marie had turned me into a loner. I still liked being with people and knew how to enjoy myself but I needed to be alone for a certain amount of time each day. I needed to sit and think things through, things I refrained from discussing with the other girls. My dilemma isolated me.

I had no trouble finding accommodation. My sister, Cathy, and most of her friends were leaving Bristol so there were plenty of flats I could move into. My mother had wanted me to return home but I couldn't even think about going so far away from the hospital — not yet anyway.

So once again I was packing.

~

On the Saturday before I left, I took Marie into Taunton with some friends. We had a delightful day. We took her to our usual haunts and spent the rest of the afternoon at the park. Off she went along the paths, loving the freedom, stopping to check once in a while that we were still there. Later in the afternoon when we arrived back at the hospital we took it in turns to give Marie a piggy back up the drive. She laughed uncontrollably as we raced with her. The nurses kissed her goodbye and headed towards the nurses' home. I went on to Marie's ward. Sister Green was sitting in the day room with one of the children on her knee. I couldn't speak so I smiled at her and took Marie into the bathroom to undress her. Sitting her on the locker I started to undo her shoes. She was watching me fold her clothes.

'I wonder where we'll go from here, Marie?' I said sadly. She still had the big scab on her forehead so I told her, 'When I see you again that's going to be better!' She laughed. She didn't really know what I was talking about — but she knew from my voice I was having fun with her. I'd been so good, I'd tried so hard not to cry and now here I was with the tears running down my face. Sister Green came in. That made me worse. I thought of all the awful warnings I'd had about her, yet she'd been nothing but kind and supportive towards me.

'She'll miss you, won't she?' she asked, passing me Marie's night-dress. 'You will come back and see her, won't you?' I was so relieved to hear I would still be welcome.

'Of course I will, Sister. I'll come back whenever I can.'

'I thought you liked working here?' she asked me, leaning on the locker top.

'I do, Sister, but I find it difficult trying to avoid Marie all the time and besides if I continued to work at the hospital I wouldn't be able to see her at weekends any more.'

'I hadn't thought about that, and I suppose with her being at school throughout the week you'd hardly see her, would you?' I shook my head. I thanked her for always being so kind and making me welcome. Soon after, I kissed Marie goodbye and left.

~

Walking through the day room on my way out a little boy was sitting watching the television.

'Goodbye nurse,' he said softly.

'Goodbye,' I replied. 'See you soon.' It was the little boy I'd seen with the large head when Marie had first been admitted. He'd horrified me then: now I hardly noticed. I had been the one with the handicap, not him.

# 5

~

I HAD BEEN back to visit Marie several times and found it much easier not working at the hospital. Yet I still wasn't happy about her living there.

My family were worried about me because I was no longer in a residential job and I lived in a flat. My mum came to stay for a week, trying desperately to talk me into going home with her, but I wouldn't. I was afraid of moving so far from Marie. Cathy tried next with her long letter about how wonderful London was and how I would love living there. Next came my Aunty Terry. She stayed for another week and almost talked me into going home but not quite. I needed a little more time. However, after six months, I packed up my boyfriend and my belongings and moved back home. I regretted the move almost immediately because of the distance which now separated me from Marie. I became very mixed up and unhappy. People kept telling me to forget about her, that she'd be all right and she was far too much responsibility for someone so young. I had given up arguing. How could I explain how close we were — how when I heard a cat cry in the night I thought about Marie lying in her cot with the sad little light watching over her from the end of the dormitory.

One evening I was talking to my younger sister, Liz. Like two conspirators we plotted and planned, covering many avenues in the hope of rescuing Marie. Perhaps Marie's mum would adopt me, making me Marie's sister, enabling me then to bring her out of hospital. No, we decided, that was no good. Then I had a brain-wave!

'Hey Liz, I wonder if they would transfer Marie to a hospital here?' That would have been too much to expect. Wouldn't it?

After thinking of nothing else for several days I finally sat down and wrote a letter to Dr Bakker at Taunton, telling him of my concern for Marie, since I was so far away, and wondering about the possibility of a transfer. I tried not to imagine how wonderful it would be.

A week later I received a reply. I was shaking as I opened the letter. I had to read it twice: I couldn't believe what he was telling me.

'What is he saying?' Liz asked as she came running down the stairs. I handed her the letter and watched her face as she read it. Looking at me with eyes that were about to pop, she said: 'Oh Mish, they're looking into it for you!'

I was stunned....

~

Christmas came and went. While I was anxiously awaiting news from Taunton I was busy job hunting and managed to get on a one-year course in a residential school for physically handicapped children. In the meantime I'd written to Dr Bakker again asking him if there had been any developments, only to receive a reply from a Dr Prentice telling me that Dr Bakker had left and there was no trace of my previous letter. My heart sank. I had thought it was too good to be true. I thought they'd start to ignore me now that I lived so far away, expecting me to lose interest, but I wouldn't. I wrote to Dr Prentice explaining the situation and sending a copy of my previous letter to Dr Bakker. I was delighted when I received a reply a week later saying he was looking into the possibilities for me and was awaiting observations from the parents.

'Oh well,' I thought, 'at least he hasn't said no.'

~

The following week I started my new job. I arrived at the big old-fashioned school on the sea front and as the sea air filled my nostrils I had the feeling I was going to like this job. I was a trainee housemother, looking after boys aged 5-16. I was looking forward to the challenge!

I thoroughly enjoyed my job but I was very worried about Marie. I had not visited her for three months. My poor mum! On the nights I was sleeping at the school I would ring home when I went off duty.

'Is there any mail, mum?' I would ask anxiously, but more often than not there wasn't.

Towards the middle of February a letter arrived from the hospital. I had telephoned them the previous week enquiring after Marie. Dr Prentice had written to say my telephone enquiry had been passed on to him and he was still awaiting observations from the parents.

I was telling my friend at work about my plight. 'I need to go to Taunton,' I told her, 'and I can't afford the train fare. Will you hitch with me?' I asked cautiously. I knew the route because I'd hitched up and down to Bristol with Cathy, but I would not hitch alone for obvious reasons.

'OK,' Sue replied. 'You arrange it with the hospital and then let me know when you want to go.'

The following week we left my mum's at 5 a.m. having gone there from work the previous evening. It was the middle of March and the fog was thick as we stood on the motorway shivering. Soon a lorry pulled up.

'Where are you going?' the driver asked as we climbed up into the warm cab.

'We want to go to Taunton,' I told him.

'Well, I'm only going as far as Birmingham so I'll drop you off and you can get another lift.'

'Oh great!' I said, 'we're hoping to get there for two o'clock because we have to be back in Liverpool tonight.'

He looked at me like I'd suddenly grown two heads. 'You're coming all the way back tonight?' he asked incredulously. We nodded. 'You must be bloody mad,' he muttered, 'you'll never do it.'

'We will!' I whispered to Sue when I saw the worried look on her face.

~

The sun was shining when we reached the hospital at 1.45. Walking up the drive we waved to some of the patients and nurses I knew who were going for walks.

'Hello,' one of the nurses shouted cheerfully, 'have you come to see your little girl?'

'Yes,' I answered feeling excited as we neared the ward. The children were playing outside so we went through the day room and out into the garden. I greeted the deputy ward sister. Marie spotted us from the other end of the lawn. With great squeals of delight she stood up and came staggering over. I picked her up and swung her around. The look on her face told me she knew I would come back. I was shocked. I hadn't seen her for five months. I'd even wondered if she'd recognise me. How wrong I had been.

One of the children had taken Sue's hand and was trying to pull her across the garden. Tickling Marie I strolled over to the deputy ward sister with her: 'Is it all right to take Marie for a walk, Sister?'

'Yes,' she answered, 'but under no circumstances is she to go out of the hospital grounds.' Leaving the ward with Marie and Sue, I was nonplussed.

'What a strange thing to say,' I said to Sue outside, 'Something must be wrong. They know I'm only visiting for an hour and why should I take Marie outside the hospital: besides, I would ask their permission first. I always have done.'

We found a bench to sit on. I looked at Marie sitting on my lap. Her sad little face and the lump told me of the hours she still spent banging her head. After a few minutes' rest, with Marie holding both our hands we continued our little walk. Somebody knocked on the window as we passed the ward next to Marie's. I was surprised to see it was Sister Green. She opened the window.

'Hello, Sister. What are you doing on this ward?' I asked.

'I've been moved,' she said sadly.

'That's a shame. I'll bet all the children will miss you.'

'They'll soon get used to somebody else,' she said modestly, but as I left her my eyes stung. She loved those children. I knew they would miss her. She had looked after them so well. Finding a bench we sat down again. I studied Marie's appearance, as I had never seen her look like this before. She had brown leather spastic boots on, and a horrible-looking eczema all over her head, and the lump still on her forehead, of course. I was frightened by what the ward sister had said to me about taking Marie out and saddened by Sister Green's move. I could already see the difference in Marie's appearance. Unfortunately it was this ward sister who had always had Marie put on her cot when she was waiting for me to take her out. I felt very insecure as I realised that she was now in charge of the ward.

'I think I'll go and see Matron,' I said to Sue. 'I need to know where I stand.' I wiped my eyes and blew my nose in an effort to compose myself. I carried Marie into Matron's office. I told her what Sister had said to me.

'You're not going to stop me from seeing her, are you?' I asked her frantically.

'Of course not, Michelle.' She was as kind to me as she'd always been. 'I think Sister was just making sure,' she added, trying to be diplomatic. I then told her of my plans to have Marie transferred.

'Don't build your hopes up too much,' she told me gently, 'in case her mother objects.'

I was happier leaving Matron's office than I had been going in! I started to relax after her reassurances that I was still welcome and they were not going to interfere in the transfer.

I finally said goodbye to my little friend before setting off on our long journey home. We did make it — but only just.

~

When Sue and I arrived back at the home where we worked, we were busy telling the staff there what had happened.

'They'll never agree to it,' one of the housemothers said. 'Even if they do, who do you think will accept her up here? You're not even a relation. And what if you lose interest and don't visit?' she said with a snigger. 'You must be mad.'

'I won't stop visiting her,' I said defensively, but I hadn't really given any thought to how the hospital up here would react.

'Anyway,' she added as she stood up to go on duty, 'you're not old enough.' She'd hit the nail on the head.

~

Because maturity was not on my side, I was wary about making any formal application to the hospital in Liverpool in case they refused. I started to wonder how I could get inside the walls without them knowing my reason for it.

One Saturday when I arrived home from work I asked my younger brothers and sisters if they would help me. John, Liz and Peter were sitting watching TV.

'The only thing is, I don't want the staff to know the reason for our visit,' I announced.

'Why not?' Liz asked me, puzzled.

'Because I don't know if Marie will be allowed to go yet and until I do I'd like to keep a low profile. Will you go and sort your old toys out?' I asked them, 'and then we can pretend we're just visiting and taking toys for the children. When we're on the ward I can have a look around and see what the place is like.'

Ten minutes later we were ready to go...

'Right then,' I said, looking gratefully at their offerings, 'don't forget you must look around the ward and remember anything you see so you can tell me when we get outside.'

We cut through the park at the back of my mum's on our way to the bus stop. I looked at the kids as they turned their backs to the wind, with their toys tucked under their arms. Liz was 14, John was 12 and Peter was 10.

The bus dropped us right outside the hospital but we were unable to see over the high wall surrounding it. We walked through the gates past the lodge as though we knew where we were going. We went into the first ward we came to. A nurse approached when we entered the day room. I smiled innocently and told him we'd brought some toys for the children. Before I could say anything else, one of the patients, a teenage boy, went up to Liz and put his arms around her. Liz was completely caught off her guard. It was her first time on a mental handicap ward. The nurse then diplomatically escorted us out of the ward to the dining room where we were very kindly given tea and biscuits. The two boys laughed and teased Liz who was still red with embarrassment. I thought the whole thing was hilarious; a complete waste of time. I wondered how I'd got us into this silly situation.

'Maybe we can try again next week, Mish,' Peter said, trying to sound optimistic.

'I can bring my soldiers along,' John added enthusiastically. They made me laugh.

'No, that's OK. I think it might look a little obvious if we start coming every week with toys: besides, you'll have none left. I'll have to think of something else,' I told them. 'The wards are usually chaotic enough on a Saturday without Liz going in and getting all the boys excited.' Poor Liz! John and Peter broke into peals of laughter and she didn't live it down for weeks.

Not long after I returned from Taunton I received a letter from Dr Prentice. Judging from its contents I gathered Matron had spoken to him after my visit. In the letter he stated that Marie's mother's permission was required for a transfer and he was still waiting to hear from her.

I was grateful to the doctor for keeping me informed. I had never met him and I thought he was very good to write to me as often as he did. Marie's mother had not visited her for two years: previous to that she had only seen her once or twice. I was concerned that she might never go to the hospital again and I could be waiting for years and years for her to make a decision.

It wasn't long before I was plotting and scheming again. This time I was taking a very serious step. I took Marie's grandfather's obituary out of my letter box. 'Did I find this for a reason? Was I given it for a purpose?' That evening I went over to visit my sister, Maureen. It was almost Sara's bedtime and she sat snugly on my knee. She was a beautiful little child with jet black hair and huge blue eyes. I showed Maureen the newspaper cutting.

'Do you think I should write to Marie's grandmother?' I asked.

'It's up to you, isn't it?' she answered. 'You have to do what you think is best.'

'Well,' I said wearily, 'I'm fed up: I'm sick of watching my p's and q's and always being frightened of upsetting people in case they stop me from visiting Marie. It's such a strain because I'm so direct by nature and they could stop me from seeing her tomorrow.'

'Yes,' she agreed, 'but the staff are good to you, aren't they? I thought you could just go in and see Marie at any time.'

'But it isn't just that!' I said angrily. 'Of course they're good to me: they always have been. But what happens if Matron leaves and somebody with different ideas and attitudes comes along? I'm not playing games and there's no security in it for Marie or myself.'

I decided to write to Marie's grandmother. I knew I could blow my chances with Marie but felt I had no choice. It seemed awful to be opening up old wounds for Marie's family, and I hoped they would see that I was acting in Marie's interest. I had discovered the obituary in such a strange way that I felt it had to be for a reason.

When I wrote to Marie's nan I explained how I'd looked after Marie for some time, told her of the potential I thought Marie had and how I thought she would benefit from living near me, explaining that Marie's mother's permission was needed for the transfer. I posted my letter that same evening, feeling very scared as I put it in the box. I walked back home in the rain.

Returning to work the following day I was glad to be distracted by a new arrival. The poor boy had been given the grand title of 'maladjusted' — in other words, he had a mind of his own! After unpacking his few belongings we both went for a walk along the beach. Sitting on the sand I watched him dancing in and out of the water and forgetting his grievances with the world that did not want him. I thought about some of the other children at the school too: there was Jonathan who, at six, was proudly showing me how he could change his colostomy bag himself, and Peter who struggled every morning to put on his own callipers, and then there was Paul who with the slightest knock to one of his limbs bravely smiled and tried not to show the pain he was in as his blood failed to clot and slowly poured into his joints until they were so swollen he was usually taken to hospital. I thought about Marie on her ward and all the other children in care — and decided that one day I would open my own children's home.

~

Three days later I walked into my mum's place after work and as usual my eyes went over to the mantlepiece where any mail was usually left for me. I looked closely at the blue envelope: it had a Taunton postmark. My heart started to pound. Picking up the envelope that held Marie's future inside I ran upstairs to my room. I closed the door and sat down on my bed. 'Please God,' I prayed, 'let everything be all right,' and I slowly opened the envelope. The news was good! I went rushing back down the stairs calling for my mother. Everybody came out of the living room with faces full of fear.

'Look,' I shouted, 'it's from Marie's nan.' Sitting down on the stairs I told them my news. 'She thinks Marie's mum would be very grateful for me to have Marie moved, and look,' I yelled waving the letter, 'she's sent Marie's mum's address.'

No more sneaking around! I was so relieved.

'Where are you going?' my mum asked as I put my coat on.

'I'm going to tell Maureen!' I ran out of the house and danced through the park in the rain towards the bus stop.

49

# 6
~

'GOSH, IT doesn't seem like we were here a month ago, does it?' Sue said as we left Marie's hospital once again. 'Sister's not very friendly towards you, is she?'

I grinned knowingly. 'She never has been,' I told her, 'but I couldn't care less. I just wouldn't give her any room to complain about me. Thank God Sister Green has only just been moved.' I dreaded to think how different things would have been had she never been there. Then she asked me the dreaded question.

'Do you think Marie's mum will reply to your letter?'

'I don't know. Marie's nan said since I'd written to her she'd moved and hadn't received any mail. Maybe she's waiting for my letter to be sent on.' We crossed the busy road to our familiar hitching spot. Reaching in my bag I found the remains of our sandwiches and melted chocolate. We were starving and starting to feel tired.

'Is Marie always dressed that way?' Sue asked as she tucked into a sandwich. 'I mean, what do they do with all the clothes you buy for her?'

'They go on hangers in the wardrobe. I could never understand this when I worked there. Sometimes the patients looked so tatty and it was really so unnecessary because they had some lovely clothes.'

'You'd think they'd make an effort with her, wouldn't you?' she said in disgust.

'I think, like everything else, it all depends on who's in charge of the ward,' I said, thinking of the linen cupboard stacked to the ceiling with new clothes that were never worn.

~

A week later I finally received a letter from Marie's mum. It is very difficult for me to put into words how I felt as I kept reading it. She finished with:

'From your letter I realise you love Marie very much and I know you'll give her all the love you possibly can. It seems strange for someone else to say they want your child, but under the circumstances you may be able to give something to Marie, which I may never have the chance to, and I would in no way wish to stop her chance of happiness.'

And so Sonia and I started writing to each other and arranged to meet in Taunton on Whit Sunday. She had also authorised Marie's transfer with the hospital.

My mother was worried. She felt that I was too young to have such responsibility. 'You should enjoy life more!' were her words.

'Gosh, Mum, I'm nineteen,' I laughed, 'and I do enjoy life.'

'But it's all work,' she said sadly; 'worrying about other people all the time. What about you? I just want you to have some life, that's all; I think you deserve a lot.'

I can see now what an awfully worrying time it must have been for her. I'd met Marie when I was almost seventeen and my mother had watched me worrying and fretting over the past two years. I smiled, recollecting the letter she'd sent to the hospital with my train fare inside. I hadn't gone home, I had followed the path destiny had laid down for me. Or was it God?

~

Dr Prentice was away the weekend I met Marie's mother and grand-mother at the railway station in Taunton. Boy, was I nervous! I'd spent six hours on the train from Liverpool with nothing to do but worry. 'What if they don't like me. What if we just can't get along.' I needn't have worried — we had so much to talk about we got on like a house on fire. We were so comfortable together I felt like I'd known her for years. Exchanging letters had helped.

It seemed strange being back in Taunton, passing familiar places full of memories and never realising we'd almost passed Marie's nan's place on our Saturday trips to the park. Strange again, to be walking side by side with Marie's mother as if it were the most natural thing in the world.

The next morning Sonia and I travelled by bus to the hospital to collect Marie for the day. She was one brave lady to make that journey with me. Putting her own feelings aside, she walked with me in the sunshine to see her little girl.

Marie looked so pretty in her new clothes. She was so excited to be leaving the hospital her feet hardly touched the floor as she ran in between us.

'Do you think she's improved at all since she came here?' Sonia asked when we sat waiting for the bus.

'Yes,' I replied bouncing Marie gently on my knee, 'but it isn't a marked improvement. She can feed herself now but she's still in nappies and there's no speech at all. I think she could do better,' I told her honestly. 'She still pulls hair and bangs her head and screeches a lot: she has to find another way of communicating.'

We had a lovely day — a special kind of day that one remembers forever.

The school was closing down for two weeks in the summer and I had mentioned to Marie's mother that I would like to have Marie for a holiday. With her permission I wrote to Dr Prentice with my request. It was eight weeks away. I started counting the days, thinking how wonderful it would be to tuck Marie up in bed at night.

~

'What's the matter?' my mum asked when she came into my room one morning with yet another letter.

'It's from the doctor at Taunton,' I answered quietly. 'Marie can't be transferred unless I'm her legal guardian. It's never going to happen,' I said despondently. 'Just when it seems to get nearer, something crops up and it seems so far away.' My mum went downstairs to make a cup of tea and I followed her into the hall.

'What are you doing now?' she asked me when I picked up the Yellow Pages book by the phone.

'I'm going to ring a solicitor,' I told her. 'I'm only asking if there is anything I can do,' I added when I saw the worried look on her face. I picked one out at random: they were all the same to me. I was given an appointment for the following afternoon. My mum was standing by the phone.

'Are you sure this is what you want to do?' she asked when I hung up.

'Of course it is,' I told her warily. 'But whether I'll be allowed to or not is a different matter,' I groaned looking up to heaven.

'I'll come with you then,' she said with a little twinkle in her eye, 'There must be something he can do.' Yahoo! At long last my wonderful mother was convinced about my seriousness and was going to help me...

~

Meanwhile, back at work, we still had lectures every Monday which were quite interesting, and sometimes our social worker arranged to take a group of students on a visit to a home or hospital to see other children in care and the facilities that were provided for them. One particular visit which sticks in my mind was to a general hospital where there was a long stay ward for several handicapped children.

Entering the ward we were greeted by the ward sister who took us to see the children, lying like dolls on top of cots.

'Why are they here?' one of the housemothers asked. 'Don't their parents want them?'

'Some of the little mites have never known their mothers,' Sister said gravely.

'It's cruel, isn't it?' one of the girls whispered to me. 'If I had a child like that I would look after it myself,' she told me indignantly.

'Look at that little girl's head,' some idiot said tactlessly. 'Why is it so big?' Sister then went on to explain about hydrocephalus. The little girl lying on her cot followed us with her eyes when we moved on until we were out of sight.

'Do you leave them on their cots all day?' I asked, and immediately realised I'd said the wrong thing. 'I suppose they're too handicapped to do anything with, are they?' I asked her, knowing I was talking a load of rubbish but not wanting to sound too critical — which I often did unintentionally. I slowly left the group and tried to imagine what life was like for those little children when they lay looking at the ceiling all day.

'God, it was awful, wasn't it?' somebody asked when we got outside. 'The way people just dump their children. They should be made to look after them,' she cried as she looked around our group for approval.

'Children don't just go into care because their parents don't want them,' I told her, unable to keep my mouth closed any longer. 'Some parents just can't cope: you don't know all the circumstances.' I thought of all the mums I'd met. 'Maybe those who can cope have been made to feel that they can't and have been convinced that the child is better off in care.' I knew I was too involved with it all because of Marie and took it all too seriously. Whenever possible I said nothing but sometimes I found it difficult and must have sounded like a know-all. Maybe if the girls had known about my relationship with Marie they'd have made allowances for my intolerance, but I didn't really talk about Marie except to close friends. I was afraid of being a bore.

~

The weeks went by and I was busy preparing for Marie's holiday. I had arranged with Matron to stay overnight in the nurses' home so we could have an early start the following day. However, when I arrived at the hospital to collect Marie, Matron was off and nobody knew anything about it. 'Oh no,' I thought as I looked at the stranger in her chair. 'Not now. Not when we're nearly there.'

'Who gave you permission?' the stranger asked, obviously thinking

I'd made a mistake.

'Matron and Dr Prentice,' I told him.

'Are you certain?' he enquired.

'Actually, I think I have the doctor's letter on me,' I answered reaching in my bag.

'If I could just see it?' he said, and reached over the desk for me to hand it to him. Luckily for me I had taken it, though it hadn't been for any special purpose.

An hour later I was sitting in the nurses' home talking with some friends when Wendy came off duty from Marie's ward.

'Sister's angry,' she said with some amusement, 'she said she didn't know anything about Marie's holiday and she's had to rush getting Marie's things ready for tomorrow.'

I could understand her anger at the inconvenience, but I would have thought her enthusiasm for Marie having a holiday would have over-ridden all of that. However, her attitude did not surprise me. I was well aware that she objected to my relationship with Marie.

~

Needless to say, we had two glorious weeks. Everybody had heard so much about Marie and welcomed her with open arms. She watched my little niece Sara playing for hours but I was never far away because of Marie's unpredictability and the grip she had when she pulled hair. She still screeched at bedtime, but settled down after a while.

My sister Liz watched Marie while I wrote a quick letter. That morning I had received a letter from Dr Prentice suggesting I contact Dr Rogerson at the Liverpool hospital because she might see Marie while she was staying with us.

~

Our holiday flew. Two days before Marie was due to return to Taunton I took her to see Dr Rogerson. It was a gloriously sunny morning. I sat Marie in Sara's pram and pushed her, with Liz accompanying me for moral support. The hospital was a mile from Maureen's but it was easier to walk than to get on a bus. Liz and I laughed when we approached the hospital thinking of our last visit with the toys and how it had all gone wrong. We found our way to out-patients and I left Liz in the waiting room when I went in to see the doctor. I was still a little apprehensive about doctors after my experience a few years previously, when Marie was taken from me. I felt very nervous. Marie sat on my knee, and Dr Rogerson stacked a few blocks up on her desk arousing Marie's interest immediately. She slid off my knee and approached the desk. She was not interested in building anything as she spread the blocks across the table — she preferred banging them, enjoying the noise they made. Marie suddenly pretended to sneeze with excitement. This was something she had started to do on her holiday: I was very glad that she was at least imitating people.

'Bless you!' I said cheerfully.

'Don't have her doing that, dear,' Dr Rogerson said to my surprise. She looked at me from behind her desk. 'After all, you don't want her spitting on people, do you?' She knocked the wind right out of my sails! I cleared my throat.

'No,' I answered quietly, not really understanding what she meant.

'Now dear,' she said, as our interview was obviously coming to an end, 'there is a residential school opening soon. Would you like me to put her name down for it?' I nodded. 'In the meantime I will put Marie's name on the waiting list for a bed here and let you know when there is a vacancy.'

I was very pleased with the way our interview had gone and breathed a sigh of relief outside as I sat Marie in her pram and told Liz what had happened. 'Just think,' I told Liz, smiling, 'no more trips down to Taunton. She'll be living here soon and be able to come home every weekend.' I took Marie's cardigan off as we passed the hospital lodge. The weather was scorching and as I stopped in front of her pram she looked at me and smiled. Her face was so alive that I was transfixed for a moment. If she hadn't been dribbling you wouldn't have known there was anything wrong with her. Her holiday was almost at an end and I knew she had enjoyed it — we all had — and she'd had so much attention and been fussed by everybody. Her hair was going yellow in the sun and she'd gone a lovely golden brown, her blue and white cotton dress with flowers on made such a change from the hospital crimplene I was so used to seeing her in. As I folded her cardigan into my bag I wondered what Dr Rogerson had meant and it slowly dawned on me. In my ignorance I had thought that if Marie was able to copy anything it was good, but what I hadn't realised was that whatever we tried to teach her had to be appropriate for Marie. What good did it do her if she sneezed on people? Of course it did her no good, and I was so grateful to Dr Rogerson for pointing this out to me.

~

I took Marie back on the train but I didn't feel too bad about it because I knew it wouldn't be long before she came up for good. I had taken Sara's pram back to Taunton with us and as we reached the bus stop outside the hospital I was glad I'd brought it as I pushed her up that familiar drive. However it wasn't long before I was walking back down it again as Sister had greeted me at the door, taking Marie and her case from me and saying goodbye to me as she walked Marie across the day room, making it obvious I wasn't welcome. Ten minutes later she drove past me in her car as I walked down the drive carrying Marie's folded up pram. I hadn't expected to spend the afternoon on the ward but a cup of tea would have been welcome after our 250 mile journey.

I soon got back into the swing of things at work and was busily distracted looking after the boys. I was still writing to Marie's mum and the hospital regarding the transfer and one day I had an unexpected surprise. It was a letter from Dr Rogerson saying there was a vacancy at the Liverpool hospital on December 29th. That meant I could bring her home for Christmas! I laughed and I cried. I just couldn't believe it.

My friends at work were delighted with the news and, never needing much of an excuse anyway, we all trotted off to the pub after work to celebrate.

I was collecting clothes for Marie and bought her a little something each week so she would have plenty when she was admitted to her new hospital. Four weeks before Christmas I received a letter from Marie's mum which almost made my heart stop.

'I went to Sandhill last week to see Marie and am going again this coming week so I will find out her shoe size for you. When I went out last week they fetched Marie back from school to the ward. You would never think she had any nice clothes, the dress she had on was terrible, far too small, and the cardigan was fit for the dustbin. I was quite shocked. The sister said they never put decent clothes on them for school, silly. No wonder you mentioned her clothes always looked new — she never gets the chance to wear them. I felt quite upset seeing her like that, Michelle. Makes you wonder doesn't it?

'They told me that she was going to Liverpool in January but they didn't know about you having her for Christmas. Haven't you mentioned it yet? Sister also said they had a very difficult time with Marie when you brought her back from Liverpool in August and she gets tantrums, throws her food down and was uncontrollable: if she didn't feed herself, her food was taken away. I thought she looked very thin. I don't think she's been eating, Michelle, 'cause they won't feed her. She is walking much better but has made no headway with speech.

'I hope she will improve when she gets to Liverpool, Michelle. You don't think the move will upset her do you? I know that sister does not like the idea of her going. She kept saying, "come out more often and get used to her". Anybody would think I didn't know how to look after her. Still, Michelle, Dr Prentice never queried her being transferred did he?'

'You should report that ward sister!' Sue said through gritted teeth when she handed me back the letter. 'Did they tell you Marie was upset when you phoned?'

'They never mentioned it,' I said in amazement. I could hardly speak.

'Maybe she missed you when she went back to the hospital after her holiday,' Sue said. 'Did she eat her food for you?'

'She was as good as gold,' I told her. 'And when you think about it, Sue, she's only questioning her surroundings isn't she?' Even though Marie's behaviour wasn't good, I thought it was quite natural.

'I didn't know Sister didn't want her to come,' Sue said, 'but then I suppose when you think of the reception we get when we go to the hospital it doesn't really surprise me.'

'True,' I said, because it didn't surprise me either, 'but it's a bit bloody late for Sister to be voicing her doubts. She should discuss it with Dr Prentice, not Marie's mum. She's not being very fair.' I wondered what was going to happen next. We stood up to go back on duty.

'Poor Marie,' Sue said. 'If you hadn't written to Marie's mum you'd never have known how upset she was, would you?' I shook my head and followed her out of the dining room.

'By the way, have you arranged when you're collecting Marie yet?' she asked me.

'Yes,' I told her eagerly. 'We finish on December 22nd and my train leaves for Taunton at midnight and arrives at 8 a.m. the following morning.'

'That's great!' Sue said sincerely.

'That is, of course, providing there are no disasters in between and everything goes all right.'

'Will you see Marie's mum when you go, because she's living back in Taunton isn't she?'

'She's collecting Marie with me.'

'It's funny the way she's suddenly taken an interest, isn't it?' Sue asked me cautiously.

'Not really,' I told her: 'it's nice that she's enjoying Marie for a little while. There's no pressure on her, you see, I've taken over the responsibility and she knows Marie will be leaving the area soon.'

~

It was the middle of December: no news was good news! I gathered sister had failed to change Marie's mum's mind. My training course had almost come to an end, so once again I was busy packing and taking some of my possessions home on my days off. On this particular evening when I went into the staff dining room for some supper I could tell they were up to something. My eye caught a big doll's pram in the corner. I walked across to admire it.

'Isn't that gorgeous,' I whispered. 'Whose is it?' They all burst out laughing.

'It's Marie's,' one of the girls said to my surprise. 'It was mine when I was a little girl and I thought with her coming home and all that you might like it for her.' I was overwhelmed at her kindness and returning to the pram I inspected it more closely. It was a huge old doll's pram and in the bottom it had slats across like a baby's pram. These could be lifted out to reveal a little compartment. When I turned back to the group they were all highly amused because for the first time since I'd met them I was speechless!

On my next day off I took Marie's clothes to my Aunty Terry's where we were going to stay before rushing back to Liverpool to buy my train ticket and the rest of my presents. At work the children had already gone home for the holiday and on the last day we were all sitting around trying to kill time as we waited for the evening to come. Some of the staff were trying to talk me into going to a party. They laughed when I said I'd love to but that I had to go and collect Marie from Taunton as though it was a big inconvenience! What a send off I had that evening when I was once again overwhelmed by the kindness and generosity of the staff as they handed me a watch and records, and they'd all bought Christmas presents for Marie, piling them into my bag. It was great to be alive...

~

At five minutes past midnight the train left Liverpool. It was almost empty and I sat back to enjoy the peacefulness as I looked out into the night. I was so thankful for the way things had turned out, but I no longer believed that destiny was responsible. There had been too many coincidences in my life; I wondered if there really was a God. I had been so lucky, and everything seemed to fall into place as though there was something inside me that guided me and told me what to do.

At 3 a.m. I sat shivering in the waiting room at Cardiff, waiting for my connection. No sounds came from anywhere as I sat alone, but I wasn't afraid. I was too pre-occupied with my own thoughts as I kept trying to glimpse into the future.

The following morning Marie's mum and I were finally heading up the hospital drive. I looked around for the last time and wondered how many times I'd trekked up and down it carrying Marie. She was ready when we went on the ward and ran towards me with her arms outstretched instinctively for me to pick her up.

'Hello!' I said. 'Look who's come to see you.' Sonia leaned over and kissed Marie tenderly. Marie obviously thought I was her mother and

Sonia accepted this without question though no doubt it hurt at times; I was always conscious that she shouldn't feel left out. Marie was doing peek-a-boo with her hands while we waited for Sister to fetch her clothes from the office.

She looked beautiful in her little light blue coat with the navy blue velvet collar. Sister came into the ward with her things. When I put Marie down she immediately reached for me to pick her up again. I thanked Sister as I took the case and we walked towards the door. She never looked my way. I was obviously taking Marie against her will.

~

Marie's mum stood on the platform waving to us as the train left Taunton, watching her little girl going to start a new life. She was wiping the tears from her face. We waved sadly to each other until she was out of sight.

'Come on, Marie,' I said. 'Let's take your coat off.' I rubbed her cold little hands trying to make her warm again before sitting her on my knee for the long journey ahead. The train was packed, since it was Christmas time and I tightened my arms protectively around her and kissed her cold cheek as she giggled happily and looked around the compartment at various people. Perhaps they felt her eyes upon them as they glanced up and quickly looked away feeling uncomfortable and not knowing how to react to her. I was singing inside: I felt so happy and there was nobody to tell. I wanted to say, 'Please don't look away. She's been so hard to get; it's such a special day. She's one of thousands who live alone, surrounded by people, in a place they call home....'

# 7
~

B Y THE TIME I carried Marie off the train at Crewe, night had fallen.
I pulled her little hat over her ears to protect her from the cold.
Walking along the platform I noticed someone waving to us: it
was my Auntie Terry! With Marie on one arm and the suitcase on the
other I rushed forward to meet her. Over the years Terry had heard so
much about Marie and now she was finally about to see her. I had no
doubts at all that Marie would steal her heart — a heart Terry gave so
freely to everybody she met. I put my case down and waved to the boys
who were heading towards us making great efforts not to bump into
people. Struggling with the case between them, they laughed shyly at
Marie when they noticed the blue and white Everton hat Terry had
knitted for her. Marie was grinding her teeth as she looked about her
anxiously.

Terry approached us. Standing there in the bitter cold she kissed
Marie and lifted her into her arms. Her eyes were full of tears as she
gave her an affectionate squeeze and I could tell that she was just too
choked to speak.

'Well?' I said expectantly, trying to cheer her up. 'What do you
think?'

'Suffering Jesus, Michelle, she's gorgeous,' was her characteristic
reply. 'I mean ... how could you not love a child like that?'

'She's been so good, Terry, she just sat on my knee all the way.'

'That's because she knows you care about her, Michelle. She knows
who's good to her and who isn't.'

Marie held onto our hands when we walked out of the station,
banging her feet on the ground, enjoying the sound of her new boots.
Our train didn't stop at Winsford where Terry lived so we'd had to get
off a stop earlier. And despite the fact that Terry had been working all
day, she'd gone home, collected the boys and got a taxi to meet us.

I don't know who was more bewildered — Marie or I — as we drove
through the snowy streets to where we were to spend our first
Christmas together. At long, long last, a dream had become reality.

~

I plonked myself wearily on the couch without a care in the world and sat back to enjoy the peace. Looking over at Marie's toys I'd left in the corner of Terry's living room, I noticed her stack had grown considerably higher. Terry filled the kettle in the kitchen before coming in to sit with me.

'Trish came up today,' she said, 'and she brought presents from everyone for Marie.' I took Marie's hand and strolled to the corner of the room. Stooping down with Marie at my side, my eye caught a beautifully-coloured box and inside was a fabulously multi-coloured wooden train with three carriages that held coloured shapes: that was from Maureen. On top of the box a big grey donkey smiled at me from the back of the pile: it was from Trish. I lifted it out for Marie to see.

'Look, Marie!' I said holding the donkey by its ears and pretending to take it for a walk. She followed me around the room giggling quietly. When I offered it to her she wouldn't hold it herself, she liked to be entertained rather than to entertain.

Terry couldn't take her eyes off Marie and looked on sadly as Marie struggled to put the food into her mouth at meal times. She loved the bones of her and thoroughly spoilt her. At bedtime, Marie cried. I brought her down, then took her back up but when I sat her on the bed she was looking at the wallpaper and screeching. We knew it was natural for Marie to be upset but she seemed so frightened and kept looking at the big pink flowers on Terry's bedroom wall.

'Don't you like them, love?' Terry asked her. 'They're bloody horrible, aren't they? I never did like this paper,' she said as she reached for the top of the strip and started to pull it off. My horrified protests at the inconvenience we were causing were soon silenced, as Terry said, 'Oh for Jesus' sake, it's only bleeding wallpaper!'

~

After a few days Marie was walking her donkey around the house, making a clicking noise like a horse as she wandered from room to room holding it by its ears.

When Christmas was over and it was almost time for Marie to go to her new hospital, I took her to my mum's house for a couple of days. Of course everybody was delighted to see her. I was surprised that Marie remembered them all from her previous visit last summer. She clapped her hands noisily as they greeted her with kisses.

~

It was snowing when we finally left for the hospital, and unfortunately we arrived there fifteen minutes late because of the effect the bad weather had on public transport. Trudging through the hospital gates in the snow I felt incredibly sad. I shouldn't have, I know. There were so many plusses to Marie's move. It was what I'd always wanted — I just wished I could have looked after her myself. Case in one hand and Marie on the other I headed towards Ward C.

'You're late,' Sister said when we entered the ward. She was down at the other end feeding one of the children.

'Sorry,' I said as I undid Marie's coat, 'the buses are running slow.' I tried to sound cheerful. 'Look at the children playing, Marie,' I remarked, thinking what a lousy welcome we had received so far. Nobody came over to us.

'Where shall I put Marie's case, Sister?' I took Marie's hand and walked down the ward towards her.

'On the bed, dear,' she replied. 'Just leave it there and a nurse will see to it.' I sat Marie on the chair by her bed and started taking off her boots which were wet with melted snow.

'Nurse will see to her, dear,' Sister shouted over to me. 'And don't visit for a few weeks, will you dear, because we want to give her time to settle in.'

'There must be something wrong with me,' I thought as I left the ward. 'This is supposed to be a wonderful day and I feel dreadful.' Joining the long queue outside the hospital gates, I waited for the bus home. I fought off the doom and gloom. If only I'd known then that within five months Marie would be living with me.

'You were quick,' Liz said when I walked into my mum's. 'I thought they'd have to kick you off the ward tonight.' I sat down and lit a cigarette.

'Gosh, Liz,' I said after a while, 'I hope Marie's going to be okay. They weren't very friendly but then maybe they were just busy.'

'What was it like?' Liz asked.

'I didn't really notice, Liz. I was too nervous, believe it or not. I was almost tempted to tell the ward sister how ignorant I thought she was but that wouldn't have helped Marie, would it?' I said, shrugging my shoulders.

~

Life of course went on, and with Marie being left to settle in her new environment I started my new job with my old friend Sue, as a housemother. Ironically I returned to the convent where I'd first worked when I left school. Sue and I were in charge of about thirty toddlers along with a young helper and a nun. I didn't see Sue very often because we were on opposite shifts and met maybe once a week. Our interview had been very promising, with great emphasis, on the nuns' part, of the need for decent childcare. There had been many changes for the better during my absence and I was looking forward to working as one of a team of childcare staff. However, the changes were superficial and both Sue and I were treated like maids. I was worn out from the time I went on duty to when I finished. The Sister in charge of our nursery was worn out too. She was very bad-tempered and shouted and slammed doors all the time. She had no feelings whatsoever for the children and they flinched whenever she went near them in case they got a slap. We were all nervous wrecks.

Going on duty at 7.30 in the morning I'd walk into a dining room to thirty silent little children, struggling to eat a breakfast that had been cooked the evening before. Relieved to see a friendly face they'd all start to speak to me at once.

'Silence!' Sister would holler at them. 'I am the mother of this house and always remember that!' The children would continue to eat their breakfast in a deafening silence. To make matters worse we were not allowed to have the lights on after 7.30 in the morning to avoid wasting electricity. It was pretty bleak. After breakfast we made the beds. Bedwetters had to stand at the end of theirs to teach them a lesson: another appalling cruelty...

~

I next saw Marie two weeks after she had been admitted to the hospital. She was sitting on the ward floor watching one of the children through its cot.

'Yoo-hoo!' I teased as I hid behind the door. She came shuffling over to investigate on her bottom. Laughing together we went back into the ward.

'We weren't given all the facts about her when she was admitted,' Sister stated. I wondered where I'd heard that remark before and remembered Sister Green saying it on my first visit to Taunton. She went on: 'We were told she was toilet trained and she isn't.'

'I think they were going to start Marie with it, Sister,' I began but she walked away before I could finish.

'Hiya Marie,' I whispered. I was glad that Sister hadn't moaned about anything else. 'Do you like it here?' I asked as I inspected her for little signs of I don't know what. I was hungry to know how she was doing but nobody seemed interested enough to talk to me.

'Had to move her cot next to the office window,' Sister said, breaking in on my thoughts as she stuck her head around the office door to me. 'She's noisy at night, isn't she?'

'She always has been, Sister,' I said in amusement but before I'd finished she'd disappeared again. I didn't know how to cope with their obvious hostility. Once again I was concerned that if they didn't like me they'd take it out on Marie. I wondered if their reason for this was because Marie was quite active and most of the children were very physically handicapped. There was another hospital up the road where I'd first met Dr Rogerson but after seeing them both I preferred the smaller of the two, thinking that with fewer patients the standard of care would be better. Maybe the staff felt that Marie was hard work but she was only there until a place was free in a residential school.

I decided to ignore them in the hope that they would eventually see I had Marie's interest at heart but I did find this rather difficult at times. I always did the right thing — phoning before I visited and not going at meal times because they were usually busy and they didn't like visitors on the ward then, although it could have been quite a help to them if their attitude had been different.

I visited Marie every week but on different days because I worked shifts and didn't always have the same days off. This didn't create any problems with the school because the teachers encouraged relatives to visit and take the children out at any time, but Matron had this policy about visiting whereby parents had to put their request in writing two days before taking the child out. My friend Sue was very supportive and whenever possible would swap a day off with me enabling me to plan well in advance. Sometimes I only just made it with my written request because I hadn't known until the last minute when I would be free. I was told the reason for such rigid rules was for the child to be passed fit to go out by the doctor.

The teachers made me very welcome and were always eager to speak to me as soon as I went into the school. One day when I went into the big hall all of the children were sitting on rubber mats and the teachers were singing to them. On seeing me Marie jumped up straight away so I sneaked to the back of the hall with her so as not to disturb the happy little group. Later, she was sitting on my knee while I was talking with one of the teaching staff. I got Marie an old doll out of the toy box and she immediately started to bang it on the back. The teacher frowned.

'I've noticed her doing that often,' she said: 'she's obviously been hit on the back some time in her previous home.'

'Oh no!' I said grinning, 'Look, she's getting the doll's wind up. She remembers this from living with babies for so long.' I gave Marie a hug. I was delighted about this and lots of other little things she was trying to do.

One day Marie and I were standing at the window in my mum's watching the snow fall.

'Look, Marie,' I said pointing out of the window. 'Look at the snow.' To my utter amazement she suddenly said 'Look.' I thought I hadn't heard her correctly when she repeated it. It was a week before her eighth birthday.

Each time I took her out for the day she would hold my hand and off we'd run through the hospital gates towards the bus stop. I always told Marie when she reached the kerbs so her feet wouldn't get all twisted up and she'd walk off them properly.

'Jump,' I said to her as she laughed and squealed excitedly. She repeated that word too! Whenever I took her home I always put on the records because we both loved music.

'Listen, Marie,' I'd say as her little face lit up and she started to clap her hands: it wasn't long before she was saying, 'Nisten.'

The only explanation I could give for her sudden speech was the attention she got from us all. We talked to her as though she was normal even though she hardly ever responded. For some strange reason she started calling me 'Mam.' Sometimes when I went onto the ward one of the nurses might shout 'Here's your mam, Marie,' but it felt very strange and moving to hear her address me. Another new word was, 'Gor gone,' but only when people hid from her. She never requested anything or looked for toys that suddenly disappeared. Whenever we stopped singing she would say 'Again.' She seemed to pick up words when she was very stimulated.

She loved going to visit Terry on the train. My kind-hearted aunt had become a new and very welcome dimension in Marie's life. A bond had developed between them which lasted for the next twenty years.

Marie got on surprisingly well with Sara, Maureen's little girl whom she'd met the previous year. Because of Marie's placid nature and Sara being a bossy three-year-old they seemed to complement each other. Marie never interfered in Sara's play and was quite happy to watch. Sara on the other hand tended to mother Marie, finding her toys to play with and wiping her mouth with a tissue when she dribbled. We still had the problem of hair pulling but more often than not Marie couldn't help herself and although we could stop it we couldn't always prevent it. Sometimes Marie pulled Sara's hair if she was angry but most often she did it just for effect. I could tell from the way she watched Sara's mouth as if fascinated, just as you'd push a button on a doll and it cried, Marie pulled Sara's hair and she screamed.

If it was a warm afternoon I would sometimes take them both to the park. Sara would always cry to sit in her pram if Marie was in it and I had to try to squeeze them both in.

'Move your feet over,' I would say as I lifted Sara up into the pram but Marie didn't really understand and I usually ended up doing for or with her, what I had requested her to do herself.

'Here's some bread for the ducks,' Maureen would say as she placed it in Marie's lap. 'You'd better keep hold of it, hadn't you, Sara, or Marie will eat it before we get there.' Off we'd go. The two girls in similar hats that Terry had knitted for them — Sara's was red and white for Liverpool and Marie's was blue and white for Everton. Reaching the park gates I'd lift them out of the pram. Marie toddled off after Sara who ran like the clappers towards the lake, and on reaching it she excitedly fed the ducks as they quacked around her ankles, while Marie fed herself.

Unfortunately Marie had a habit of sitting down anywhere when she got tired. She just plonked on the ground with her legs splayed out; it didn't matter where — dog muck, bird muck, she never noticed.

'Come on Marie, up off the floor,' I would say and usually had to stand her up, telling her how good she was as though she'd done it herself. She'd spent most of her life indoors — she had a lot to learn.

Once on our way back from Stanley Park Marie had lost one of her shoes. I didn't notice until we'd reached the gates, and gazing back across the field I didn't know where to start looking. Fortunately I found it by the lake under a bench and picked it up breathing a sigh of relief. I had only bought them the previous week and I didn't have the money to buy her any more. I was wondering how to tell the ward sister and dreaded her reaction. I didn't realise until this incident how uncomfortable I felt with the ward staff, how I was always careful not to upset them. Sometimes I'd go to collect Marie and they would say she couldn't go out because of illness on the ward. Nobody had bothered to telephone me, they just waited until I arrived. Marie's hair was growing onto her shoulders and I used to do her hair in little pig tails. One day when I went to collect her she came running up to me with her hair cropped really short. I went to Sister's office. She was indifferent to me as ever when I said, 'Who cut Marie's hair?'

'Staff Nurse took Marie to town on her day off,' she said casually, 'and she took her into the hairdresser's.' What could I say? Staff Nurse wanted Marie's hair cut so she'd had it done. I wondered if other parents were treated like this and realised why I never saw any on the ward. I don't think they had anything against me personally. I think they just couldn't be bothered with visitors, mistaking any interest shown in the ward routines as interference. I was beginning to understand what a skilled job nursing really was, how it wasn't enough to care about the children — it involved other people too. I wondered how many parents didn't visit because they didn't feel welcome, how many nurses thought they didn't visit because they didn't care: the doctors no doubt think that parents have lost interest and the parents (feeling full of guilt) won't approach the doctors to talk things over because they think the ward staff are quite justified in their attitude. And so we all misunderstand each other. I had also noticed in the last few places I'd worked how there always seemed to be friction between the different departments — between education, childcare and nursing staff. They never seemed to work together, but rather as if one always resented the other. One day the teachers wanted to take the children out in the snow but when Sister was asked she refused permission. So what did the teachers do? They got a large plastic sheet and took some snow in to the children! The teachers were eager to stimulate the children and let them experience as much as possible: the ward staff were concerned that illness would sweep through the wards because of it. Both departments had their reasons and I could see both their points, but sometimes the child in care is the child in the middle.

Sometimes I felt the nursing staff did their utmost to cold shoulder me. Some days I felt really miserable leaving the ward. What probably annoyed them most about me was my outward tolerance to their ignorant behaviour. I was at their mercy; they pulled my strings. I couldn't afford to fall out with them. On the other hand I was no fool. They knew I saw right through them and wouldn't give them the satisfaction of complaining about me. On Marie's birthday for example, Maureen and I went to collect her at 11.30 as arranged so she could have a little party at home. Arriving on the ward we were casually told there was illness on the ward and Marie couldn't go out. I'd left all her presents and cards at home. We stayed for a little while until the trolley was brought in for lunch, and then we left. Maureen was disgusted: 'They should be ashamed of themselves,' she said when we got outside. Poor Marie had followed us to the door and we could hear her crying at the other side of it.

'I shan't leave her there,' I told Maureen firmly. 'I shall find somewhere to live and look after her myself.'

~

Years later when I met up with some of those nurses they showed great surprise that I had continued to care for Marie, saying that because I had been so young and she was so handicapped they felt I would have lost interest in her not long after she'd been transferred to Liverpool. It takes all sorts...

Things were growing increasingly difficult at work. Always a sufferer from tonsillitis, I was struck with it almost every other week. I couldn't go off sick because there was no staff cover. Sue had been off sick for quite a while with laryngitis and hadn't been replaced, making things pretty grim. The social worker who'd been in charge of our residential course rang to see how we were getting on in our new 'careers.' She was outraged when we told her the conditions under which we worked, and she complained to the Mother Superior at the convent. A week later Sister was moved, and replaced by a truly amazing woman. Working in the midlands for the past eighteen years with teenagers, she had only been informed the day before she came to us that she was being moved. She was understandably very hurt and did not know how she was going to cope with a bunch of tiny children. We laughed at the absurdity of it all. She was great fun to be with. Even the children started to relax and became noisy and mischievous! However she didn't stay long and was sent to a new children's unit at the convent in Wales. Not long after she left, I had a lovely letter from her telling me she had met some staff and children from the Bristol convent who'd remembered me. She also invited me to go to Wales to run the new unit with her. I was naturally very flattered, but at the time changes were taking place in my life too so I had to decline her offer.

I'd recently returned from a week's holiday in Lincolnshire where my sister Cathy had an old schoolhouse. She lived in London for most of the time while she studied at the Royal College of Art and returned home for long weekends and holidays. We spent a wonderful week together. Going for long walks and then resting when I wanted, I was soon able to unwind, and spent many nights sitting around the log fire in the schoolhouse talking with Cathy and her husband. The night before I left I was filling Cathy in about Marie's hospital, how she was waiting to go to residential school and my plans for the future. I had known months ago that I would never leave Marie in any hospital. At the end of the day they were all institutions run by institutionalised people. I was looking for a place to rent in Liverpool so I could bring her home to live with me. Cathy and Raynor listened with great interest and when I'd finished Cathy said: 'Listen! why don't you bring Marie here to live instead of living in Liverpool with her?'

I couldn't believe my ears. 'You mean for me to live here with her?' I asked incredulously. She nodded. I looked at the fire and watched the flames dancing around the logs.

'But wouldn't you mind?' I asked them quietly.

'Of course not,' Cathy's husband said. 'In fact it will be nice to have someone living here while we're in London. Just so long as you remember that the roof leaks and we have no bath or inside toilet, but ahh!' he said grandly, 'we do have a tin bath and one can get water from a tap in the back shed.'

'Well,' I said, convinced, 'what more could one have asked for?'

~

Marie left the hospital a month later on June 2nd, 1972. Just before she left her assessment by the Clinical Educational Psychologist showed: *Mental age*, 20 months: *Hearing and speech*, 17 months: *Locomotive*, 21 months: *Hand/eye co-ordination*, 20 months: *Performance*, 21 months.

She was $8^1/4$ years old.

# 8
~

J UST BEFORE I left the convent my mother rang me one evening and
said a reporter had been making enquiries about me, for a Sunday
newspaper article and was interested in writing about my interest
in Marie. It turned out that Cathy's husband had written to them
after seeing Marie's photograph being used in one of their newspapers
to raise money for handicapped children. He had explained about our
relationship and my hopes for Marie and asked if they could help in
any way. My feelings about this were mixed, the strongest one being
that I didn't want to do it. Keeping an open mind I arranged to meet
the journalist one evening after work. He made me an offer I couldn't
refuse. He told me that if I would do an article for them they would
pay me £300. Being my usual impulsive self I didn't really think about
the article, as soon as he mentioned the money all I thought was that I
could bring Marie out of hospital and live off the money for a while
until I got sorted out. He asked me some rather silly questions, like
whether I was looking after this child to avoid having relationships
with men. I'd never heard anything so absurd in all my life! I didn't
think it was any of his business, so I had no intention of telling him that
I had a boyfriend. He could think whatever his tiny little mind let him.
Then he said: 'I can understand somebody old looking after her, but
not someone young like you. And why this particular child?' I counted
to ten before answering.

'But that's a bit like asking why your wife married you when you
don't appeal to me, isn't it?' I asked him, thinking how much can be
learned about people from the questions they ask. He laughed, and for
every question he asked me I fired three back.

I don't know why people expected me to be some kind of mouse or
social misfit because I took an interest in Marie, as though children like
her could only be used to fill empty gaps in people's lives. I didn't think
I was giving up my life to look after her, as some people suggested. I
didn't think she was a bind. I loved her company and cared very much
about her. I hoped I could give her a better life than she'd had so far
because she was entitled to it. The interviewer wasn't convinced at first
— typical journalist, never quite trusting anybody. However, later on

we became great friends and looked back in amusement at our first meeting.

By now I was walking on air! My family and friends were very supportive and there were only a few people who were doubtful. In a way, even they were quite helpful, because I was able to appreciate difficulties that might arise in the future. I wasn't a bit worried. I always felt that things would work out all right. People's main concern seemed to be: 'What will happen to Marie when she gets older?' I suppose I appeared cocky and arrogant, but on reflection I couldn't have done it if I'd been any other way. I wasn't playing games with her. I was the best offer she'd had — the only offer, in fact. I wasn't offering a bed of roses. I was far from domesticated, hated cooking, cleaning and any other household chores. In short I was saying: 'if you have nowhere else to live then you come and live with me. I'll look after you. Maybe others could do better but I promise you I will do the best I can', and how proud I feel to have been given the chance.

~

Cathy was at the schoolhouse when I arrived with Marie, busily making beds and preparing food. I changed Marie's nappy: she had her lunch and toddled off outside into the schoolyard dragging her doll after her by the hair. Up and down, up and down she walked listening intently to the noise her shoes made. We watched her through the kitchen window although she wasn't aware of this and would frequently walk back into the house to check that we were still there.

'The reporter is coming to do the article next week,' I told Cathy as I screwed up my face with dread.

'Oh it won't be all that bad,' she laughed. 'Besides, nobody knows you here.'

'That's true,' I told her, 'but I hope it won't be too sentimental, you know, "Poor lonely woman".' I giggled.

'They won't say that,' she said, laughing again.

'I hope not,' I told her, 'because there are many other children like Marie who would benefit from living at home given the opportunity. So much depends upon how the article is presented, because, who knows, it may encourage other people to consider offering a home and love to a handicapped child.'

~

Marie was in her element. Two of Cathy's friends came to stay so there were five adults to give her attention and within a few days she had us all peeling grapes, or nearly. That first evening I put her to bed but

70

after five minutes she was still screaming, so I told Cathy I would go to bed because Marie did not like being on her own. Her look said I was a dope! Her mouth said: 'All right, but you can't be doing this every night. You're going to need a break from her.'

'Oh well...' I mumbled, 'just tonight.' As soon as I went into the bedroom Marie stopped screeching and laughed happily. She snuggled under the covers when I got into my bed and soon fell fast asleep. The following evening when Marie went to bed she screeched loudly again but fortunately Cathy wasn't around to question my hasty exit. This makes things easier, I told myself as I ran up the stairs to join Marie. When I reached the top it was only to see Cathy sitting outside Marie's bedroom door.

'What are you doing?' I whispered, although there was no need to whisper for Marie was making so much noise you wouldn't have heard a bomb going off. 'I'm waiting for you,' Cathy said. She looked like a big rag doll sitting on the floor with her long dark curly hair falling about her shoulders. 'Just leave her to cry for a while, she'll soon get tired.'

I was shocked. 'Oh no! I can't do that. She's upset, and what if she should hurt herself?'

'Just try it,' Cathy repeated.

I reluctantly agreed and joined Cathy on the floor, cringing each time Marie smacked her own face, longing to pick her up but realising I would have to persevere as it was impractical to go to bed with her every night. After what seemed like hours (ten minutes!) the screaming began to fade and the silence somehow seemed louder. 'Is she all right?' I thought. 'What if she's knocked herself out,' but she broke my thoughts with another scream. The screams were less urgent now, the panic had disappeared from them and they were like a last wary attempt. When Marie was quiet we both crept downstairs and went out into the garden. I waited until Cathy was distracted (coward that I was) before I crept back up the stairs again. I was worried in case Marie had knocked herself unconscious. I quietly turned the handle and very slowly opened the door and immediately the little devil came out from under the covers and started to scream again. 'Oh no,' I thought as she dived across the bed to be picked up. She had been asleep and in my anxiety I had woken her. 'I'll have to be firm,' I kept telling myself as I gently put Marie back into bed, thinking how hard it must sometimes be for parents of handicapped children.

'Go to sleep, there's a good girl,' I whispered. She started to scream again as I closed the door behind me. Five minutes later there was silence and so every night after that Marie went to bed on her own until eventually she was asleep under the blankets before I reached the bottom stairs. (Thanks, Cathy!)

~

Cathy and her husband had returned to London after the weekend so we were now on our own. I was grateful that they had been there when we'd first arrived, otherwise there was no telling how our nights might have ended up!

The reporter arrived and we managed to get through the interview. We spent another day with the photographer before going to the TV studios in Bristol to do a commercial for the newspaper feature. I found it a very gruelling experience and hated every minute of it, as I'm sure the cameramen did as they wiped the sweat off their foreheads when it was all finished. I realise now I should have put my own feelings aside and co-operated a bit more but I felt the emphasis was on me rather than on Marie and I wasn't very happy about it.

The day before our article appeared in the newspaper Marie and I watched the TV commercial with the elderly couple next door. I laughed when I saw it — had I blinked I'd have missed it, and it had taken the whole morning to do. The scene was of Marie and myself walking alongside a waterfall and I had to pick her up after I counted ten and swing her around. Poor Marie screamed. The location was all wrong — it was noisy and she was terrified as they kept shouting 'cut' and I tried not to swear at them.

It wasn't long before Cathy and her husband were back at the schoolhouse for the summer. On the day the article appeared Raynor had gone to London for the day.

'Did you enjoy yourself?' I asked him on his return. He looked at me wide eyed.

'I just couldn't get away from you,' he laughed. 'Everywhere I went you were watching me.'

'What do you mean?'

'There are posters of you on all the newspaper placards, pictures of you and Marie. They're even on the boards outside the shops.'

'What does it say on the poster?' I asked in amazement.

'This year's most moving love story,' he said tentatively looking across at Cathy. I felt so embarrassed.

'Oh no: it's too mushy!' I told him. I left the house and went across the fields for a walk.

~

After a few days I started to realise that the article hadn't been on children in care: it had been about my relationship with Marie. I understood why it had to be a bit mushy and although I had quite a few letters from people who read the newspaper, I knew it would eventually die down. I did one more article for *Woman's Own* but I refused any more offers after that. I just wanted to be left alone to look after Marie.

I loved being a mum. I found that because of her institutional life Marie would waken at the crack of dawn and climb across the bed to cuddle up with me. I was awake instantly, never quite used to our situation and always marvelling at the fact that Marie was now home with me. Off we would go downstairs. Marie was always chuckling. I suppose she couldn't believe the attention she was getting now. I talked to her all the time as though she understood everything I was saying. She watched every move I made. Her eyes would follow me from the cooker to the cupboard, watching what I put where. She appeared to be intrigued by everything that was happening around her. It was as though she was seeing everything for the first time, and indeed she was in many instances. She still had her tantrums but they weren't as frequent and if she started her screeching I always sat her on a chair to prevent her from banging her head on the floor. She would then probably try pulling her hair out or smacking her face, screeching as loudly as she could. She no longer wore nappies around the house and on most occasions we were successful with the pot. This surprised me as it seemed to happen so quickly, making me wonder why it had not been achieved sooner. I always knew Marie would be much happier at home but I never thought she would improve so much. Her speech was progressing and she was able to say simple words in order to make her needs understood. 'No,' was her favourite. She talked to her doll most of the time, pretending to feed it or change its nappy. She would always chatter after meals and imitate conversations in her own way. She was still fascinated with the mirrors, and was starting to be a little more adventurous in her play. She would sit trying to thread laces or simply look at the reflection of a picture in a book. Without the mirror she was unable to stimulate this kind of play and would wait for me to amuse her instead. However there were times when I had to put the mirror away. When people came into the room, instead of Marie turning round to look at them as they greeted her she would search for that person's reflection in the mirror and once discovered she would be satisfied and continue her play. She could be quite anti-social.

After being at home for six weeks the scab on her forehead had started to clear up because she wasn't allowed to bang her head on the floor. I thought how wonderful life was as I brushed her hair back from her forehead and she looked at her reflection in the mirror. One evening I sat on our little kitchen step watching her sitting in the old tin bath, and I thought how lucky I was to have her at home. She washed her doll's face meticulously with soap before ducking it into the water. She would then break into peals of laughter as she brought her doll slowly to the surface shouting 'BOO!' She seemed much more alert and her face was so full of expression.

We gradually established a daily routine. I had found our biggest problem since Marie came home was the hair pulling which she usually did for attention. For example, if my friends came with their children Marie would reach out quite unexpectedly and pull someone's hair. I found this quite difficult to handle and in other people's company spent most of my time watching over Marie or telling her off, which must have been quite boring for people. After a while I realised that even if I told her off she was still getting attention so I decided that the next time she did this I would put her in another room to see if it made any difference. I was careful to leave the door open because of her fear of being enclosed. It didn't work at first but when she started to realise she got more attention when she didn't pull hair than when she did, her behaviour improved. There were times when she was so angry she couldn't help doing it and would pull her hand away quickly, regretting her impulsive action. At times like this I pretended not to notice because she really hadn't been able to help herself. Sometimes she'd put her hand out towards someone and suddenly stop, then we all clapped and cheered and told her how good she was. She'd laugh and clap her hands with pleasure.

Two weeks before the summer holidays Marie started her new day school. I felt it was a nice time for her to start because of the six weeks' holiday, and thought it would give her a little taste of what was to come. I would have preferred for her to have gone part time, and knew they would have problems with her. The school was ten miles away and Marie shared transport with three other children who were picked up at various points along the way. I felt that Marie was very confused with this new routine because it was the first time in her life she'd gone to school away from where she lived. However the headmaster wanted her to go full time: I thought it was too long a day to be away from home at first. I did ask whether I could call in and see Marie at some time during the day, or go in with her for odd days. I thought we needed to work very closely together with her. But no; he wanted to do things his way without any help from me. During Marie's first few days when I rang to see how she was, the headmaster told me she'd been screeching at lunch time and they'd had to feed her.

'Can't you just leave her?' I asked him, 'because she eats all right at home and when she sees you won't feed her she'll probably attempt to feed herself.' I must have touched a raw nerve!

'It's all right for you,' he told me angrily. 'What you've done is given her an ideal situation, but it's an unnatural one and you've just made it difficult for everyone else.'

I thought that if we shared our experiences in looking after Marie then we wouldn't have these problems but if he was going to shut me out then they were inevitable because she was unable to communicate for herself. I didn't pay too much attention to his criticism. If I took everything people said to me to heart, I'd have given up my interest in Marie years ago. I was glad when the school holidays arrived.

Life in the schoolhouse was pleasant but I didn't know if we could survive the winters there. It was obviously going to be very cold and damp. I put my name down for a council house. I'd talked it over with Cathy and Raynor and they both agreed it was a good idea. Arriving home I went to tell Cathy but she was out with Marie. Looking out of the schoolroom windows across the field I could see Marie bobbing up and down on Cathy's shoulders on their way home. I went out to meet them. The cows were out (much to Marie's delight). We just had to watch she didn't sit in a cow pat. It was mid-afternoon and very hot so we sat under a tree in the shade. Marie decided to roll over; she was showing off in front of the cows so I jumped up and ran on ahead to make sure the path was clear. She was tossing over non stop, flashing her bright pink knickers every time her bottom went into the air until she got tired. She relished being out in the open, going for walks or sometimes pushing her doll's pram around the field. I longed for a home of our own with some land where she could play freely but I knew that short of winning the pools this was an impossible dream.

~

I was beginning to realise a little of what it was like being the mother of a handicapped child, although I didn't feel the sorrow or the guilt that some parents feel about their children. Most people I met thought I was Marie's mother: their reactions were mixed. Some of them offered me unwanted advice, usually about Marie's future. One day we'd been sitting in the park when a lady joined us on the bench. Before I knew it the lady was telling me that I should let Marie go, that she didn't belong in the community and that I should consider her needs and not my own.

That evening when we were almost home I lifted Marie over the stile into the field. She usually took off then and made her way to the house as I walked behind her. She had her wellington boots on and I watched her little spastic legs as she tried to run across the field squealing with delight. I thanked God that I looked after her and that she wasn't 'hidden away' because it was obvious to me that she just loved the air that she breathed.

I was building up a nice circle of friends and lots of people recognised us anyway because of the newspaper article. Even Charlie the bus driver beeped his horn when he passed us. Tuesday was our day into town. A bit of shopping, a nice cup of tea in the café and then the bus back home. Marie really enjoyed this experience but when we arrived at the bus station she screeched like mad if we had to wait for the bus. Once it arrived she did the same thing as the queue slowly moved forward. More often than not the well-meaning people would stand back to let her on first.

'You little monkey,' I used to whisper to her but she would just laugh as she climbed the steps, like royalty going on ahead of everyone. After weeks of doing this I realised I wasn't doing Marie much good so I sat her in the bus shelter with me and told her to stop shouting or I wouldn't take her onto the bus. I knew it was hard for her but she had to learn to be a little more civil as it would be easier for her in the long run. It was difficult for her because she had always reacted to situations in this way, so that it was now second nature. It took weeks, but eventually instead of screeching in the queue she would stamp her foot and stick her neck out in anger and impatience — but she was clever enough to know if she started screeching she would not be allowed on the bus.

Just before winter set in I was offered a job by the Social Services looking after two mentally handicapped adults. The job was only temporary until a more mature person was found, but it suited me to work there through the cold winter and it was also nearer the school. Trish was living in the schoolhouse with us so Marie and I stayed in between the two houses. She had been at the same school for about nine months but I did find the Headmaster's attitude somewhat peculiar. One day a letter came home from the school. It was dated the previous day, and went like this:

'Marie was sick (vomiting) at school today. I think from the smell of her clothing you had a cleaning up period before she left home this morning.'

I wondered if he talked to all the parents like this. I was very angry that he should think I would wipe vomit off Marie's clothes and send her to school. She only had to look tired and I kept her at home. I'd had enough of him. The next day I went to the Education Department and asked to see the director. The good man saw me straight away and listened to what I had to say. Firstly, I told him I was concerned that the Headmaster's personal feelings about me being allowed to look after Marie were interfering with her welfare at school. Secondly, I asked him what was the point in feeding Marie at school when she could feed herself at home and finally, what was the point of her going to school at all if the school and I didn't work on her problems between us. He was very nice and said he could see my point and would have a word with the Headmaster. Shortly after this the Headmaster sent for me. He was very angry.

'You should have approached me first,' he said to my astonishment. I thought of all the times I'd asked if I could go into the school.

'Just you remember this,' he said, pointing his finger at me, 'the only thing anyone can sack me for is sexual assault or physical abuse.' After he'd had his little say he told me I could go into the school for two afternoons a week to see what they were doing in the classroom with Marie. I don't know why he was so surprised at the steps I had taken, since it's a parent's right if he or she isn't happy with the child's school, but I don't know why on earth he thought I was trying to get him sacked.

Looking back today my one big regret is that I ever sent Marie to a special school. I thought it was compulsory for her to attend and it wasn't. It was my experience that these schools are not only a waste of time and money, but that they are counter-productive in that they segregate and isolate the handicapped child from the rest of the community.

When I went into the school the children had just eaten their lunches and were playing in the hall with no adult supervision. There was a window at the end of the hall which looked into the staff room enabling the staff to observe the children to a certain point, but they couldn't see around corners and were unable to see a little boy of about twelve giving a boy of about six a long, lingering kiss as he sat on his knee. There were chairs stacked too high for safety around the walls and none of the children had anything to do. When I asked the Headmaster why the children were left alone he told me that sometimes children feel too inhibited when the staff are around all the time. I was quite concerned about the lack of supervision. I could well see how Marie spent her lunch hours screeching if there were no adults in sight. And there was I getting the blame for everything because of the unstable life I was providing!

# 9
~

WE MANAGED to survive quite happily over the next few years. I have many happy memories and many sad ones. How many of us would trade in our past for a new one? Would we obliterate those painful moments and disastrous mistakes, stop at the crossroad and take a long look before we decided which path to take? My marriage was one of them. It lasted two years and broke up when Marie was twelve. I am very reluctant to write about my first husband because he loved Marie so much, but in the end I think she took up so much of my time that it killed our relationship.

We had been honest with each other from the start. He told me that although he loved Marie and would give her most of his attention he would never give all of himself. I asked him never to make me choose between them, because had I chosen him, I could not build happiness on someone else's misery. So when the going got tough... Yet we had endured so much together.

Marie had been jealous of my husband at first and pinched or pulled his hair whenever he sat near her, but it wasn't long before she was holding his hand on a Saturday morning and going down to the snooker hall with him. She used to sit on a chair with a packet of crisps and watch him playing.

'Hiya!' she'd shout when she arrived back home and sometimes she'd have a bunch of daffodils in her hand that he'd bought for me. Sometimes when he was going fishing he'd chase me around the house with a bowl of maggots and she'd run after him screaming with laughter at the fun of it all.

The only serious problem we had with her was at meal times when she suddenly started throwing her food. She was so bad we dreaded sitting down to a meal with her because she just refused to eat. I was baffled by this and thought that Marie must be unhappy at home, especially when I rang the school and they weren't having any problems. She had changed schools by this time and I had a very good relationship with the staff. But Marie would no sooner be sat down at the table when she would chuck her plate anywhere, at the wall, on the floor, up at the ceiling and as much as we tried to ignore it I would end up smacking her and sending her out of the room. If we didn't react to her she would pick up handfuls of food and wipe them all over our arms or just squash them in her fingers. I was at my wits' end with her. After weeks of this we decided smacking was no good, especially when she continued to be naughty, so we decided to ignore her completely. This was very difficult because I didn't even coax her with her food. I felt there had been too much importance attached to it and so we let her sling it or do whatever she wanted with it, but she wasn't allowed to leave the table and had to sit through the meal with us. I let her make whatever mess she wanted and when the meal was over and I started to clear the table I would say quite casually: 'Come on Marie, clear up your mess.' I handed her a little bin. My eyes stung as I'd watch her discreetly, bending down tutting to herself in disgust at the mess she'd made. Bored at being unable to manipulate us, she eventually decided it was more fun to sit at the table and eat with us. It was only a year later that I learned she was being fed at school. If the teachers didn't feed her she would push her food onto the floor and scream, creating such a disturbance in the dining room. Naturally Marie had been confused when she had come home from school and tried the same thing with us and we'd reacted in a completely different way.

I found most professional people in the field of mental handicap very patronising. They always made me aware of what I couldn't give Marie rather than what I had been able to give her. My age meant the odds were stacked against me. For example I didn't think it mattered where Marie was, so much as who was looking after her and how she was managed in terms of acceptable behaviour. I thought she was a very happy, healthy little girl and her behaviour problems were very superficial. However if she was in a group situation when she wanted attention immediately, her old habits would quickly surface, and of course I got the blame.

~

It was during this time I met someone who was to have a great influence on my life. Marie had started having epileptic fits and my GP recommended that I see a specialist with her. Although I agreed to this I was a little dubious about the meeting. I was unsure about her reaction to my bringing Marie out of hospital and expected to walk into a lecture on how selfish I had been. However when I did meet the specialist I was pleasantly surprised and realised that my fears had been unfounded. I liked her immediately. The first jolt for me was when she asked if it was all right to speak in front of Marie. How wonderful it was to meet someone who was so sensitive to Marie's feelings that she didn't claim to know all about her at a glance. It was so refreshing for me. Strangely enough, in all the years I've had Marie she was the only 'professional' person ever to ask me that question. Generally people just go ahead and talk about her and sometimes it's been just as well Marie has not understood. Dr Kidd became my anchor. She gave Marie some blocks to play with which she'd borrowed from her little girl. We watched Marie as she looked at them from different angles. She shook them as she tried to discover whether they made any noises. We talked of Marie's progress since she had come to live with me and I told Dr Kidd that she still pulled hair sometimes at school. She said it was probably Marie's way of objecting to having to go along with a group for most of the day. As we drove home in the ambulance I was feeling secretly relieved I'd met this marvellous woman: it helped enormously to have someone looking over my shoulder. She also made me feel very 'normal' and applauded the steps I'd taken in bringing Marie out of hospital.

I soon discovered there was a local playgroup for mentally handi-capped children, of which I took full advantage during holidays. It enabled Marie to keep in touch with other children, often popping in for a cup of coffee. It was here that I got to know some of the mums and we'd have a little natter as we sat watching the children play. There was a little boy called Julian and as soon as Marie saw him she would smile with pleasure and follow him around. She would sometimes take his hand and walk around the garden with him. They were a strange little pair — hardly any communication between them but they always seemed to be near each other. One day when I was talking to Julian's mum I suddenly had an idea.

'Would you let Julian come up to our house for the afternoon?' I asked her. She looked at me and smiled: 'You must be mad,' she said: 'I can't even cope with one of them and you want them both together!'

I laughed at her honesty. 'But it's different for you,' I told her, hoping she wasn't offended: 'I think maybe if I had three other children I probably wouldn't be able to cope either, but I only have Marie so it's easier for me. We'd be doing each other a favour.'

Unconvinced, she sat there grinning at me: 'How can I be doing you a favour by letting you have Julian for the afternoon?'

'Because Marie gets a bit lonely when she's off school and it keeps her in touch with other children. Just let's try it,' I said, 'and we'll see how it goes.'

We did try it and it worked out very well. After a while Julian came to us for odd weekends during school holidays which we all thor-oughly enjoyed. Julian walked around the house for most of the day, tapping the doors and laughing as if it was tremendous fun. Marie usually helped me because she was a bit more alert than Julian. She would do simple things like fetching a nappy for me or attempting to fold his clothes when we undressed him.

Whenever Julian came for a weekend his parents always insisted on paying me. I found this very difficult to handle at first. However, once I put my own feelings aside I could see that by refusing their money I was making them feel obliged to me and once I accepted his keep his parents felt easier about approaching me. Once this was seen to work I started to have other children to stay. It was great fun.

~

After my marriage broke up I spent time in Liverpool. I worked at a hospital once again, but this time in the Physio department as an aide. I enjoyed my work, especially in the mornings when we took the children into the hydrotherapy pool. They yelled and shouted play-fully, stimulated by the water, enjoying the freedom their swimming aids provided for their normally immobile bodies. In the afternoons we collected the children from the wards and brought them to the physiotherapy unit where we did the appropriate exercises with them.

My job worked out very well, particularly during Marie's school holidays. I used to take her to work with me each morning where she'd either stay in the unit with me or go and play on the wards. I had no pangs about this: had Marie not approved of this arrangement she'd have been the first to let everybody know. She liked watching the nurses feed and change the more severely handicapped children, following them around the ward for most of the day. When I went to fetch her after work in the afternoons she'd come running over to me with her monkey dangling by its foot. Sometimes she'd greet me with: 'Oh mam, nauzy girl!' I would pretend to be cross. She was so funny and would tut in disgust imitating the nurse. Other times she'd be sitting on the chair in Sister's office swinging her legs and would rush out to meet me saying: 'Bye now!' and off we'd go hand in hand for the bus home.

I had a good social life, since my family were so near. Liz, John or Peter often collected Marie and took her home for tea. They were all grown up by this time and could take her off on their own. Marie loved them all: as far as she was aware they were her family. We were still regular visitors to my Aunt Terry's too. Spending so much time at Terry's over the years I knew most of her friends and neighbours. It was at Terry's house that I met John: he used to deliver meat in those days and would stay for a cup of tea and a natter. One thing we both had in common was that we adored children. And then something happened which kind of threw us together.

I was working in the hospital where Marie had lived when she'd first come to Liverpool. Our physiotherapist was based in the other hospital along the road and would come over to see us whenever she could. Most of the time however, myself and the other two helpers, Jean and Sandra, were left on our own, once we had been shown the individual exercises for each of the children. We usually had four children twice a day, staying for about an hour each period, and because they were such a small group they more or less had a one-to-one relationship. When we had done the exercises with them we gave them orange juice and biscuits. They seemed to respond more to the rustle of the packet than they did to any of our treatments, smiling from ear to ear as they jerked their legs in excitement. It was the highlight of their day.

In my group there was a little girl called Sophie: she was ten years old. Sophie was blind as well as mentally retarded and was unable to walk unless she held on to somebody's hand. She looked younger than her age with her curly fair hair and big blue eyes. The nurses were all fond of Sophie and they all agreed that she was too bright to be on that ward and needed to be with more active and talkative children. They were also more aware than anybody that Sister's priority for cleanliness left them hardly any time to play with the children, but they never complained. If ever they came over to the unit they would prolong their stay as they played with the children and made the most of their freedom. We took advantage of this and picked their brains as we tried to find out more about their likes and dislikes. There was Richard who, apart from being severely mentally handicapped, had the most awful asthma attacks. He would sit on the floor wheezing and deriving great comfort from the towelling bib he took everywhere with him. Then there was Rachel in her wheelchair, who flinched every time a man went near her because of the beatings her father gave her when she was younger. We nicknamed her giggler because that was all she did for most of the time, as she sat beside Audrey who giggled too in between her frequent *petit mal* fits.

The first time Sophie came into our unit she was accompanied by one of the nurses who hardly took her eyes off the child while she sat amongst the other children. I was soon to learn why when Sophie reached out and grabbed one of the children by the hair. The nurse jumped up and quickly came to the rescue telling Sophie how naughty she was.

'Fuck off, you stupid git,' Sophie told her, obviously resentful at being chastised. You could have heard a pin drop as we all looked at each other open-mouthed. I don't know where she'd picked up this language, but she used it quite appropriately. She never smiled: whether she was happy or angry she always wore the same serious expression. When she got to know myself and the other physio staff she seemed to enjoy her daily visits. When she wasn't being aggressive she was quite a pleasant little girl.

Sophie was a little girl who needed to strengthen her legs by walking about as much as possible. She loved the individual attention and was only too happy to stroll around the unit as I held onto both her hands counting up to ten. She would imitate my voice and tell herself how clever she was.

'Is the sun shining?' she would ask sometimes, having been used to daily reports on the weather because of her blindness. If it was a sunny day she would then say: 'Do you think you could take me for a walk in the sunshine?' How could anybody resist such a request?

She always wore little green pumps and a coat that was three times too small. Many a time, she went to scratch me and pull my hair but after watching the nurses with her I started to get wise and kept hold of her hands as I lifted her up. If I kept talking to her and let go sometimes she was so preoccupied that she forgot to do it. If she suddenly remembered and raised her hands I would take hold of them as I continued talking, ignoring what she was trying to do. This certainly did not stop her but her attacks on me were less frequent. Because her attacks on the other children were so vicious, whenever she was on the ward she had to sit in a huge play pen on her own. Unless she had a one-to-one relationship with a nurse this was inevitable but I felt desperately sad for her when I went to collect her. Sometimes when I went onto the ward to fetch her she would be sitting in the corner of the play pen with her legs crossed and head drooping onto her chest just like a discarded puppet.

'Hello Sophie,' I would whisper as I sneaked up on her. She would immediately come to life with her barrage of questions as I lifted her out of her play pen. I felt that because she spent so long in her play pen with no physical contact then it was only to be expected that she would be attacking people. The longer she stayed in hospital the more difficult her problems would become until they were so serious she might not be accepted anywhere. Despite the obvious affection the nursing staff had for her she needed a lot more scope to develop although her age was against any great change.

It was about this time that I started to enquire about Sophie's history. She was born in 1968 and needed an immediate operation to remove a lump on her neck, a cystic encephalocele. A Spitz Halter valve was inserted to assist drainage of the cerebral fluid. Sophie went to live at home soon after the operation, where she stayed until she was eighteen months of age. During this time her mother had a miscarriage and a nervous breakdown and Sophie was then admitted to a residential nursery. There was no contact from her parents except for an occasional visit from her grandmother. By the time Sophie was two years old she had outgrown the nursery and an alternative home had to be found. She was then admitted to a rather large children's home some sixty miles from where she lived. This home, for severely physically and mentally handicapped children, had about 150 beds, mostly cot cases. Sophie only stayed there for two years and at the age of four was moved into a local authority home for mentally handicapped children in her own area. The home was mostly for short stay children and the staff had great difficulty in preventing Sophie from attacking other children. Four years later, when they could no longer cope with her vicious behaviour, she was admitted to the hospital where I met her.

I could not understand how a child who had spent all of her life in care under the supervision of skilled staff could end up with such serious behaviour problems. I felt a great affinity with her. I knew I had to do something positive to try to improve the quality of her life.

News came that the little hospital school was closing down and that the children would be transferred to the big hospital along the road where it was thought they'd benefit from better educational facilities. I had reservations about Sophie being transferred there and felt that going onto a larger ward would take her to the point of no return.

I had a word with Sophie's teacher and told her of the children's home which was shortly to open, feeling that Sophie would benefit from being in a smaller unit. I also had a word with the hospital social worker who met with enthusiasm my request to take Sophie home for occasional weekends. I was invited to Sophie's next case conference to put my proposals forward to Dr Arya, the hospital consultant. I was over the moon. I couldn't help noticing, not for the first time, how the older professionals seemed so optimistic and were always willing to try anything that might lead to the child having some kind of life out in the community.

By the time the case conference had come around my job had finished. Dr Arya gave me his permission to take Sophie home for weekends and school holidays and recommended that when she went to her new home I continued with this support. Sophie's area social worker agreed, as did the hospital social worker. Matron was absent and the ward sister said that of course it would have to be cleared with Matron — until Dr Arya reminded her that it was he who ran the hospital and not the Matron. BRAVO!

Sophie's area social worker was about to retire and had brought along her replacement. I knew the Fostering Officer in Liverpool because I had recently fostered a young mentally handicapped boy at weekends to give his mum a break, so I rang him and told him the good news. He was very keen to get the ball rolling and two days later he'd sorted it all out and sent me a copy of a letter confirming this. The letter had been sent to Sophie's area social worker and went as follows:

'Further to our conversation this morning, I am writing to confirm that we have no objections to your linking Sophie Jones with our foster parent, Miss Shearon, on the basis of overnight and weekend stays. If, however, the contact proves fruitful and you are considering making a long-term placement we would want to be involved in the decision making. Perhaps it would be useful if I were to attend any reviews as Miss Shearon's Liaison Officer.

'I enclose a form which I would ask you to complete so that the Consortium may keep an up-to-date record of inter-agency links. Could you also confirm in writing that your authority will accept responsibility both for the supervision and the financing of this link? Perhaps you could do this when you return the Consortium form?

'I do hope this contact works out well.'

~

Unfortunately Matron was not very pleased. In fact, she hit the roof.

I telephoned her a week after the conference to see if I could bring Sophie home for one night.

'Who do you think you are?' she asked me angrily: 'just walking in here and taking a child to a strange place — removing her from people who care about her, and expecting her to adjust.'

'Sophie knows me.' I told her. 'I've had her almost every day for the last few months.'

'Who gave you permission to do this?' she enquired.

'Dr Arya said I could at Sophie's case conference.'

She got worse! 'What were you doing at the case conference?'

'I was invited,' I told her warily.

'If you want to take her out I want two days notice in writing, [as if I could ever forget] and I'll see Dr Arya about this.'

I posted my letter the same day. Two days later I received the following reply:

'Dear Miss Shearon,

'Thank you for your letter received this morning requesting permission to take Sophie Jones out for the day on Friday.

'I am writing to inform you that Sophie is to be transferred to Dr Barnardo's, tomorrow, Wednesday, and I would advise that you give her a settling in period before you approach the Superintendent with a view to taking her out.

'I should also like you to approach Sophie's grandmother who loves her very much and takes her out.

'I am glad my assessment of Sophie proved to be correct.'

~

I was mortified. Sophie's move was far too sudden without any introductory periods. I felt very sad for her and hoped she would be able to cope. She was also starting her new school the following Monday.

Months later I was talking to the nurse from Sophie's ward. 'I felt like a Judas as I took her off the ward, handing her over to the two strangers at the car, just like that,' she told me, 'it was heartbreaking.'

~

Following the Matron's words of wisdom I did as I was advised and kept my distance. After two weeks I rang the Superintendent at the unit and was told that Sophie hadn't settled as well as expected.

'Can I visit her some time?' I asked, but she told me she'd like Sophie to have more time to settle. I disagreed but kept my thoughts to myself. Had I been in her position I'd have asked all the ward staff to visit, knowing that Sophie probably felt a bit lost. Then came the thunderbolt. She told me Sophie's social worker had left instructions with the staff that nobody from her past was to take her out for at least six months, in order to help her realise where her home was. 'Poor kid!' I thought when I hung up.

I was a little confused myself. Everything had been sorted with regards to my having Sophie for weekends: there had obviously been a change of plan, no doubt precipitated by Sophie's new social worker who'd obviously taken over the case. That afternoon I emulsioned away my anxieties and transformed Marie's bedroom into a dusky pink to match her bedroom suite, telling myself I was getting niggled over nothing.

Terry, my aunt, was very upset when I told her. She was one of life's crusaders when it came down to children being neglected. She was outraged that somebody had the power to implement such extreme restrictions on little Sophie's life. She had no time for social workers anyway: 'They want shooting — the bloody lot of them,' she always used to say.

~

At the end of Sophie's third week, with a little gentle persuasion I was allowed to visit. I was greeted by a rather miserable looking housemother.

'Who gave you permission to come?' she asked to my surprise.

'It was arranged yesterday,' I told her: 'they must have forgotten to tell you.' She continued to stand there like a jailer.

'Who have you come to see?' I was still standing on the step in the bloody cold.

'Sophie Jones.' Once I had been vetted she stood aside and let me in the front door. I followed her through the hall and into their sitting room. I smiled when I saw Sophie: she was sitting on a chair in the corner with her head down.

'Hello Sophie,' I said cheerfully and lifted her up to sit her on my knee.

'Hello,' she answered quietly without her usual spark, her little head drooping onto her chest. Her goosebumped arms and legs were freezing. I tried to ignore her chilly looking cotton dress which was open to the waist with nothing underneath it. She still had her little green pumps on with one of the ribbons missing and a pair of ankle socks. It was the first week in November.

The home had only been open three weeks and the six children in Sophie's unit were all trying to cope with their new moves in different ways. I recognised two little boys from the large hospital, one of whom was throwing Fisher Price toys aimlessly. The other was almost bouncing off the walls with pent-up energy, having been used to the open space of the hospital.

Holding onto Sophie's little hands I stood her up and walked her around the room. Two housemothers and a psychologist were sitting in the corner of the room with a pretty little girl who had Downs Syndrome. They were obviously enchanted with her and as I glanced over at them one of the housemothers looked at Sophie in surprise.

'I didn't know she could walk,' she said, nudging the person next to her.

'Oh, she's quite a busy little bee,' I told them. 'She enjoys being on her feet. Usually counts to ten as she walks, don't you Sophie?' I asked her. There was no reply. Sophie remained silent and kept her head down.

'Hasn't she got any decent clothes?' I asked, hoping my directness wouldn't offend them. One of the staff shook her head: 'We've been trying to get money out of her Social Services but they won't budge and she's hardly got anything.' I glanced down at Sophie as we stood hand in hand, hoping she wouldn't get too withdrawn as she tried to cope with her new environment. Strange as it may seem, I was worried because she had stopped scratching and pulling hair. My intuition told me this 'problem' had stopped too soon to be for the right reasons and daft as it may seem, I think it would have helped her if she'd brought her play pen with her and been weaned out of it, so to speak.

My attempts to strike up any conversation with the housemothers had failed. I was hoping they would bombard me with questions about her but nobody seemed that interested.

I bit my lip as I left the home, trying to hide my disappointment. It had been so different to what I had expected — and so had Sophie.

~

Try as I might I couldn't get Sophie out of my mind. Marie and I went to Terry's for the weekend and we met John. I had still not received any official notice that Sophie would not be placed with me at weekends or school holidays. I just had to sit tight and wait. However, on my next visit John came with me.

The children had just returned from a walk and poor Sophie was still dressed for a summer's day as she sat huddled in the chair with her legs crossed. The two little boys from the big hospital were a bundle of fun but I watched with growing concern at the way the toys flew across the room. I was very worried for Sophie's safety. I must have met a different shift on this day because the housemothers were more pleasant and chatty when they came in and out of the room to take the children to the toilet, etc. Poor Sophie: she seemed just as quiet as before, if not quieter.

'She's perished, Mish,' John said gently squeezing her hand. 'And find out what size shoes she takes and we'll go and buy her some. She can't walk about like this,' he whispered so as not to offend the staff.

Looking back now I suppose we could have left the money for the staff to buy her shoes but I was afraid the problem would then be that nobody was going to the shops.

We guessed her size (because she wasn't allowed out) and bought her a little pair of Clarks blue shoes. I told the man in the shop that the child was ill in bed and he very cleverly suggested that if the shoes did not fit, I could draw Sophie's feet on a piece of cardboard. This tip came in very useful because the shoes *were* too small. John eventually handed the right size into the home one evening on his way to see me. It was 6.30 and Sophie was in bed. Despite John's request to ring and let us know if the shoes fitted, nobody bothered. In fact, nobody phoned for the next two weeks. Still concerned about the child's apathy I rang her social worker. I explained as patiently as I could about how withdrawn I thought she was and that she needed a bit more individual attention. He flatly refused my request to bring her home one afternoon a week, insisting that she needed six months to settle down. With great difficulty I managed not to argue with him. I wanted to leave the door open, and I had the feeling if I said any more he would have slammed it in my face. I decided to pay her grandmother a visit. I had intended doing this on the recommendation of the hospital social worker but I was afraid that her new social worker would see it as overstepping him. I knew I was skating on very thin ice.

As it happened Sophie's grandmother made me very welcome and was glad of news of her little grand-daughter, although I couldn't bring myself to tell her how withdrawn she was. I left my address with her and told her that I would like to look after Sophie at home, and to contact me if ever they would consider this. She said she would. I knew that if the social worker were to find out I had made this request directly to Sophie's family, then I'd blown it.

At the end of the day my hands were tied. There was only so much I could do without the co-operation and support of the decision makers. It was very frustrating indeed. It was also very sad.

I decided to stop visiting Sophie until her six months were up. Resentment was creeping in from the care staff: not being a relative or calling in an official capacity I was just a bloody nuisance. I was also frightened of preventing the staff from getting to know Sophie, and afraid they might resent her instead. I can see now it was a dreadful mistake.

I wondered whether Sophie's social worker saw all his clients twice a year and planned their lives six months in advance to keep his files in order. I was very shocked at his freedom to pull the child's strings any way he wanted. One thing was clear to me — Sophie was being exploited because of her handicap, instead of being protected as she should.

I was sorry that John had been thrown in at the deep end and witnessed such callous treatment. It was his first experience of children in care and bureaucracy. His life was never the same again!

# 10
~

WHEN I HAD finally rung the home after Sophie's settling period was over I was informed by the Superintendent that she had been very ill and was in the hospital for sick children.

'What has happened to her?' I asked.

'She just stopped eating and drinking,' the housemother replied, 'and she lost so much weight she was almost dehydrated by the time she was admitted to the hospital.'

I was stunned. Thanking her quietly I hung up.

My enquiries at the children's hospital didn't get very far. The nurse told me that Sophie had been discharged from there too and had been sent to the big hospital for the mentally handicapped.

'What was wrong with her?' I asked anxiously.

'I'm afraid I'm not allowed to say,' she said, much to my annoyance. 'That's confidential information.'

By the time I found out which ward she was on at the big hospital, I was shaking when I asked the nurse how she was.

'She's still very ill,' she answered, and waited for me to speak. I bit my lip as I tried to get my thoughts together and continue the conversation.

'Is it all right if I visit her?' I asked. 'I could come in tomorrow.'

'Well...' she answered despondently, 'if you used to know her before she was ill, be prepared for a shock.' I hung up thinking what a strange thing that was to say.

When John and I went to the hospital the next afternoon, no amount of preparation would have lessened the shock of what we saw. Walking into the day room I searched dozens of little faces, smiling when I recognised some of the children I'd taken for physiotherapy — but I couldn't see Sophie.

The nurse we had just spoken to in the office came in to join us.

'Where is she?' I enquired trying to make myself heard above the background noise of the children.

'There she is,' she replied pointing to the side of me. Looking down I gasped in horror at the little scrap of skin and bone that was lying on the bean chair. She was like someone from the Third World. I had seen her already and hadn't recognised her.

'What's happened to her?' I whispered to the nurse. Stooping down I lifted her out of the bean chair. I was choked. She had lost so much weight and could no longer sit up on her own, let alone walk. The nurse shrugged her shoulders: 'I told you to be prepared for a shock, didn't I?' she asked me gently. 'As far as any of us know she became very dehydrated after refusing drinks for about four weeks.'

I cannot describe how I felt. I knew they were personal feelings that I had to deal with myself but I will never forget the sorrow that clouded over me as I gently rocked Sophie in my arms. This was her third home since she'd first left the hospital the previous year, going from one stranger to the next. She was just another lonely child in care.... Poor John had turned white with shock as he looked at what was left of the little girl whose hand he had held as she'd walked for him only a few months before. My heart ached for her. I was angry that she was in such a noisy and impersonal environment when she was still obviously very ill — so ill in fact that she was only being fed on watered orange juice. We took her into the dormitory where I put her on her bed. She was freezing: her legs were bare and I stifled a sob as I thought about the empty bedroom at home.

Sophie's hair had been cut very closely to her head as if she'd had some kind of operation. I was aware that she had a Spitz Halter valve down the side of her head, which assisted in draining the cerebral fluid, and wondered if complications had arisen over this. Sometimes a valve could become blocked or misplaced, but careful observation by staff should detect this straight away. For example, if a child became lethargic or her eyes suddenly became glazed then she would need to be admitted to a hospital immediately, in case the valve needed to be corrected. Even though all the signs of Sophie's present condition indicated a blocked valve, I put the idea straight out of my head, never imagining it could have gone undetected by the people in whose care she was.

A nurse came into the dormitory to where we sat beside Sophie's cot. There was a little shelf above the cot. The nurse reached up and took down a jug of orange juice and got a little teaspoon from her pocket.

'Open wide,' she said cheerfully. I watched full of anguish as the orange juice ran down Sophie's mouth onto the back of her neck: the nurse hadn't even bothered to sit her up.

I left the hospital in tears. So that was the extent of Sophie's 'special care' — cold, watered-down orange juice. It was deplorable.

To me Sophie had died. I knew she would never again pull my hair as I told her how pretty she was and that no more sounds would ever pass her little lips. The only comfort I could find was that God had taken her spirit and left her breathing body behind as an example to us all to treat children in care with a little more tenderness and understanding.

The next morning I was still shaking when I rang the hospital social worker. She didn't know what had happened and said she would not like to commit herself, adding that one didn't know what had gone on in the child's mind.

I wanted to ring Sophie's own social worker but kept putting it off because I did not trust myself to speak to him. When I eventually rang I almost regretted it as I listened to his cool voice on the other end of the line.

'Oh yes, she's been ill, hasn't she?'

'Have you seen her?' I asked him.

'Well,' he said casually, 'I haven't had the chance yet, what with one thing and another.' I bit my lip to stop me from vomiting abuse down the phone.

'But she was in the hospital for sick children for two months,' I said incredulously. 'Are you telling me that you didn't visit her once?' He started to sound a bit irritated with me.

'Like I said,' he replied, 'what with one thing and another.' I suddenly changed my attitude knowing that it would serve no purpose to antagonise him. I told him I realised how busy he must be. I was revolted at my lack of sincerity and was becoming a master at keeping my cool. He refused my request to look after Sophie at home, telling me that she was in the best possible hands and was receiving expert care.

'Don't you think she has a right to live in an ordinary home like any other child?' I asked him. I knew I was wasting my time: we were on different wavelengths.

I visited Sophie that afternoon, stopping at the jewellers on the way to the hospital to buy her a Saint Christopher medal. She had looked so lonely when we'd left her lying on the bed in the middle of an empty dormitory the previous day: this time, when I left her I tied the Saint Christopher medal and chain around her cot and somehow she didn't seem so alone. Strolling out of the hospital against the cold March wind I looked towards the out-patients clinic and could see Dr Arya through the window. When I arrived home I rang him. I trusted his judgement: he'd been very fair with me in the past. I felt that if he would not let me bring Sophie home it would be for genuine reasons. He invited me to his clinic the following afternoon where he explained Sophie's future was to be decided at a conference the following week. He invited me along.

In the meantime I continued to visit Sophie on her ward and found it an enormous strain to be pleasant when I could not really accept what had happened. My discreet enquiries about the events which had led up to this serious physical deterioration came up against a barrier of silent officials who managed to convince most people that Sophie had a condition whereby she became dehydrated very quickly. People's acceptance of this situation left me wondering at my own sanity. The reason for my interest was not so that I could point the finger at people, but to bring to light the mistakes that had been made — otherwise how could people learn from them if they were hushed up to protect the carers? Was anybody answerable for Sophie's precious life?

Most of the ward staff were pleasant, but unfortunately there is always one bad egg and it's that bad egg that tends to get everybody else a bad name. She was not a senior member of the ward staff but was still left in charge occasionally. One day when I went onto the ward she was sitting in front of the TV knitting as the children crawled around her feet. That mightn't have been too bad, but she also had a cigarette hanging out of her mouth. Unfortunately when she was in charge her attitude tended to rub off on the other nurses. She treated me with casual disregard: I'm sure she thought if she ignored me for long enough I would go away. I never criticised her, and nor did we communicate very much. Sometimes our eyes would meet, and they said it all: after all, the eyes are the windows of the soul.

~

The day of the conference my stomach was in knots as I sat watching the various people arriving. The two housemothers from the home, the hospital social worker, the physiotherapist and several other 'professional' people. When Sophie's area social worker arrived he went into Sister's office with Dr Arya where I could see them through the glass. I was edgy as I stood looking out of the window. I could see a nurse in the distance pushing a child in a large buggy: as they got nearer I could see it was Sophie. Is there no end to this child's suffering? I screamed inside. I watched her being wheeled through the snow. She had on a little pair of ankle socks and a sleeveless cotton dress with a poncho on top. I wondered whether the nurse would dress her own children like that. If she had they'd have been taken off her and put into care!

When Sophie arrived I sat her on my knee. She was perished, and immediately closed her icy hand around my finger. Her social worker didn't come into the conference. I could hear him arguing with Dr Arya in the office. Within minutes he walked out, shouting at Dr Arya and slamming the door behind him. He went out of the building and I never saw him again. I listened to one of the staff from the home say they were prepared to keep Sophie's bed for the next six months when one of the hospital staff spoke: 'Just for my own information,' she said addressing the staff from the home, 'before Sophie was admitted to the children's hospital did it occur to any of you to measure her head?' They both shook their heads. I then realised why Sophie's illness had been treated as 'confidential' — as someone later confirmed, she had suffered a valve closure. She had been so dehydrated by the time she left the home her weight was a mere 1 stone 8 pounds.

Unfortunately when Dr Arya put forward my request to look after the child at home some of the staff took it as personal criticism of their care. I was not very popular with the physiotherapist who'd been my boss at one time. Our difference hadn't been that serious — I had simply objected to her request to have a child admitted to hospital just for physiotherapy, when during the child's stay she would receive hardly any treatment at all. She was an exhibitionist and these requests which usually took place in conferences at the out-patients' clinic were purely an attempt to assert herself amongst her colleagues and unfairly misled the parents. It was the physiotherapist who spoke out when Dr Arya told her of my proposal.

'Actually,' she said smugly, 'it's a pity the person who cares about her the most isn't here to represent her.' The knitting nurse from Sophie's ward sitting next to her nodded her head in agreement. It was a few seconds before I realised they were talking about an old nurse from Sophie's ward with whom I kept in touch and who gave me her blessings with the child because she was not in a position to look after her.

'I don't mind taking a back seat if somebody else wants to look after her,' I told them. People started coughing and shuffling about. They had embarrassed everyone with their pettiness. Dr Arya was obviously irritated with them and told them that I was representing Sophie. The meeting moved on with everybody putting their various proposals forward. I listened expressionless while the physiotherapist recommended that Sophie should stay in hospital for at least another six months because she needed intensive physiotherapy. I knew then that I had no chance. The final recommendation from Dr Arya was at least another six months in hospital because she was too ill to be discharged. I was given permission to visit whenever I wanted.

It was with a lump in my throat that I quietly accepted his decision. It wasn't in Sophie's interest that she was staying: it was in their own.

When the conference came to an end I shuddered when I saw the knitting nurse wheeling Sophie's buggy in to push her back to the ward.

'Do you want a lift?' I asked her, trying to make an effort. 'It'll save you having to go out in the snow.' She willingly accepted.

We continued to visit Sophie and on the days there was a ward sister on duty I was usually made welcome and the atmosphere on the ward was pleasant. On other days things were very different. I would leave the ward full of anguish and frustration.

A week after the conference John and I had arranged with the ward sister to visit Sophie. When we arrived mid-morning, it was to find the poor child lying on the bean chair in the middle of a noisy day room. She looked so vulnerable as she lay there with her big blue eyes unaware of the chaos around her. There were two children sprawled out on the floor next to her with their little heads resting on her bean chair. My stomach turned when I lifted her up: I noticed teeth marks across her fingers. Needless to say, the knitting nurse was in charge. When she came in I asked her if she'd seen Sophie's fingers.

'Oh,' she said casually, 'one of the other children must have bitten her. I'll have to keep an eye on her in the future.'

~

It seemed strange being on the other side of the fence. I wondered how many attempts at moving people out of hospital had failed and one of the reasons for this was that like Sophie's social worker, officials lacked the skill and understanding needed in helping that person adjust to the change.

I knew this incident had not helped the nurses' attitudes to the benefits of community life. Some were smug: others had been so alarmed at Sophie's physical deterioration, they were convinced it was through lack of nursing care. Who could blame them?

Two months later, a representative from the home assessed Sophie and came to the conclusion that she was too severely handicapped to return to them. They had to let her bed go. She was on the scrap heap now. Still — she'd been everywhere else: it was the only place left.

Over the next few weeks John and I continued to visit Sophie. When Marie came with us she would lose herself in the dormitory and put her monkey to bed. She walked around like she owned the place.

Each day Sophie was getting a little stronger. I was thrilled when I went onto the ward and she was propped up in her feeding chair, wearing the little blue shoes that John had bought her.

'She looks nice today,' I told the nurse.

'They brought her things yesterday,' she told me, looking disgusted. 'They didn't even ask to see her.'

'You mean the staff from the home?' I asked.

She nodded. 'They just dumped her things in the office and went.'

'But their job is done now,' I told her. 'Sophie's your department, and besides,' I added, 'maybe they didn't feel welcome.' The nurse stopped dead in her tracks and looked at me.

'We didn't say they couldn't see her,' she told me defensively.

'Maybe not,' I said, 'but did you say they could?'

'No,' she said quietly.

'Well then,' I told her, 'you probably just misunderstood each other.'

~

By this time Marie was almost fourteen and I was twenty-six. The hospital had been, and still was, my backbone. The short-term care available for Marie at the hospital was the only means of support I had. Any plans to fill in the gap for community care would take a long, long time before they catered for the Maries and Sophies of this world. They were way down the priority list. I don't believe using the hospital for Marie did her any harm, at least not on a short-term basis. Besides, I would always be looking over Marie's shoulder wherever she went, not that she needed me now. Her wilfulness and lack of tolerance in situations that she disliked meant that she would always be last in the queue and first on the bus. I wouldn't want it any other way: she was one of the lucky ones.

~

It was after this dreadful experience with Sophie that John and I decided to return to Lincolnshire where property was cheap and set up a foster home for the profoundly handicapped child, being more convinced than ever of the desperate need for this type of care.

~

Sophie was eventually moved to a ward for delicate children later on in 1979. She stayed there for 4½ years until an adventurous hospital social worker started a scheme for some of the hospital children to be fostered out into families at weekends. Sophie eventually found her little piece of heaven on earth but unfortunately, after six wonderful months in that foster home with tender loving parents, she died. She was sixteen years old.

# FROM THE FAMILY ALBUM

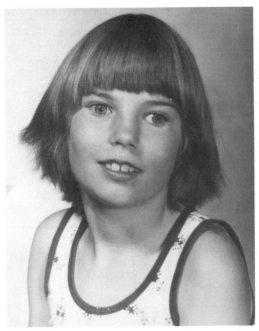

*Left:* 10-year-old Marie's school photo.

*Below:* Playing and learning: Marie at 8, outside the old schoolhouse.

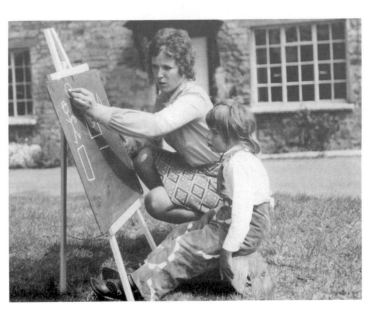

*Left:* Enjoying water play

*Above:* On the phone, 1973

*Above right:* A walk in the park. Liverpool 1978

*Below right:* Happy together — the first week 8-year-old Marie came to live with Michelle

Growing together

*Above:* Michelle (17) with Marie (5) in Bristol — photographed by 7-year-old Morgan!

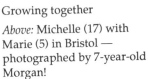

*Opposite:* July 1981, Marie at sixteen, with Michelle, who was eight months pregant with Patrick.

*Above right:* Anna's third birthday, one week before Marie's 21st.

*Below:* 1989, celebrating Marie's return to the ATC after a six-year wait.

# 11

~

W HEN WE FIRST moved to Lincolnshire we bought a cosy two-
bedroomed house in a little terrace of about twelve houses.
Although we wanted a large house to take in more children,
property prices were way out of our range. One evening when John
returned from work he looked deep in thought.

'What's up?' I asked him as I helped Marie tidy away her new toys.

'I've just had a thought,' he said, not really enlightening me at all. I
stopped what I was doing and looked across the room at him. He hung
up his coat and sat down.

'How much do you reckon that house up the road is?' he asked.

'Do you mean the one three doors away?'

'Yep,' he answered. I didn't have a clue and I told him so.

'I think I'll go and find out,' he said standing up. I dived into the
kitchen in response to the pan's coughs and splutters as the stew spilled
over onto the stove. When I returned to the room he had gone. Marie
was looking at me expectantly.

'Come on then, it's tea time,' I told her. Laughing happily she went
to get her bib off the door.

'I think John's gone off his rocker, Marie.' She laughed again,
knowing by my tone that I was joking. I could hear John's muffled voice
on the phone in the other room. My curiosity was killing me.

'Hey Mish,' he said, suddenly appearing in the room again, 'how
would you like a house for £1,200?' I was incredulous.

'What!' I said stupidly, holding Marie's plate in mid air as I stopped
to look at him. The smell of the food must have tantalized her nostrils
as she patiently waited. 'It can't be,' I finally said.

'It is,' he replied, 'and I'm going to get the keys to have a look.' Before
I could say any more he was out the door and gone.

~

Two weeks later we were the owners of another house. We wheeled
and dealed with the private owners and managed to get a private
mortgage. The idea of buying the house was in case one came up for

sale either side of it in the future. We would then try to buy it and knock the two houses into one. And that would be our big house for the kids.

We couldn't believe it when, six months later, the house we had been waiting for came on the market.

We knew the man who owned it. When John went to see him I remember I was on my hands and knees wiping Marie's hot chocolate off the carpet. Although Marie had improved enormously since coming to live at home I didn't kid myself about the severity of her handicap. The reason her drinking chocolate was on the floor was because she had stood up forgetting her cup was still on her lap. She stood over me tutting.

'Never mind, Marie,' I said sympathetically. Even though I never scolded her I always pointed it out. She would continue tutting as if someone else had done it. Although she understood simple instructions she still got confused about things. For example if I asked her to wipe her mouth sometimes she would take her hair out of her eyes and vice versa, depending on how switched on she was at the time.

'Hey Marie, that reminds me,' I said, 'I've got to take you to the doctor's tomorrow. That'll be fun and games, won't it?' I rubbed her hair playfully. I loathed taking her to the doctor's and having to wait in a crowded *quiet* waiting room, because Marie always seemed to take the floor. She would be sitting next to me as she looked around the room when suddenly someone would walk in and I'd think, 'Oh no' when I'd notice them wearing a pair of large earrings or something which would attract Marie's attention. I just used to sit tight and hope she wouldn't notice — some hope!

'Oh mam!' she would say without any discretion and being the coward I was I would pretend not to hear. She would then try again, shouting: 'Oh Mish!' and if that wasn't enough, she would add, 'Buddee-ell.' Once, in the waiting room a man sneezed. 'Ot- dya-say?' Marie shouted over. Everyone looked up to see who was talking as she added, 'Essuse you!' I thought situations like this were hilarious. I dreaded them most because after Marie'd had her little say she would be quite serious again and I was always left laughing on my own. I loved her sense of humour. After eight years of living with her, she still brought an enormous amount of pleasure and satisfaction.

When John returned he was full of beans. The house had been modernised which meant that if we knocked the two houses into one, one side had a bathroom and the other didn't: it couldn't have been better.

Two months later we had the keys. It was a dream come true.

~

We had already introduced ourselves to the social worker at the local hospital for the handicapped. She had visited us several times and responded to our plans with great enthusiasm. I also wrote to the local fostering officer telling her that we would like to register as foster parents with a view to fostering handicapped children. Unfortunately people became suspicious because we specified what type of children we wanted. When I said the child didn't have to walk or feed himself or be toilet trained I was met with raised eyebrows. One particular social worker said that sometimes they're easier to look after when they don't walk because you don't have to be running all over the place after them. I hadn't really thought of it like that: I told him so too. It got worse.

'I suppose if they don't walk you'll get the mobility allowance too?'

'I don't think foster parents are entitled to it,' I said as calmly as I could.

When I told John what had happened he was livid.

'The thing is,' I groaned, 'if you ask for children from hospital there are going to be those that don't walk, don't feed themselves and are incontinent, but if they have to reach all those standards before they can leave then they'll be there forever. There are people who'll take the bright kids. What about the others?'

'I thought people would jump at the idea,' John said sadly.

'So did I,' I replied, 'so did I.'

~

When I eventually rang the Fostering Officer she had never received my letter. She came to meet me, filled in some forms and was sending off for my notes and references from up north.

That evening when Marie arrived home from school I took her to meet John from work. I was bubbling to the brim. Sitting on the wall in the car park I checked on Marie occasionally as she walked up and down on the pebbly driveway. When he finally appeared I filled him in on the events of the day. He was clearly delighted.

On the way home we called into the pet shop to buy a goldfish. I tried to arouse Marie's interest but she wasn't impressed and tried to put her foot through the glass because she was feeling impatient. I was used to this kind of behaviour and just kept her far enough from the glass to avoid her outstretched leg. We were looking at the lizards in the tank. I turned around to check on Marie, and saw a man bending down quite near to her, looking in the aquarium. As I stood near him and before I could stop her, Marie put her hand up the back of his T-shirt to tickle him and the poor man got such a fright he nearly went through the glass. We laughed all the way home as she skipped in between us. We bumped into a woman I had met at the doctor's months ago.

'Isn't it sad?' she said looking at Marie, 'it must be heartbreaking for you — and she's so pretty.'

'You must be joking,' I wanted to say because there was nothing sad about Marie. We burst out laughing again as Marie screwed up her face in an attempt to wink at the woman.

~

We were starting to make plans for having the renovations done on the house.

'Have you worked out what's going to be done yet?' I asked John one evening as he sat on the bathroom step watching me bath Marie.

'I think I'll ask the builders to concentrate on the outside of the house and I'll knock out the dividing walls inside.'

I had arranged with Yvonne for Marie to go into the hospital for a week so we were all set to go. The day she went in I had two rooms to get cleared so John could start work. I often find that when Marie goes away I go through a kind of pattern. The first day I start to do little things that I would not normally do when she was with me — like lying in bed or soaking in the bath for two hours. The second day is just a nice change: the third day I start to miss her. This time, however, I was so busy I didn't have time to miss her as I rolled up the carpets and covered the chairs with dust sheets. I cleared all her toys into black bags and stacked them in her bedroom upstairs.

'It's like doing an inventory,' I said to John as I climbed the stairs for the third time: 'I didn't realise she had accumulated so much.'

By Friday evening we were almost ready. The builders were coming in the following morning and John was busy getting his tools sorted out. I missed Marie. I felt she should have been involved with our little project. Standing in the kitchen pouring the coffee I knew I was only being sentimental — that she'd probably be screeching and pulling her hair out because she was bored.

The next morning I was jumping up and down like a big kid as the first brick fell out and we could actually see into next door. Slowly, brick by brick the dividing wall crumbled to the floor, and John refused to stop until it was finished and our two houses became one. I did my little bit — moved some rubble out of his way and supplied the tea and sandwiches. We spent the following day clearing up the mess but it was worth it, I thought, as I spat out the dust from my mouth.

On the Monday the electricians came in and started rewiring the house as one. At the same time John was knocking out the upstairs wall to make an opening into next door. It was great: our house was suddenly twice the size and we had two stairways.

'That's lucky,' I said to John. 'In a way this house is safer than having one big one: how many houses do you buy with two stairways?' It was like a fire escape.

When I think of the wasted journeys I had, traipsing up and down the stairs with cups of tea for John, only to discover when I reached the top he'd gone down the other side. We laughed about it and thought of all the fun Marie would have as she went on her little walks about the house.

~

The Fostering Officer called the day before Marie was due home. I think we overpowered her with our enthusiasm as we trailed after her from room to room explaining what we hoped to offer. Unfortunately, she had other things on her mind. She asked us if we would consider taking a little three-year-old boy. He was living in a foster home and, because of his difficult behaviour, was classed as unfosterable. I gulped. The little boy's name was Richard: he was in need of a long-term foster home. We said it was not really what we wanted to do but we'd give it some thought. When she had gone I was thrown into confusion as I sat on top of the ladder painting the playroom wall.

'Poor kid,' John said, 'he sounds like a little monster.' I laughed as I watched him plastering the holes the electricians had left behind.

'Three-year-olds are little monsters,' I told him, 'but it shouldn't make them unfosterable.'

I hoped they used us as a last resort because I was sure he could do better than be put in a house with mentally handicapped children. It would be different if he'd been our own child, but this little boy was already disadvantaged by coming from a broken home. I felt it would leave him a bit vulnerable to outside prejudices — mainly from children at school.

That evening we put the finishing touches to the playroom. We laid the carpet and brought in Marie's light blue piano that we'd bought her the previous year for her birthday. This brought her hours of pleasure as she sat banging the keys, usually with Joey placed on top of it watching her. He was the seventh monkey I'd bought for her over the years but I don't think she was aware of this as I discreetly swapped the old for the new when they were too battered to repair. By the time we had finished it was just past midnight.

'I can't wait to see Marie,' John said straightening Marie's piano against the wall. 'Mind you,' he added, 'she probably won't notice any difference.'

'Oh she will!' I told him, surprised at this statement. 'On second thoughts,' I said backing down, 'she'll notice we've moved her piano.'

It was hard to tell sometimes just what Marie noticed and what she missed. She reacted to things differently from what we would call 'normal'. For instance if someone entered the room she might express her joy by kissing her piano or some other object of her excitement. It was obvious when she was happy but she almost lived in a little world of her own at times. She was very affectionate but did not show this in exactly the same way as we would.

One thing about Marie was that we could never take her for granted, though after living with her for so long we could usually tell at a glance what kind of mood she was in. Either way, she kept us on our toes. We could be sitting in a café enjoying lunch and if someone came in with a noisy child she would put her spoon down and refuse to eat. Whenever she did this we left her, accepting that if anything upset her she couldn't eat. To have forced her would have made her very angry, and she'd probably have slung her plate across the table. I just had to keep talking to her now and again to distract her attention from the noisy child. If for example I whispered: 'Isn't that little girl naughty, Marie?' she would laugh quite loudly with tears in her eyes. As long as she laughed she was releasing some of her tension. To avoid this kind of situation all the time would have been impossible — it was part of everyday living. I was happy that Marie was at least able to sit through it.

Even in a dozy mood her little idiosyncrasies kept us on our toes. She was enchanted by the strangest things. Often I found myself checking on her as I followed her eyes, and more often than not she would be staring at somebody. It could even be an object — the top of a sauce bottle or a man's buttonhole in his jacket. She delighted at the things most of us would ignore. Past experiences told me to distract her because it isn't always obvious to other people what is wrong with her. Some people got offended and thought she was just being rude. I learnt my lesson some years ago when I was travelling on a London underground with her and I heard someone say: 'I'll fucking punch her in a minute.' I quickly glanced up from my book to see where the threat was coming from. There was a group of coloured girls looking our way. I was shocked to see they were talking about Marie. She had been sitting staring at them, like she usually does with coloured people and one of the girls was getting quite angry with her and hadn't realised (I think!) that Marie was mentally handicapped. I quietly told Marie to stop staring. Closing my book I took her hand and stood up to go. Fortunately the next stop had been ours anyway!

We collected Marie the following morning and received our usual noisy welcome when we entered the ward.

'She's as lively as a cricket today,' Sister said as she came out of her office, 'she hasn't stopped singing since we brought her own clothes out of the wardrobe and she realised she was going home.' By this time Marie had latched onto our hands and was halfway between laughing and crying. She kept requesting to go on the bus. In fact we owned an old transit van, but anything that wasn't a car was a bus to Marie.

'Has she been all right?' I asked Sister.

'Most of the time she's been fine,' she replied. She was getting Marie's drugs out of the cabinet. 'She gets a bit noisy at times with her screeching,' she said, returning the cabinet keys to her pocket. 'But then that's Marie, isn't it?' she grinned.

'You don't think she's emotionally disturbed then?' I joked.

She raised her eyebrows and shook her head: 'Well,' she pondered, 'that depends on your perception of her!'

On Marie's last visit to the hospital we had been unable to collect her and had arranged for her to travel with the hospital transport. When she was due home Sister had telephoned me. I could hear Marie singing in the background.

'I'm sorry, Mrs Daly,' she said, 'but while I was having my lunch the ambulance arrived to collect Marie and they refused to take her because she was screeching. They said she was too emotionally disturbed. Listen to her — can you hear her singing her head off?' she asked.

Even though Marie was not particularly distressed, the ambulance driver's attitude didn't surprise me. I knew the drama Marie was capable of creating. I also knew it was purely for effect and she had no deep-rooted emotional hang ups. One of the reasons I liked using the hospital was because the staff knew and accepted her. I had every confidence in them. And until an alternative was found, it was all I had.

We collected Marie after all that day, stopping at a café on the way home.

'She's got lots of bruises this time, hasn't she?' John remarked. I watched him cutting up Marie's sausages.

'I know,' I replied looking at Marie's elbows across the table. 'I wish she would look down when she walked.' When we had collected Marie one of the nurses told us she was tripping over the patients' feet all the time; her poor arms and legs were black and blue.

~

When we arrived home Marie's reaction was as we'd expected. I walked into the house ahead of her, searching her face as she walked past the opening into next door — she didn't even notice. As usual she went straight to the kitchen.

'Hey Marie,' I said glancing over at John, 'come on, show a little enthusiasm. What do you think of your new home?'

'Disdits?' she said in response to my appeal. 'Doose,' she further requested when something suddenly caught her eye and she broke into a smile. 'Pallo,' she chirped as she looked past me through the opening into the corner. John and I grinned as we watched her cross the room and walk up the step into next door — she leaned over her piano and kissed it!

# 12

## ~

O VER THE next few weeks we had many different social workers calling to our home. John and I must have seemed a strange pair — very naive, two people with their heads in the clouds who wanted to change the world. A few of the social workers were mildly interested: the others were just plain curious. 'Why mentally handicapped children?' most of them asked, 'Don't you think all children in care are handicapped?'

The Fostering Officer called to see us. She had received my references by this time and said she wondered if I was too qualified to foster (whatever that was supposed to mean!).

Many meetings were held in an effort to decide how best they could use us. We were not invited to these meetings and were just given little tittle-tattles from the various visitors who called. Then Yvonne, the hospital social worker, came to see us. She had been making enquiries about having a little boy who lived at the hospital placed with us. She called straight from a meeting with the local social workers who told her that when Richard, their three-year-old, was placed with us then we could not have any more children for at least three to six months. They were also telling her to back off, that she was on their territory, that we were their foster parents and not hers. I found their attitude very disappointing and hoped things would improve. Some hope!

Our little 'unfosterable' foster child was a great success. I was told there would be no parental contact, and yet his mother came to see him quite often. The two of us devised a plan and she spent every other afternoon combining her efforts with mine in trying to 'tame' him. After eleven weeks Richard waved us goodbye as he walked up the road holding his mum and dad's hand: he was going home for good. He was the one and only child the local Social Services ever placed with us.

## ~

I have always been a great fan of the Beatles. Like many people around the world, I was devastated when I heard John Lennon had been shot dead. It was also the day my pregnancy was confirmed. John and I were naturally delighted with the news, but I remember the day being tinged with sadness for the loss of such a charismatic and humane person.

Being pregnant made me more determined than ever to continue our struggle to foster. The baby, to me, was a gift from God: it was also a test of our convictions. I was unshakable.

When Marie was almost sixteen and due to leave school, we were looking at what was available for her in the form of day care. The Social Services are responsible for providing day facilities in the community for the mentally handicapped when they leave school and are no longer the responsibility of the Education Department. This facility is in the form of an ATC (Adult Training Centre). Because more mentally handicapped people are living in the community, the Social Services are slowly recognising the need for special units for people like Marie who need maximum attention. Their response to this need (in our area) was what they called an ISU (Intensive Support Unit) which had recently been built onto the ATC.

When I had discussed Marie's future with her teacher she told me she didn't think Marie would like it in the ISU and would be better occupied watching people in the main workshop where there was a little more activity. I felt that going into the unit could have been to Marie's advantage, depending on the skill and understanding of the staff. I knew from experience that if Marie is in a situation that she dislikes she can revert right back to her old habits very quickly. I knew the workshop would be too noisy for her and she'd probably spend most of her day screeching.

~

The ISU was a new, pre-fabricated building standing apart from the main workshop. When John and I had visited it there was a group of handicapped people watching TV. One of the instructors came and introduced himself and explained a little more about how the unit was run.

It was built for ten people but only had six, which meant lots of attention for everyone. We were shown various programmes on the wall which represented the day's activities. TV programmes were watched throughout the day — some lasting only five minutes, but everyone had to sit and watch them. I thought they would have problems with Marie over this: she had never responded very much to the TV. I hoped a lot of what they did was optional because when people leave school, even if they are mentally handicapped they have the same rights as everyone else and should be allowed a certain amount of freedom in how they choose to occupy themselves.

The instructor then told us the names of the people in the unit, telling us whose parents were over-protective when he came to each person. I was starting to feel disappointed as I listened to him discuss the people and their parents so casually. We eventually left the unit feeling very unimpressed, and decided to look for an alternative. I was just so thankful that Marie had left the watchful eye of the Education Department and no longer had to be dumped in the nearest special school every day.

Since Richard had gone home nobody from our local Social Services approached us. I had made it clear to them when Richard first arrived that we would only accept mentally handicapped children in the future, and they just didn't have any.

One day I rang the British Fostering Society and they told me of an organisation with children who were difficult to place. They had representatives all over the country (called Bookholders). The book was full of difficult to place children with photographs and a little information about each child. You then took the name and number of the child you selected and contacted the agency, who gave you the name and address of the child's social worker. The child we enquired after was from Birmingham. Her social worker was very relieved when we contacted her: she was about to remove the child's photo from the book because she'd had no enquiries.

Karen was fourteen. She had hydrocephalus and could only walk with the aid of a calliper. She was living in a home for 'normal' children and would have to leave there when she was sixteen. Karen's social worker was very enthusiastic and suggested we travel to Birmingham to meet Karen.

The following Sunday at 8 a.m. Marie was sitting in the back of the van with her monkey on her knee as we set off for Birmingham. By this time I was 6½ months pregnant and knew it was too late to place anybody before the baby was born. The introduction was with a view to a placement after the baby had arrived.

There were so many aspects to look at when a child was being placed with us. One of them, of course, was how Marie would get along with the child. We had seen a photo of Karen and knew what to expect. Of course there was no way of preparing Marie because of her limited understanding so we just had to keep our fingers crossed.

We arrived at the home just before lunch and were able to see Karen straight away. Immediately, she took Marie by the hand and invited us to see her bedroom. Karen had a bedroom of her own, mainly because she soiled her bed at night (which we had not been told about), which was unpleasant for the other children if she shared a bedroom with them. I thought this was a bit sad. She seemed to stand apart from the other children and was aware enough to sense it. Sitting together on her bed Karen smiled at Marie.

'I went to the baths yesterday,' Karen said shyly.

'Baff,' Marie repeated, her face lighting up.

'Don't talk daft,' Karen told her, 'how can you go to the baths today when there's no school?'

But Marie continued to laugh, thinking Karen had told her she was going to school.

We had our lunch with Karen. The staff made a great fuss of Marie and gave her an extra chair for her monkey so it could join us at the table. She ate her lunch and everybody laughed when she asked for more.

Karen was full of conversation. I don't think she was aware of the reason for our visit. We eventually said our goodbyes and thanked the staff for making us so welcome. They were all obviously very fond of Karen and concerned about her future.

That was the first and last we saw of her. A few weeks later her social worker rang to thank us for our interest, but said that, unfortunately, after having a meeting with the powers that be, they had decided they couldn't see the point in Karen coming to live with us. They reckoned that if we were going to be looking after a few handicapped children then she might as well stay where she was. I felt sorry for Karen's social worker, I think she was as disappointed as us. I could see their point but felt that while they were searching for their ideal home they should leave all the doors open in case they were unsuccessful.

'I don't believe it,' John said angrily. 'How do they all sleep at night?'

'A lot more comfortably than they would if she were fostered,' I replied.

~

Yvonne, the hospital social worker, was still an enthusiastic visitor to our home. She always had her ears open for us. She phoned one afternoon: 'Michelle, someone is looking for a foster home for a handicapped child at present living in a children's home.' She made arrangements for the child's social worker to visit us.

I couldn't wait for John to return from work that evening so that when he asked me the usual question 'Any news?' I could answer, 'Yes!'

However, after our introductions, John's time off work, etc., they rang to say it had been decided in a meeting not to go ahead. Again, they were looking for an ideal family and until they found one the child would remain in the children's home.

Some time around the middle of June 1981 there was a TV documentary about the appalling conditions in a hospital in Surrey. It told of the lack of facilities for the patients who spent most of their days unoccupied on over-crowded wards or in the hospital compound, due to staff shortages. It showed a mentally handicapped boy who was tied to a post on a ward because of his hyper-activity, which, due to staff shortages and lack of supervision, was all they could do to contain him.

The producer's name was Nigel Evans. I applauded him. It was the most honest and natural presentation of a hospital that I had ever seen. The facts spoke for themselves. He pointed no finger at the nurses and put the blame where it belonged — with the hospital management.

Over the next few weeks I listened in amusement as some brushed it off with a pinch of salt as an exaggerated piece of propaganda. They had obviously not ventured very far through any hospital gates. And I still maintain today that Nigel Evans did more for the cause of mental handicap than anybody before or after him ever did. The only mistake he made was being brutally honest.

# 13

~

I N THE MIDDLE of August, when our baby was two weeks overdue, the doctors decided to induce me. I eventually had a little boy delivered by Caesarean section. I couldn't believe he was ours when I looked at him through sleepy eyes, stroking his little mop of silky black hair. He'd been worth all those hours of agonising labour — until after refusing to be dragged out by forceps the doctors decided to delve in and get him. We called him Patrick!

For the first time in my life I had a taste of what it was like to be in someone else's hands. Mind you, for the first few days they must have found me pretty strange too. As most of us know, nothing, but nothing, comes in the way of the hospital routine. It just took some getting used to (with a few compromises here and there!)

I seemed to spend the first few days always looking for my baby. I'd go to the telephone and on my return my baby was missing from the end of my bed. Perhaps there'd be a cleaner outside my room or a nurse walking past.

'Who's taken my little boy?' I'd ask incredulously.

'He's probably in the nursery,' someone would say indifferently.

'What's he doing there?' I'd ask. I was not aggressive or angry — I was just bewildered that the babies were always being whipped away from mothers who'd waited so long to have them.

'It's bed rest,' the nurse might say sympathetically.

'Too bad!' I'd tell her and go and retrieve my son. It was difficult being assertive as I was, in such a vulnerable position. I could have done without the aggravation, and no doubt the nursing staff could have done without such an awkward mother.

Understandably I was not allowed to bath Patrick or change his nappy until I'd had the clips removed from my stomach. When he was three days old it was time for his bath and I looked forward to seeing him in the water. Mid-morning the nursery nurse came into my room looking very bright and cheerful.

'Can I borrow Patrick to do a show bath for the other mums?' she asked.

'Of course you can,' I answered.

'The only thing is, you won't be able to come and watch because I already have enough mums.'

I thought she was joking but she didn't smile; she was serious.

'You mean you want to take my baby for a show bath and there's no room for me to watch?'

'I'm sorry,' she told me indignantly, 'but it's just too crowded. I can always ask someone else,' she added impatiently.

'You do that,' I told her and she was gone. I felt vulnerable because I knew I had upset her. That same day I had to have bed rest in the afternoon. I wheeled Patrick to the side of my bed so I could see his little face, when a nurse came breezing in.

'Don't put your baby there,' she told me. 'They go at the end of your beds.' She moved Patrick's little trolley and walked out. Half an hour later another midwife came around with the obstetrician. After enquiring after my health the midwife gave me some advice: 'Why don't you try to get to know your baby a bit more,' she suggested and wheeled Patrick's trolley to the side of my bed. 'After all,' she said looking towards the obstetrician for his approval, 'that's what it's all about, isn't it?' I could have died with embarrassment.

The evenings were the hardest for me. As soon as the bossy auxiliaries started shoving open the doors of our rooms and removing the flowers I knew it was almost time for Patrick to be taken away and brought back the next morning. I couldn't understand why he had to go. Obviously the staff had lots of sensible reasons for doing this and each night I would make an effort as I prepared for his departure, telling myself how lucky I was to have a baby etc., but it didn't help. I would lie in the dimly lit room looking out into the night. When I wasn't pining for my little baby I was worrying over Marie. I was very upset that she had been unable to share the experience with us and had no idea that I'd had a baby. She was in fact in a hospital just up the road from me, both of us twenty miles from home. The ward sister was very kind and understanding: 'Would you like me to bring her to see you?' she offered kindly. I shook my head because whenever I thought or talked about her I was too choked to speak. I knew a visit to me in hospital would have thrown her into confusion and until I took the baby home she would not know he was a new member of our family. I decided to sign myself out. The ward sister was mortified. One of my stitches had not closed up, resulting in a little hole in my wound which needed daily dressings as it bled throughout the day. It was partly my own fault. There was a smashing bunch of mums in and when I wasn't crying I was laughing my head off. This of course pulled the clips on my stomach which were like staples and sometimes I'd be holding my stomach in agony because I couldn't stop laughing.

'If I let you have a private room at the end of the corridor and keep

Patrick with you all night, will you stay for a few more days?' Sister asked seriously.

I accepted her kind offer, and once I started looking after Patrick on my own I started to relax a little. The mums came down to visit me and I went back up to the ward with Patrick in his little trolley. Sometimes we'd meet a group of doctors: 'Good morning Mrs Daly, are you doing your rounds?' they used to joke.

I went home when Patrick was twelve days old.

~

Next morning I was pacing the floor as I waited for Marie to arrive. Coming through the front door she did a double take when she caught sight of the pram in the corner of the room.

'Go asneep,' she whispered tenderly. Neck outstretched in an effort to see, she crossed the room and peeped into the pram. She was of course, completely surprised: I think she'd half expected to find her monkey in it.

Within days we had become accustomed to our little addition and life went on as usual. Marie would sit on the chair for hours at the side of the baby's pram, holding his bottle when his feed was due and tutting in disgust when I changed his nappy. She tapped his back very gently while I held him, trying to bring up his wind. When all his little needs were seen to she would sit looking miserable as she once again guarded his pram waiting for the next burst of activity.

From the start I had to tell Marie not to touch Patrick's pram: she had no sense of danger and could quite easily hurt him. She understood this rule which was why I never panicked when I left her in the room alone with him for a minute, because she usually did as I asked her.

I could not go out of the room and leave Patrick sitting on his bean chair or in his baby bouncer, because in the bean chair Marie could quite easily sit on him without realising it. She has almost done it to Sam, Liz's little boy, and we had just caught her in time. If I left Patrick in his bouncing chair it was likely that Marie would trip over him because she didn't look where she was going. So although she would do as I asked her, I couldn't leave her to use her initiative because she didn't have any. She was never allowed to put the monkey in Patrick's pram when it was empty because I knew she would probably do the same thing when Patrick was in it.

We enjoyed the last of the summer, spending most of it taking Patrick for walks: Marie always pushed him while I hung onto the side — (like the Nanny!). People said the strangest things. I had been warned over and over to expect Marie to be jealous, but knowing Marie the way I did I knew she would be so involved in helping me with his little needs that the advantages of Patrick far outweighed any disadvantages. People also said the oddest things to us when they met us in the street. For example: 'Is the baby all right?' and when I answered 'yes' they would say something like: 'I bet you were relieved, weren't you?' It took me quite a long time to realise they were actually asking me if my baby was handicapped like my daughter. Another question was 'What are you going to do with her now? Are you still going to keep her?' Marie would look at people, sometimes smiling as she held onto Patrick's pram. I was glad that she was so mentally retarded because I knew that some people's cruel words could never hurt her.

My friend's little boy started coming to us before and after school to fit in with his mother's working hours. Marie recognised him from her old school straight away, laughing happily when he arrived each morning. By this time I was looking for someone to help me at home. Our young paper girl was ideal, especially when I saw her trailing up the street each evening with groups of children following her. I made her an offer she couldn't refuse so she gave up her job and came in to help before and after school hours.

Patrick had many names — Marie called him 'Packwick', little John called him 'Battery' — and things worked out surprisingly well in our lively (sometimes chaotic) home. When John arrived home in the evening I didn't get a look in as he took over with the kids: we both loved having them around.

My mum came to stay, bringing my niece, Sara. Patrick was instantly dethroned by Marie and as usual I couldn't get a postcard between the two girls. I teased Sara: 'I bet you don't remember when she used to pull your hair when you were little, do you?'

'Oh yes I do!' she'd answer, cringing from the memory with mock horror.

It was during this time I wondered if Marie missed the company of other children because she was at home with me all day. She was also putting on weight which was not good for her balance. Our GP had put her on the pill to regulate her periods: she was so short the slightest increase in weight was noticeable.

That weekend we were in the *Sunday Press*. A friend had written an article about the apathy from our local social workers, and how we had empty beds waiting to be filled. Unfortunately, the issue which sparked off the story was not mentioned ('The Silent Minority' TV documentary produced by Nigel Evans). However, the article stimulated various reactions and two days later the Fostering Officer called to see us from the head office at Lincoln. He apologised for the way we had been treated and said that the Lincoln office were going to take us under their wing, and we would bypass the local Social Services.

Having worked with his wife in a village for the mentally handicapped while having two little children of their own, he could well understand our enthusiasm, telling us that we'd have his backing with whatever we wanted to do. This was very good news for us and also gave Yvonne, the hospital social worker, the green light to get involved in our scheme.

She rang one day informing us that her colleague at the hospital was looking for a long term foster home for a thirteen-year-old girl.

'Do you think this is the third time lucky?' I joked.

'Let's hope so,' she replied.

John was pleased with the news but both of us had learnt that a number of things could go wrong, although I was quietly optimistic.

~

Judy had a mental age of about 2½ and had lived in a hospital since she was five. Previous to that she had lived at home. After years of living in the hospital it was felt that Judy would benefit from a more homely environment. After an introductory weekend she was admitted to a home for mentally handicapped children. She was 11½.

Most of the children had been at the home for a long time and were familiar with the social standards expected by the staff. Instead of these children being moved on to foster homes to make room for the Judys of this world, they tended to be permanent residents.

Unfortunately, because of Judy's behaviour problems and (I think) her difficulty in adapting to such a different environment after such a short introductory period, the staff at the home decided after a six month trial that they could not cope with her, and she went back to live in the hospital.

When Judy came to visit us she was accompanied by one of the nurses who was doing a case study on her. She didn't walk through the door when she entered the room — she came in like a gust of wind dragging Chris, her social worker, with her. She stood in the middle of the floor with her long wavy ginger hair falling in ringlets down her back, a fringe almost covering her eyes. Her nose was running and she'd rubbed it all over her face which didn't exactly make a pleasant sight but she looked a bundle of fun as she stood there laughing at us with one finger stuck in her mouth as if she was about to make a decision.

'Well,' Judy's social worker said as he headed for the front door, 'I'll collect her in an hour.'

'Coward,' I teased as I watched Judy clear the top of the piano with a sweep of her arm.

In a way it was a relief having her nurse around to see how he dealt with her but unfortunately when Judy (who was very excited and showing off) tipped the record player over and started ripping the pictures off the wall he didn't seem to notice: he was rolling a cigarette.

'Does she understand what you tell her?' I asked him. I was watching her throwing the lid of the record player up at the wall so it bounced back down again. Her eyes were full of mischief. She looked at each of our faces to see what effect she had on us.

'Well,' he said, licking the cigarette paper and sealing it, 'sometimes.'

I laughed as I looked across the room to John thinking what a great help *he* was.

~

Marie thought everything Judy did was hilarious and her loud approval only seemed to encourage Judy to be all the more silly.

'Would you like the records on, Judy?' John asked her. She immediately responded to him with a smile and stood back to make room for him.

'She doesn't speak at all,' the nurse said as if he suddenly remembered the purpose of his visit.

'She gets by all the same though, doesn't she?' John said. Judy was insisting that the records he played had different coloured labels.

The hours flew, and by the time Chris returned, Judy had us all running around in circles. She did the daftest things just to make sure she had our undivided attention.

By the time it came to having Judy overnight, Christmas had come and gone and little John, my friend's son, had now left us to take up his long-awaited place at residential school. It was a cold January morning when I collected Judy from her ward. She strutted on ahead of me to the van, insisting on carrying her own case while I said goodbye to the nurses.

She was so different to what we had expected — much calmer than before. John dropped us off at home before going to fill up the van with petrol. Marie was giggling quietly: 'A kiss,' she kept saying to Judy, offering her cheek.

'Why don't you show Judy your toys, Marie?' I suggested on my way into the kitchen to switch on the oven. They both followed me and stood in the doorway. Marie seized her opportunity.

'Doose,' she ordered as I took Patrick's bottle from the fridge and dipped it into hot water.

'Would you like some juice too?' I asked Judy as she stood holding Marie's hand. She smiled in response and followed me with her eyes to see what I was doing. Her face was full of expression — because of her lack of speech she was used to using it to communicate with people.

We had three cots around the house for Patrick — one in his bedroom and one in each of the downstairs rooms. This meant we could have him around for most of the time. After the girls had a drink I could hear Patrick cooing to them where they were standing by his cot looking down at him. When his bottle was ready I joined them and lifted him out over the bars. Judy looked at me questioningly but Marie was gone into the sitting room to the chair where she prepared herself to watch me feed him. She never tired of things she liked. When Judy entered the room with me Marie beckoned to her: 'Shub ober,' as she made room for her on the same chair. Marie loved to share and was very good natured: she was never jealous and loved the stimulation sharing brought her.

When Patrick was fed and I was putting out lunch, Marie took her apron off the door, which she did mechanically after years of habit, and gave it to John to tie on her. We rooted out one for Judy and she was soon sitting cheerfully at Marie's side in one of my spotted overalls.

The meal passed with surprising calm. Only once when I asked Judy to wipe her mouth did she try to test us. She threw back her head to laugh at us, letting the food pour out of either side of her mouth. We ignored her after that: she was obviously doing it for effect.

During the afternoon she sat with Marie at the table doing jigsaws. John and I were amazed at her capabilities. She studied the picture intensely before tackling the pieces.

'Again,' Marie requested each time she completed a puzzle and Judy happily obliged, smiling at her new friend who sat holding a monkey.

I didn't leave her alone with Patrick for obvious reasons and whenever I was feeding him or changing his nappy she sat with Marie on the chair watching me. At tea time when Marie and I took Patrick upstairs to bath him, John took Judy to the shop for some sweets and to let her have a glimpse of the neighbourhood. She resented bitterly the fact that she had to hold his hand, and in an attempt to bite his fingers she had bitten her own. She lay on the floor in the shop trying to be as noisy and disruptive as possible, becoming more distressed when John didn't panic and drag her up off the floor but instead walked out of the shop.

'Gosh, that was brave of you,' I remarked.

'It wasn't really, Mish, it was bloody stupid because she didn't follow me out of the shop. Instead she got up off the floor and ran behind the counter wanting to play with the bacon slicer.' Judy suddenly threw her head back and laughed when she saw my startled expression: she'd been listening to John's account of what happened and was tickled pink.

The rest of the evening we spent pottering about the house. The two girls complemented each other. Judy enjoyed the novelty of having all the toys around her, being able to play with whatever she wanted whenever she wanted. Marie enjoyed sitting and watching, stretching her neck occasionally when Judy blocked her view.

One of Judy's habits, and the only thing we really objected to, was her constant hair chewing. When I told her to take it out of her mouth she became quite agitated and blew raspberries at me. Later on when they were in their nightclothes watching TV, sensible John sat Judy on a chair in front of him and brushed her hair down her back, making it less available for her mouth.

After Judy spent three successful weekends with us she came for half term. She really was no trouble. She seemed to appreciate everything we did for her. Her favourite pastime since she'd first arrived was dressing and undressing an old doll she'd found in the toy box. She did this for hours and never seemed to tire of it so I sorted out some baby clothes and put them in a carrier bag for her which she kept at the side of her chair. But if any of us went near her she stopped what she was doing and held her doll tightly so we couldn't take it from her. She eventually realised it was her doll and, unlike living on a ward, she didn't have to share it with lots of other children. On the day Judy was to return to the hospital, Chris, her social worker, called and seeing she was so happy, arranged for her to stay with us. We laughed at the surprised look on Judy's face when she stood up to leave with him before realising she didn't have to go. Her face was a picture as she stood there wringing her hands with pleasure.

'Are you going to say goodbye to Chris?' I asked her as John went to see him out. Infected by our laughter she strutted across the floor and pushed poor Chris over the step as she tried to close the door on him. It was all taken in good fun. Chris walked down the path pretending to be disgusted as he straightened his leather jacket.

When Chris had left I watched Judy curiously as she approached the cupboard in the playroom and lifted out some magazines. Standing there holding Patrick, I was intrigued. From the bottom of the pile she brought out a carrier bag: in it was her old doll that she had obviously been hiding until her next visit...

We were now into February 1982.

# 14
~

TRIPS HOME to Liverpool in our old transit van were quite a regular event. Friday nights when John arrived home from work we'd be packed and ready. Bottles, nappies, steriliser, wheelchair, toys and children would all be waiting eagerly to be loaded into the van.

My family were scattered throughout Liverpool and Cheshire. Waiting patiently for us to arrive, they never knew how many children I was going to turn up with. They were well used to me and made us all most welcome. Flying visits were all we could manage but they were worth the effort. Returning home on Sunday we were a little tired but refreshed.

Judy was settling very well — so well in fact that she was starting to put us to the test. She hated the sound of a firm voice and would flare up at the least sign of any disapproval of her behaviour, using her screeching as a weapon against us. Her biggest difficulty seemed to be having to cope with our slower pace after being used to the hospital's inevitable routine which was so rigid, especially at meal times. She could be sitting quite happily eating her lunch but if she caught sight of her pudding she would shovel the rest of the food into her mouth. Any comment from John or myself to slow down brought screeches of resentment which were so loud that I had to move her from the table. Then we felt guilty in case Judy saw it as another rejection. However our clever little Judy didn't mind one bit: in fact the arrangement suited her fine. Peeping through the door after a particularly noisy commotion I saw her sitting watching the TV. She'd turned it on and left the sound off! I smiled at her shrewdness. I sneaked back to the table to tell John. We both laughed at her spirit.

Marie took it all with a pinch of salt but only because we made light of it and kept distracting her. Having Judy around made me realise how difficult it must have sometimes been for Marie at school. Over the years I had learnt she could cope with noise but only with the help of someone steering her through it. I have learnt a lot through Marie: the most rewarding thing she has taught me is about people's individuality, and how to accept and respect it. Both John and I had agreed to be very careful with Judy and only disapprove of her behaviour when it was intolerable to avoid her feeling yet another rejection. Our expectation of fostering was not to have a group of perfect children. On the contrary we welcomed the difficult-to-place children and hoped with all our hearts that we could provide what they needed which was basically a warm and loving home. Too often I have seen children admitted to homes and hospitals where the staff have let their enthusiasm run away with them by putting the new children on 'programmes' before they have allowed themselves time to build a relationship with the child. This is simply because of their own ideas of how the child should be, and often the poor child ends up with more problems than he or she had in the first place.

We had been given surprisingly little information about Judy's behaviour problems and discovered after ringing Chris that this type of behaviour was normal for Judy. We were still trying to cope with her disruptiveness at the table and felt that by removing her all the time we were avoiding the issue. We compromised. Towards the end of the meal we brought in her pudding and allowed her to leave whatever food was on her plate providing she didn't screech. If she screeched we took it all away.

The next thing we attempted was to make her stay at the table until we'd all finished. She was usually pushing her chair back to leave before she'd finished chewing the last mouthful. She objected quite strongly to our request for her to wait and would put her hands under the table, trying to turn it over but we usually continued eating with our elbows firmly holding it down, trying to ignore her. After a while I realised once again how difficult it must have been for her and thought perhaps we were expecting a bit too much of her having to sit there with nothing to do. In the end I gave her a picture book to look through. Sitting across the table from her I was very moved when she smiled her appreciation over the top of the book as she glanced over at us.

Then there was her drinking... She liked to swallow it all down in one go. When she did this her eyes would look over the top of her cup at us as if she was rushing it before we jumped up and stopped her. She would then end up with a red face, coughing and spluttering. I felt that sometimes her behaviour was a reflection on how other people had reacted to her in the past. However, we would not allow Marie to behave like that so it wasn't really fair to let Judy. In the end we gave her a cup quarter full. She still rushed it, but it didn't have the same dramatic effect. Each time she finished we gave her another little drink. She was so pleased thinking she was having a special treat so after a few weeks we started filling her cup up again and she forgot all about the race.

Marie followed Judy everywhere, frightened of missing anything. She loved watching her play with the toys, sometimes handing Judy something to wind up.

'Come on, lazybones,' I'd tell her jokingly, 'do it yourself,' but Marie got more pleasure from watching. Most of the things Judy was able to do, Marie found most difficult: she'd never been able to fit two pieces of a jigsaw together, so Judy was very stimulating company.

When Patrick went to bed at night we'd tidy all the toys away. Judy was a great help; she was so thorough that ages after Marie and I had gone into the kitchen to make the cocoa, she was still picking bits off the carpet. She was so helpful that once she got the dish cloth and started washing the wooden panels in the sitting room. Unfortunately the cloth was full of spilt milk and I looked on in horror as the walls turned white, knowing I'd have to wait until she'd gone to bed before I set to cleaning it.

One evening John and I were developing some photographs in the kitchen. The kitchen was almost in darkness except for the low dark-room light in the corner. Marie and Judy stood in the doorway.

'What's the matter, Judy?' I asked when it became obvious she was trying to tell us something. She turned in the direction of the sitting room. I thought she'd gone to watch the TV until I heard the drawers in our desk opening. I could hear her laughing with satisfaction as she came running back into the doorway, smiling proudly and handing me a candle!

~

Patrick was five months old when Judy came to us permanently and Marie started at the local ATC. John had taken the morning off work to join us. Marie was surprisingly calm when she sat next to Patrick and I in the Manager's office after our initial interview. A social worker had rung me the previous day (at the Manager's insistence) from the local Social Services Department advising me that it was policy for all parents to be accompanied by a social worker to the Adult Training Centre. I told him if he had to be present then I would see him there. I also told him how I liked to pull my own strings. No offence was meant and I'm sure none was taken. We greeted each other the following morning and the interview began.

We were surprised to hear that Marie's old teacher had sent in a report to the Manager after a class visit to the ISU informing her that Marie had been very distressed while there. We were not aware that Marie had been to the Unit although we knew Marie's teacher had reservations about her attending there after she'd left school. Although the Unit could well have been the cause of Marie's distress I felt it was more likely that when she'd set off from school in the mini-bus she had not realised she was only going on a three-minute drive to the ATC. Knowing Marie, her loud objections would be for the abandoned mini-bus outside. I mentioned this to the Manager but she didn't appear to be listening to me. I also made a mental note to ring Marie's teacher and tell her how angry I was at not being informed of this incident. The Manager then went on to tell us how difficult we'd made things for them by keeping Marie at home, asking us if we'd been able to do anything at all with her. I resented being talked down to. However I was already aware of an icy distance between us so I said nothing. We had requested a part-time placement on the application form but they didn't bring it up for discussion, they just went ahead and made their own arrangements for her to go full-time. She was in their hands... I knew from looking around the Unit that the emphasis was on group activity and because of Marie's wilfulness and concentration I thought it would be too long a day for her to have to conform with this idea. But then, who was I to have any say in the matter?

'Good God,' John said unlocking the van in the car park, 'that was like being on the mat at school.'

'I know,' I said miserably. I was fed up with them all.

~

Having always been an early riser, busy mornings were no problem. With Patrick dressed and fed and the two girls ready to go we usually had an hour or so to bomb the playroom.

Judy was the first to depart in her taxi. Beautifully dressed in the clothes her parents bought, hair no longer falling over her face but held back with a brown velvet band, bag over her shoulder, she looked a picture. I had very tentatively introduced a diary between school and home to avoid the many misunderstandings created by verbal messages through third parties. It worked very well. In fact Judy's teacher took a great interest in her and often popped in after school for a chat.

After Judy left in the mornings I would put on Marie's coat and she would stand by the window waiting for the bus to reverse down the street.

'Not 'ere yet' she'd keep repeating impatiently. And then I would hear: 'Oh mam!' and then an even louder, 'bu-dy-ell'. I knew the bus had arrived.

Marie seemed happy enough when she arrived home in the evenings, kissing the walls and doors as she chatted to herself. I had always used a diary for Marie too, but the ATC staff met my proposal to continue with this arrangement with raised eyebrows. Reluctantly they agreed. In it I would be told when Marie needed 20p for an ice cream but not when she was coming home from the Unit two hours early, when she needed more elastics for her hair but not when she was throwing her food at them. I was given no information at all and consulted about nothing. I was later to learn that I had the reputation of an upstart. Not sending Marie straight to them from school had confirmed their beliefs, as they all wondered 'just who does she think she is?'

~

Eight weeks after Judy was placed with us another little girl arrived. Her name was Linda, and she was twelve years old. Her short black hair was a mass of knots at the back where she rocked herself to sleep at night. When she spoke there was hardly any eye contact: she looked down at the floor for most of the time. We used to tease her, saying, 'Let's see your lovely face', whenever she spoke and she would giggle shyly as she slowly raised her head to meet our eyes. However, this lack of eye contact in no way impeded her speech. She never stopped chattering. She was also very motherly and wanted to do everything for the girls so I had to explain there were some things they had to do for themselves. For example, Judy objected to Linda's kind attempts to help her with her jigsaw and she finally had to accept that although the girls were not as able as her, they were just as capable of asserting themselves and refused to accept her well-meaning bossiness. Then there was Marie whose friendly and affectionate nature appeals to most people: Linda was no exception. She looked on helplessly when Marie struggled to undress herself but I had to be firm on this because Marie, being the way she was, would quite happily let anybody do anything for her. Too often I had seen Marie put in other children's care at school with alarming results as they walked her into doors and dragged her over steps. Once on Open Day I watched helplessly while a child dragged her over a stack of wheelchairs, and the teacher wasn't even looking Marie's way as she stood up crying and was walked back to class on the hand of the brighter child.

~

'Aren't you bothered about bringing the baby up with them?' people would ask, but the girls treated Patrick like a prince and from the start I had very firmly forbidden them to touch him unless I was in the room. They accepted this so if he dropped his dummy, Judy or Linda would come running out to let me know. He had them all running around in circles. They dashed about the room trying to pick up all his baby toys and put them in his cot before he slung them all out again and they all laughed helplessly.

They each had their little jobs to do. As soon as I went to change Patrick's nappy Judy jumped up and got me his changing mat from behind his chair. Even if she was in the other room and she heard me talking to him she'd appear in the doorway to check if I needed it. Marie would hold his bottle for me but it was Linda whom I had to watch because she was always trying to pinch Patrick's clothes for her doll, which was why she always insisted on folding them.

'Oh look at this, Michelle,' she would say, holding one of his garments in the air. 'Isn't it lovely?' Then she would say, 'I think it's too small for Patrick though, don't you?'

'Hey, never mind,' I would answer playfully, 'just lay off and put them in the cot.'

'Oh okay darlin',' she would answer loudly as she laughed at her own cheek.

The three girls got on extremely well: perhaps because they were all so different they complemented each other.

Not long after Linda came to us we bought her a budgie for her birthday. She was ecstatic about it and called it 'Lion'. The day it arrived we placed it on top of the piano in its cage. Then I set to trying to arouse Marie's interest.

'Come and see the bird,' I said, almost dragging her across the playroom floor. She stood there very unimpressed before returning to sit with Judy and singing: 'Hatty-bird-day-to-you.'

Judy was different again! She was intrigued with it and wouldn't leave it alone, standing at its cage for hours and jumping back nervously if the bird so much as flapped its wings. Enjoying the sense of danger, when the bird was sitting on the far side of its cage Judy would wet her fingers and stick them through the bars, making the bird food stick to them as she tasted it. One day I heard a sudden scream and ran into the room. I nearly collapsed with laughter when I saw Judy running around the room with the bird perched on her head. She'd let it out of its cage. She'd learnt her lesson and was very careful after that incident not to get too close... There was no getting away from it — they were all a bundle of fun.

~

One day, not long after Linda had arrived, her social worker who'd recently been promoted to Fostering Officer at Lincoln rang me. She'd been to a meeting at Head Office with the fostering panel, and amongst them were two social workers from the local office. One of them had placed Richard with us and the other dealt with families of mentally handicapped people in the area. However, I was told that both these social workers had expressed their concern to the Divisional Director that John and I were allowed to foster two mentally handicapped children, and wanted to know who would take the rap if anything went wrong. The Divisional Director had apparently reminded these two social workers that we were coping with a child one of their homes had given up on. They had then both expressed their concern about the effects living with handicapped children might have on Patrick. I was mortified. I wished they'd concerned themselves with more important things and leave our son's welfare to us.

That same afternoon something happened which made Mrs Wilson's phone call seem like years ago. It was only months later I realised I should have taken them more seriously and not underestimated the lengths to which they would go to prove a point. Anyway, when we had first bought our houses one of our neighbours had expressed concern about the type of children we were going to look after, telling us it wasn't really the place for them. On this particular afternoon when I answered the doorbell she was standing on the step.

'Would your girls like these comics?' she asked, to my surprise.

'I'm sure they would,' I told her before inviting her in. You see, the girls had ignored her shyness over the weeks when they went in and out to school and usually waved to her whenever they saw her in the garden. After the comics she was always passing things in. She gave us a spare three piece suite and carpets for the little house next door we had recently purchased.

'It must cost you a fortune to furnish these places,' she told us. She was right and we were very grateful as our neighbours started taking an interest.

It was the same with shop assistants when the girls spent their pocket money. They were very shy at first and did not know how to react to the girls' overwhelming friendliness. Fortunately, it wasn't long before they were chatting back and helping them with their change, being genuinely pleased to see them.

# 15

P AST EXPERIENCE had taught me never to allow little problems to turn into big ones. My mother always said to nip them in the bud before they grew out of proportion. That was easier said than done in Marie's case. In my attempt to show the ATC staff I was not an upstart, I was turning a blind eye to things I should have pointed out.

When Marie had first started at the Unit, it was during her period. Although she'd had her pad changed, when she arrived home the soiled one was stuck down the leg of her tights having gone unnoticed by the staff. With three staff and only six handicapped people in the Unit I wondered how it had escaped the staff's attention. I let the incident pass and hoped it wouldn't happen again. On this particular day, however, I was concerned because for the last few evenings when Marie had arrived home her bra was up around her neck. I don't know how this happened but I did feel that the instructor should be made aware of it because Marie was so vulnerable and unable to protect herself in any way from being exploited. I decided to telephone the instructor.

'Do you think she's improved at all?' she asked me anxiously. I am very wary of people who feel they need to get results to show their own effectiveness. Marie was just seventeen and I didn't kid myself about her potential. Her development over the years had been very slow. Before I could speak, the instructor went on to tell me that the last time Marie had gone swimming she'd had an epileptic fit.

'But she went swimming two weeks ago,' I told her thinking we must have our wires crossed.

'Yes, that's right,' she answered.

'Why wasn't I told?' I asked her. 'Why are you only telling me now?'

'I forgot to send the diary home with her on Friday,' she told me casually, 'and when I returned after the weekend the urgency seemed to have gone out of it.'

I casually mentioned Marie's clothing. She told me she did not know how this could have happened but would look out for it in the future. I hung up wondering if she was for real!

John was very angry when I told him about Marie's fit. We were both concerned about their attitude towards the parents. Had Marie had fits every week we could have accepted it a little more but as far as we knew this was her first one. I didn't want Marie just to be supervised by the staff: I expected them to have a bit of feeling too. Both John and I finally agreed it would be a good idea to have a chat with the instructor. I sent a note in the following day suggesting this.

The day before our visit to the Unit we went to Linda and Judy's Open Day at school. It was teeming with rain when we ran through the car park and into the classroom. Patrick stole the show as all the children fussed him. We listened in amusement as Linda informed her class how she bathed and changed Patrick at night. The Deputy Headmistress popped in to say a quick hello.

'Did you know that Marie was in the hall?' she asked us. We shook our heads. Had we not had the girls in the school we'd have known nothing about Marie's visit. Naturally we went straight to the hall to greet her.

'I can't see her anywhere,' John said. We were almost at the back when I spotted her. I stopped to take John's arm to show him where she was. I was unable to speak. She was sitting with her little group. They looked so switched off from their surroundings they could have been dummies borrowed to fill empty seats, sitting in rain-soaked coats that nobody had bothered to remove for them. I fought the lump in my throat and forced a smile as I sneaked up on her putting my hands over her face for a bit of fun. I didn't even know who was accompanying them. I could see no member of staff so I removed Marie's wet coat for her and took her to sit with us further along the row.

The next afternoon, Patrick, John and I went to Marie's Unit. I hardly recognised her when I saw her sitting at a little table on her own. Her lovely long hair was tied back with a piece of string. It was a glorious day and she was sitting in her track suit with a nylon overall on top. The instructor greeted us and Marie's little face came alive when she saw us. Marie was due to go away with the Unit the following week and as requested by the staff, we'd brought her things a week earlier (for them to check she had suitable clothing for a holiday!). John handed it to the instructor and as she put it in the office we sat with Marie at her table.

It was Open Day and some of the parents were starting to arrive when in walked the Manager. John and I looked up to greet her but she walked past us, and past everybody else, without any kind of acknowledgement. Marie looked dreadfully uncomfortable sitting in the heat and when the instructor returned I asked her why Marie wore an overall.

'She sits and dribbles all day and soaks her clothes,' she said primly.

'She'll wipe her mouth if you ask her to,' I told her trying to sound helpful, 'and I can always send extra clothes with her if you want,' I offered. 'Would you mind if I take it off her? I think she's a bit too hot.' I folded Marie's overall on the back of her chair and removed the jacket of her track suit making her a bit cooler in her slacks and T-shirt. Marie kept leaning over and kissing Patrick's arm while he blew raspberries at her playfully.

'I'm pleased I've seen her with Patrick,' the instructor remarked, 'because she doesn't respond to many people, does she?' Our perceptions of Marie were obviously different. We started to walk around the Unit. Marie made me laugh when she put her arm through John's to accompany us.

I felt that Marie was out of her depth. Looking around the large bathroom I thought of all the hours of fun she would have if she'd been allowed to bath her dolls or play in some sand. I had seen her more stimulated on a hospital ward and yet here in the Unit she reminded me of an apathetic patient. However, I kept my views to myself and remarked on how nice the Unit was, because that part was true: it just seemed ideas on how to stimulate individual people were lacking.

'By the way,' the instructor said, 'the swimming will be on a Tuesday now instead of Friday.' I gulped and looked over at John. We didn't want Marie to go swimming any more but somehow I didn't think she'd understand why. She didn't. I told her we were worried after what happened the last time.

'But I apologised for that,' she said angrily, 'and what happens if she has a fit doing something else? Are you going to stop her from doing that too?' she asked with a smirk. John tried to reason with her, asking her to see it from our point of view.

'She'll have to go swimming,' she told us. 'All the group goes.'

'That doesn't matter,' I told her. 'She can have a day at home on the swimming day.' That made her very angry.

'You just remember this,' she almost snarled at us. 'I didn't have to tell you at all.' And with that bit of frightening information she left us standing in the middle of the floor and walked away.

'Round them up,' she shouted to her assistant. I looked on in amazement as the people in the Unit stood up to go over to the big hall.

The following day I wrote to the instructor telling her that if she did not feel answerable to us with regard to Marie's welfare then we were not very happy about her taking Marie on holiday. I asked her to return Marie's things.

The bag came home with Marie on the bus the next evening with a letter from the Manager asking me to keep Marie at home the following week because although the ATC was still open, the Unit would be closed.

The secret of our success was teamwork. Though we made every effort to give all of the children their fair share of attention we never forgot that unlike Marie and Patrick, who were in our sole care, Judy and Linda were in the care of the local authority with their two social workers, Carol and Chris, acting as their guardians. They were required by law to visit the two girls at least every six weeks. Their visits in fact were far more frequent, and because they were so helpful and supportive we looked forward to either of them popping in whenever they were passing.

We still came under fire, especially from social workers at the local office, not only because we fostered two mentally handicapped children but also because we were given special allowances to cover the cost of their needs. I didn't pay too much attention to what people said, but being accused of looking after handicapped people to profit from it touched a raw nerve. I mentioned it to Carol when she called one day.

'Take no notice of them,' she said in disgust. 'You've only got to look around your house to see where the money goes.' I hoped that in time the social workers would accept us and come around to our way of thinking. They refused to accept that an ordinary person like myself could cope with children who'd spent most of their lives in hospital being looked after by 'trained' nurses. I was fighting a losing battle.

At the beginning of the school holidays Rachel, John's niece, came to join our little household. She had finished her university course and was working through the summer with us before going on to teach. By this time I was two months pregnant. We were very happy with the news because we'd wanted the children close together. Rachel's presence in our family made an enormous difference to me. I had never allowed any of our helpers to look after Patrick and did everything for him myself, the reason being that in years to come I would not have to wonder if he'd had enough of my attention.

It was during the first two weeks of the holidays that Sara, my niece, came to stay and, because of the distance between our homes and the time involved in travelling, we had arranged to meet her Dad halfway to collect her. Just before we were about to leave Marie started to get cross. John had gone to fill up with petrol and she thought he had gone without us. It was amazing the way her moods swung: her perception of situations was so bad that had I tried to tell her John was coming back to collect us, she'd not have understood.

'Do you want to wait outside, Marie?' I asked as she stuck out her chin. This was the only way I could let her know she was still going. Her face creased up and she went to cover her eyes and cry. 'Oh here we go,' I groaned. 'Do you want to stay here?' I tried to sound as firm as I could because if Marie had started crying, that would have been it for hours.

'No,' she answered dramatically. Suddenly jumping up and down on the spot, she went out the front door giggling, before I could blink.

'What do you want now?' I asked when she came back into the room.

'A kiss,' she said. Pecking Rachel and I on the cheek she was gone again. Rachel looked very thoughtful after Marie had gone and I was putting on Patrick's coat.

'A penny for them?' I teased.

'It's a funny thing about Marie,' Rachel said, more to herself than any of us, and seeing my puzzled expression went on to explain. 'I know all the girls are affectionate,' she said shyly, 'and they're always kissing and hugging us, but when Marie does it it's as if she really means it.' I nodded in agreement: what a lovely thing to say.

Sara's two weeks flew. When she wasn't playing with Marie she was in the joke shop trying to find concoctions to catch us out. The itching powder was banned: we didn't mind the blue sweets, but I definitely objected to the laxative tea bags.

One day Sara was supposed to be amusing Patrick when I discovered her lying on the floor on her stomach reading a comic. In between her toes was a soft dog that he glimpsed as she slowly lifted her leg up and down to keep him amused.

'Oh isn't she cruel?' I laughed, lifting Patrick out of his cot, and catching sight of Marie's bus I shouted to Judy and Linda. They were both fascinated with the vehicle which had a lift on the back for people who couldn't cope with the steps. Marie giggled uncontrollably as she was lowered onto the ground. She was like the Queen arriving home, with everybody waiting to greet her.

Unfortunately my relationship with the ATC staff was still very strained. In an effort to improve the situation I had telephoned the Manager to arrange a meeting. She had sent me a letter telling me she was going on holiday and would contact me when she returned to arrange for us to meet. Marie still only attended the ATC four days a week, staying at home on the swimming day. This arrangement had worked out very nicely because it allowed Marie to have a day on her own with Patrick and I, though I have to admit, by this time Marie had become so used to having Judy and Linda around that she missed them if they were gone for more than a few hours.

# 16

I SHOULD HAVE known it was all too good to last. Always when least expected someone comes along and pulls the rug from under your feet. That's what happened to me anyway — it was like a giant wave sneaking up behind me, and I was too blind to see it coming. In short, my feet were pulled from under me and I was never the same again.

Carol, Linda's social worker, who had by this time been promoted to Fostering Officer, telephoned me one afternoon requesting to call and see John and I together that evening. She sounded a little subdued but I didn't pay too much attention: it was half term and I was busy with the children. Carol and I had a very good relationship and not only were we very alike, we also shared the same birthday (the same as Hitler's!). However, nothing could have prepared me for the bombshell she brought with her.

Marie had apparently been having problems at the ATC. None of the staff had notified me of this or had the decency to see if I could throw any light on the possible reasons. Instead, the Manager had asked a social worker from the local office to visit me, feeling that Marie's disturbed behaviour was due to her being very unhappy at home. She was screeching, pulling hair: they had noticed bruising on her body, she had lost weight and was very aggressive. In other words she was bored.

The District Officer at the local Social Services had refused to let any of his social workers deal with the problem and had referred it to the Director at Lincoln because he felt that Marie's problems were due to our fostering two other mentally handicapped children.

John and I were absolutely devastated. We'd had no idea. I thought that after having Marie for all these years and dealing with professionals, I was open minded and nothing would shock me: I was wrong. Carol went on to tell us that the ATC staff had been making notes of bruising on Marie's body for the last three months and the staff in the Unit felt she was seriously emotionally disturbed. They had even reported me for not allowing Marie to go swimming.

Before she left, Carol added insult to injury when she told us of the events which led up to this. The Director at Lincoln had asked Carol to look into the matter. She had then reluctantly visited the ATC and spoken with the Manager. Finally deciding the problem wasn't hers, she told the Manager to handle it herself in the proper way (i.e. by sending for me to discuss it with her). She also explained that she and another social worker visited us regularly and were quite happy with the conditions for all the children. However, the Manager did not contact me and the District Officer sent in another complaint to Lincoln. This time Carol was ordered to look into it.

We felt so humiliated, especially as we thought of all the people who had known before we did. Nobody had given us a friendly warning. Even Carol, though perhaps meaning well, had made a special twenty-mile trip from her office to discuss us with the Manager, almost driving past our home which is only five minutes drive from the ATC.

The most annoying thing was that they were describing the Marie we all knew. Had they been less arrogant and given themselves time to get to know her they'd have seen this for themselves. The lack of skill and understanding by the Unit staff seemed to defeat its whole purpose. The hardest thing to accept was the noted bruising on Marie's body. Carol was unable to enlighten us on this saying she would have to ring them and find out what they meant.

'Even if the allegations are untrue,' Carol said, 'I want you both to think very seriously about this because we have to think of our reputation in the type of foster parents that we select.' I didn't know whether to laugh or cry — or just to thank her for the vote of confidence.

Before Carol left she said she'd give us a couple of days and then she'd be back for some answers.

'No wonder the hospitals are full, Mish,' John muttered quietly, 'if people have to put up with things like this.' I nodded as I bit my lip. I was too frightened to speak.

'What kind of people are they?' he asked me, raising his voice, 'and look at you — five months pregnant.'

~

That weekend we were as miserable as sin. Early on Saturday morning we all went to the park but John and I sat like two strangers on a bench, both deep in thought as the children played around us.

I was frightened when I realised the powers social workers had. Watching our little boy running across the grass I wondered what steps they were allowed to take if ever they thought the girls were affecting him. I thought I could put up with a lot: I could not put up with this. If being a foster parent left one open to all kinds of accusations and spite then John and I obviously were not suitable candidates. Every time I looked at Marie a lump rose in my throat. I had to bully myself to try to accept that they were only doing their jobs, but it was difficult. Carol had phoned me the day before to ask our permission to visit us with a senior social worker. I was looking forward to straightening things out and clearing our names.

The dreaded Monday arrived and John took yet another afternoon off work so we could be seen together. Deep down I found it rather degrading having to explain about Marie's mental and physical condition and the behaviour problems which can arise from time to time. The senior social worker was very angry because they'd passed the buck instead of dealing directly with me. Carol then told us that Marie's bruising had been on her hands and lower arms. I was stunned.

'But she's always got bruises there from when she pinches herself if she's cross: they know that,' I said incredulously. 'So why did they suddenly start writing it down three months ago?' It slowly dawned on me that three months ago had been our disastrous Open Day when we had stopped Marie from going swimming.

We took Marie out of the ATC. At the time it seemed the only thing to do. Carol tried talking us out of it by telling us the ATC staff were quite prepared to sit around the table and talk with us but John and I were too hurt and angry and felt the situation had gone way past that stage.

'But they don't want you to remove her,' Carol said. 'She's so happy there and has improved so much.' I think that must have been the understatement of the year!

~

When you think you're as normal as the next person and then someone comes along and gives you a character assassination, it's very traumatic. I know it shouldn't be, but I found it so. The Manager had said I was difficult, unapproachable — but what threw me was being described as eccentric. I thought only elderly people acquired such descriptions. How could I, at the age of 29, be so? I was so shocked when the social worker casually gave me this information I quietly excused myself as if to check on the children. I sneaked a dictionary off the sitting room shelf, took it to the bathroom and, sitting on the edge of the bath, looked up the word 'eccentric'!

Given that period of my life again I would sit and laugh at them all. It no longer matters what they think of me, and as far as Marie goes I know they would stoop to any level in abusing their powers to prove they are the experts and are always right. It has been my experience that if you have a handicapped child, the Social Services don't like it if you don't put yourself in their hands. Even though I'd looked after Marie for ten years and had managed without their 'support' they could not accept me. Their concern was that even though we had social workers looking after the foster children's interests, there was no social worker looking after Marie's. However, sitting on the edge of the bath that day I wondered why nobody had ever told me. 'Odd, unconventional, deviates from the norm', the dictionary described me. I swilled my face so they couldn't see I'd been crying and went to join them.

Many letters were exchanged.

Despite my depression I still had enough fight in me to go and see my solicitor. He wrote to the Director at Lincoln asking for some justification for the accusations against us. A few days later we received the following reply:

'Thank you for your letter informing us of your instructions from Mrs Daly. The circumstances are that Mrs Hardy, as the Manager of the ATC, where Marie was attending, reported to the fieldworker that bruising had been noted on Marie over a period of days. Mrs Wilson, Fostering Officer who supervises two children in Mrs Daly's home, was asked to discuss the matter with Mrs Daly from the point of view that Marie was falling about more often. It was intended to discuss possible reasons for this and other matters noted in Marie's physical condition and attitude. However, Mrs Daly saw this discussion as implied criticism of her handling of Marie and regrettably in my view, has chosen to withdraw Marie from the centre.

'Mrs Wilson, with the senior social worker Mr White will be visiting Mrs Daly again and I hope it will be possible for Marie to be allowed to attend the centre once again.'

~

I felt like banging my head against a wall. The man who wrote this letter eventually came to see us and apologised for what had happened. He agreed that we should have been contacted initially by the ATC staff and he would inform them of this. He also said that a lot of water had gone under the bridge since he had written to us, adding that he would not expect Marie to return to the centre as we probably had no confidence in the staff. How right he was...

~

I looked after all the children up until three days before my second baby was due. Ideally I should have been able to go into hospital without anybody needing short-term care. It was their home too and having a baby was such a natural event for them to experience. Instead, my wonderful Irish midwife arranged for me to go into hospital a week earlier than the obstetrician had planned in order for me to organise everybody's short-term care. Even though the social workers had said I'd over-reacted I was very nervous about leaving the children at home while I was away. I had visions of returning home to find everybody had been taken into care, including Marie and Patrick. I was having another Caesarean section and expected to be in for at least two weeks. I was taking no chances.

Judy went into a children's home, Linda went to stay with her grandparents and Marie went onto her usual ward at the local hospital for mentally handicapped children. I felt such a failure.

~

Anna was born on 3rd February, 1983. She was a bonny little thing and like Patrick, had a mop of black hair. Then came all the cards, flowers and telegrams. What should have been a wonderful occasion was tinged with sadness when I thought of my little boy at home and the three girls staying in separate places.

'I want to sign myself out,' I told the ward sister the day after Anna was born. She was very kind and very shocked.

'But you can't go yet,' she told me gently, 'don't you realise you've had major surgery?'

I nodded. 'I have to go,' I told her.

'Will you at least stay and see the doctor?' she asked me anxiously.

I agreed because I didn't want anybody to think she'd upset me, and blame her. I rang John at work and put on Anna's clothes. The doctor arrived and despite her efforts to make me stay she knew I was determined to go and that I'd only waited to see her out of courtesy.

'You seem sensible enough,' she finally said, 'but please take it easy when you get home.' They must have thought I was crazy!

~

We decided to move from the area. What kind of environment was it to bring children up in if I was frightened to leave them in the house when I wasn't there?

Judy's parents were told of our plans to move up north, and they decided they did not want her to move that far from home. We were very sad about this but knew that the fourteen months she'd spent with us would have helped her enormously to adjust to a children's home. It was a very sad day for us all when we piled into our blue mini-bus to take her to the home.

We rented a house at the beginning of the summer holidays and, leaving our house on the market, we moved up north. Our new home was a lot smaller that what the children had been used to and they desperately missed the play space. Despite our great efforts, none of us liked it.

The week before Linda was due to start her new school we went to have a look around the ATC. We were very impressed. The 'students' as they called the mentally handicapped people were not looked down on from a great height: they were very much on the same level as the staff and treated with the dignity and respect they were entitled to. Instead of monotonous routines they had one free day when they did as they pleased. We explained what had happened in Lincolnshire and they accepted our decision not to have a social worker but to deal directly with them to avoid complications. We looked around their Intensive Support Unit, where Marie would most likely be going, and breathed a sigh of relief at the brightly coloured toys along the shelves. I knew straight away that she would like it and the staff would accept her for what she was without expecting her to grow up overnight and be the adult her eighteen years told them she should be.

For the first time in months, things seemed to fall into perspective. I had almost been convinced of my worthlessness and that old suspicion that comes now and again had been lurking about — had I really been selfish in bringing Marie out of hospital and had I really done her more harm than good? And slowly, ever so slowly, it dawned on me — we should have stayed where we were and fought for Marie's rights. At the time we had felt too injured ourselves.

When we arrived home John and I sat in our little kitchen. For the first time in months I felt good. I put on the kettle for some coffee.

'Where would you rather live?' I asked John as he sat doing the crossword. He put down his pen and grinned at me: 'This house is nice,' he said, 'but it's not really suitable for all of us, is it?'

Not only am I very impulsive, I am also very superstitious. Because we had not sold our house in Lincolnshire I was sure we were not meant to leave it. The funny thing was, we'd had to build the dividing walls in an attempt to sell them separately, because most potential buyers had thought they were too big.

We returned within a week, seeming like we'd only had a long summer holiday. Four days later we had the dividing walls knocked out again and the playroom painted. It was as if we'd never been away. John and I laughed as we watched the children playing. Marie was over in the corner kissing her piano: Patrick and Linda were running up one side of the stairs and down the other. My little blue-eyed Anna was cooing excitedly in my arms. Yes, it was chaos, it was good to be back.

~

The following week I took Marie to the doctor's. Strangely enough he had to leave the room for a minute. I noticed a letter on the top of Marie's notes with the Social Services' letter heading on it, so I opened it. It was from a social worker at the local office. In her letter she told my doctor how I fostered two mentally handicapped children and of the problems the ATC had been having with Marie, of the bruising that had been noted on her body and of her concern for Marie's welfare. She went on to explain that even though Carol and Chris supervised me with the two foster children in my home, there was nobody to supervise me with Marie. She finished by telling him that if he was ever worried about Marie, he should not hesitate to contact either herself or the District Officer at the local Social Services. I was devastated.

So many things were going through my mind when I strolled out of the doctor's that sunny afternoon. John and I had so many rows over social workers that I dreaded telling him. Then a kind of relief flooded over me as I realised I had not over-reacted after all. I was thankful that we had returned and shuddered as I thought how that letter would have followed me wherever I went and I'd have known nothing about it. We were obviously meant to return and finish what we had started.

# 17

I HAD BEEN foolish to think we could carry on where we had left off. Our fresh application for Marie to return to the ATC had been rejected — no vacancies. This surprised me greatly. I had been led to believe before we had left the area that there was ample space, and now I was being told Marie would have to go on a waiting list. They could give me no indication of how long the list was or where Marie was placed on it. Always the dangerous optimist, I imagined it would only be a matter of weeks: after all we still fostered a severely mentally handicapped child from the Social Services and surely, I thought, they'd wish to make life as easy as possible for us to enable the fostering to run smoothly. They couldn't have cared less. If only I'd known then that it would be six long years before Marie was once again to take her rightful place in the Unit.

The Social Services' one and only concern was for Linda's needs. Under normal circumstances that's how it should have been, but our circumstances were far from normal. Our lives had been turned upside down. With Marie at home all day, plus an eight-month-old baby and a two-year-old toddler, it was very difficult to pick up the pieces and put the past behind us. They obviously were not going to let us forget. I had made my bed and now I had to lie in it. It was a matter of rolling up my sleeves and getting on with it. We'd had so many plans for the future, so many dreams...

~

It was a very hard decision to stop fostering because we had become so attached to Linda: she was like one of our own children. Yet her presence in our home was bringing us nothing but misery as social workers walked all over us. They often called at tea time, when I would naturally be busy looking after the children and preparing the evening meal. Sometimes when John came home from work the children would be sitting around the table eating while a social worker sat on the settee sipping coffee indifferently as he whiled away the time. Knowing I'd been on my own with the three children all day and bringing no news of any kind of day care for Marie, I knew it took John all his efforts not to throw him out. It was after he left that the rows would start. Finally, after many sleepless nights and much soul-searching we asked the Social Services to find Linda another home. Linda had lived with us for two years: we had to live with that decision forever. Though the decision had been a very hard one to make, by closing the door on the Social Services we not only gained our privacy but also found our self respect.

The children, unaware of any difficulties we'd had with officials, thought Linda was returning home. They missed her terribly after she went and constantly asked me when she was coming back. Many, many times I wanted to ring up the Social Services to tell them that I was sorry, that I would put up with anything if we could just have Linda back. I was being foolish. We'd made the decision and we had to live with it.

By the time we had been back in Lincolnshire for a year, I employed a young girl to come in and help me. With only twenty months between Anna and Patrick, it was like having twins. Far from being the baby, as soon as Anna was toddling about she was kicking her nappy off and insisting on using the toilet like Patrick and Marie. Bathtime was great fun. With Marie's generous dose of bubble bath, Patrick and Anna were submerged almost to their mouths in suds. Kneeling at the side of the bath, Marie loved to help. Getting a good lather on the flannel she washed their backs and legs most thoroughly.

The children were my life. Nothing else mattered to me as long as they were happy. Years of looking after Marie had put an end to any social life John and I might have had. I was not too bothered; I had learned to create my own interests at home. I loved to read, especially biographies. I was always looking for an opportunity to sneak off to a quiet part of the house and stick my head in a book. Music was another form of escape. I was an avid record collector. From the moment I got up in the mornings the records were played for most of the day. It didn't matter how low I was feeling, music always lifted me out of my gloom. The Beatles have always been a favourite, as they are with Patrick and Anna today.

Just to remind myself there was a world outside of the house, occasionally when John came home from work I'd go and have a look around the shops on my own. Instead of testing the new perfumes on the cosmetic counter or browsing in the lingerie store, more often than not I'd find myself standing in the middle of the toy shop winding up all the Fisher Price toys!

Eventually, my helper became rather unreliable. Sometimes she'd go home for lunch and wouldn't return in the afternoon. It seemed less trouble to get on with things myself than to wait around for someone who constantly let me down. Apart from the refreshing change for the children I was quite happy on my own.

~

Despite my outward cheerfulness I was full of inner turmoil. It was Anna's second Christmas and still there was no day care for Marie. I felt so guilty. Without a doubt Patrick and Anna loved Marie, her gentle disposition and endless patience made them very loving and protective towards her. I know one of the dreaded fears of having a handicapped child is the other siblings feeling responsible for their care. But there is a great difference in enjoying a child and being burdened with her. Marie was a bind, there was no doubt about that — there were places we couldn't go and people we couldn't see, but I never told the children that. I always used the bad weather or some other excuse rather than Marie's handicap, thus avoiding her being resented. Nevertheless spending day in and out with Marie in their formative years was not part of the plans John and I had for Patrick and Anna.

Every few months I wrote reminding the Social Services that Marie was still sitting at home all day but they couldn't give a damn. It seemed ironic that they were hurting the very person they had set out to protect. They had a duty to provide day care but it seemed they were a law unto themselves. I just prayed the day would never come when I would have to put Marie in the hospital because I couldn't cope with her at home. I dared not even think about it. It would never come to that — surely it would not.

~

Although Marie was nineteen, she couldn't have been with a better age group. The house was like a toy shop and, to compensate for being housebound on some days, the playroom was also full of garden toys dominated by a big red and yellow slide in the middle of the floor. The children's constant chatter as they flitted from one curiosity to another kept Marie occupied for most of the day. Late afternoon, just when my batteries needed recharging, who came hoot-hooting cheerfully on the TV screen but Thomas the Tank Engine! Snuggling up either side of Marie on the sofa there wasn't a peep out of any of them while Thomas and his naughty friends kept them entertained.

Week after week, month after month, I would anxiously scan through the post every morning to see if there was a letter offering Marie a place in the Unit, but there never was. I knew when I looked at the children I should have put up more of a fight. Though Marie was happy she was not getting the exercise and stimulation she needed. However, to have battled with officials for Marie's day care would have used up the emotions and energy I badly needed to play the 'happy' mother.

I could also have gone to the Press. That was something else I was unable to deal with for various reasons. Not only did I hate the focus of attention and lack of privacy, I did not want the children exposed to the publicity. It was one thing to stand up for what I believed in, but there was no way the children were going to carry my banners for me.

Most days I tried not to think about the injustice of it all. On other days I felt so despondent that guilt would envelop me. If only... I hadn't been so mouthy ... if only the fostering had worked out and we'd been able to keep the girls ... if only I wasn't so direct with people.

Unable to sleep at night I would sit by the downstairs window and look out at the moon as the hours ticked slowly by. Often I felt so tired I didn't know how I was going to get through the next day but my over-active mind would not let me sleep.

Returning to bed in the early hours of the morning I used to wonder if the social workers would ever forgive me for standing up to them and refusing to be bullied. I wondered too if I would ever forgive them for making my children suffer because of their differences with me. I felt nothing but contempt for them. They treated us with casual disregard, and I accepted it.

What we really needed was someone to take on Marie's case. I knew my hands were tied and there was nothing I could do. I could fill a phone directory if I were to list the organisations I rang for help and support. Most of them gave me unwanted advice and completely missed the point. Some said it was time I 'let go'. Decent residential care for mentally handicapped adults was very hard to come by. Had I been offered decent day care resulting from a residential placement then I certainly would have considered it for Marie, but I was not. Hanging up the phone I'd regret having contacted them because they always reinforced the low opinion I already had of myself.

One day I rang the regional office of Mencap in Nottingham. I explained the situation as best as I could. There was a sigh on the other end of the phone: 'Your lot have a right reputation in Lincolnshire, you know?' He obviously didn't mince his words either.

I giggled knowingly. 'Well... it is partly my fault because I have this knack of upsetting people.' I hadn't reached this stage of my life without seeing the error of my ways. I didn't apologise to him for being me, I simply stated a fact.

'That's nonsense! Shouldn't even come into it,' he said firmly. 'You should hear the way I speak to them sometimes — but that's life, isn't it? They can't exclude someone from the local training centre because her mother does not agree with everything they say. And how long did you say your daughter has been waiting for a place?' he asked. I told him it was 1½ years. He went on: 'I know for a fact that the ATC in your area is one of the few in the country that isn't fully utilised.' He promised to write to the Social Services to ask them what they were playing at. I didn't hold my breath. I knew it could take them three months just to reply to a letter. They were, after all, a law unto themselves...

~

Every so often Marie went into the hospital for a week or two. Using the hospital was only a temporary solution to a long-term problem. With emphasis on care in the community, using the hospital to give the rest of the family a break was far from acceptable but it was all there was — and by God we were glad of it!

For Marie, two weeks on the ward was long enough before her behaviour started to deteriorate and the old behaviour problems began to surface. Yet what made the nurses' attitude different from other professional carers was their realistic acceptance of Marie and her capabilities. Her pretty looks and good manners often suggested a higher degree of intelligence than we all gave her credit for. This had been half the problem with inexperienced ego-tripping ATC staff. They had refused to accept her as she was and had their own ideas of how she should be. I had much more confidence in the nurses.

The other source of support was still my ever-faithful Aunty Terry. Marie still went to stay with her for occasional weekends and still got spoilt with kindness and adoration. Most of the children who'd looked after her protectively all those years ago when Marie had first gone to Terry's had now grown up and had children of their own. Marie was always known as 'the little girl from the newspapers,' stirring up fond memories and great warmth and affection from the local people. They all loved to see her.

Not only did it enable John and I to spend more time with Anna and Patrick, it also made a pleasant change for Marie to go and see her 'Tommin'.

~

My biggest regret was not being able to drive. I had always wanted to, yet had this terrible fear of being involved in an accident and being unable to look after Marie. When the children came along I knew I should have made more of an effort but I was just too nervous and felt I was relied on more than ever.

149

Trips to town at first had been a nightmare. With two toddlers and a handicapped child, just preparing to go was a ritual. When they eventually had their boots, hats, gloves and snowsuits on and their zips, laces, ribbons and buttons were fastened, we were ready to go.

Marie went in her wheelchair, Patrick held onto one side and Anna (supported by her reins that I held) held onto the other side as we slowly made our way to the shops.

We went at a snail's pace, stopping to inspect every little distraction along the way. Cats were the most fascinating as they ran in between the cars and hid behind the wheels. The children thought they were playing hide and seek with them and waved sadly when we had to move on.

When Anna showed signs of becoming tired I would lift her onto Marie's lap to give her little legs a rest. Marie immediately came to life. Sitting back in her chair to make room, arms outstretched she would laugh happily.

'Om on!' she'd say putting her arms protectively around Anna's waist, 'Om on, Narna,' she coaxed. Up in the comfort of Marie's arms unaware that I was still holding the reins so Anna wouldn't fall off Marie's knee, the repertoire of nursery rhymes would start as we continued our journey to town.

'Aren't they lovely?' people would remark, 'they're such happy children.' Their kind words touched me with relief. For the first time in my life I had no friends living near me. Bridget, my long time friend, lived some sixty miles away, so there wasn't really any yardstick by which to measure the children's development. I just plodded on each day and hoped for the best. Maybe if the children had been naughty and unmanageable the situation would have been easier to accept, but they were always so well behaved.

On the way home Patrick used to ride on the foot bars at the back of the wheelchair so he wouldn't feel left out. There was some weight between them!

~

Occasionally a neighbour called in for a coffee but it was usually more trouble than it was worth.

'Mum,' Patrick whispered, 'I think Marie is going to start!' I was in the kitchen making coffee for one of the old ladies in our road who'd supported our fostering plans in the early days, when Patrick came and stood in the doorway. 'Should we just ignore her?' he asked. I pulled my funny face and looked towards heaven. That always made him giggle.

'I would if I were you,' I told him, 'she's just being silly because we have a visitor.' Handing him a tin of biscuits I picked up the tray and followed Patrick into the sitting room. Marie was indeed starting. Having heard the cups rattling in the kitchen and having to wait for her drink she was sitting pinching herself on the hand. One would have thought that after all these years together either Marie would have learnt to wait or I would have mellowed and given into her — no way. It was still a battle of wills between us. Taking the lid off the biscuit tin she tried to force herself to cry. 'Oh no,' I thought 'here we go!'

'If you don't behave yourself I'll send you out of the room,' I told her firmly. She knew I meant it and decided to laugh instead. It was nice having visitors but Marie was always twice as hard to look after with her manipulative behaviour. If I hadn't checked her then, she'd have got out of hand and spoilt it for everyone. If I wanted to keep her at home I had to be very strict with her.

~

As time went by I slept less and less. I had recently received a letter from Mencap which took away what little hope I'd had. They had been informed by the Social Services that although there were vacancies in the workshop at the ATC there was no room in the Unit and because of the maximum attention Marie required the workshop would not accommodate her.

I was very upset when I read the letter. It was okay for me to struggle on at home for the last two years with Marie at home all day and two little children to look after — for the ATC staff who only worked from 9-4 Monday to Friday, she was too much hard work.

By the time John arrived home in the evening I was laughing at the hypocrisy of it all. If I hadn't laughed I'd certainly have cried. Switching off from things was becoming a bad habit with me. It was the only way I coped. For as much as I laughed and joked (and did my crying on my own) I knew I was running out of time and I had to face reality. Patrick was almost $3\frac{1}{2}$ and ready to go to nursery. I didn't want to be having to gauge Marie's moods when we were getting ready to go out in the mornings. Patrick had enough to cope with, starting a new nursery. I couldn't believe we had reached this stage and there was still no light at the end of the tunnel.

Finally in desperation John and I went to see the hospital psychiatrist. I was clutching at straws again and was hoping that if we provided the transport Marie would be allowed to go on the wards as a day patient. Even one or two days a week would have relieved some of the burden. We were prepared to give anything a go if it meant keeping Marie at home.

Although the psychiatrist was very sympathetic, he felt the twenty-mile daily journey for Marie would be too much for her to cope with and suggested we let Marie live on the ward from Monday to Friday, and have her home at weekends. We drove home in silence. Choice is a luxury — we didn't have any.

When you love one of your children as much as the other, it's heartbreaking to have to choose between them. That's how I felt, like I'd been put in the position where I had to decide who was most important. Perhaps I should have loved Marie less because she hadn't been born to me, but I didn't.

Sadness replaced my animosity towards the social workers. How could I feel angry towards such a pathetic group of people who would go to such extremes to prove a point.

~

Standing in front of the mirror wearing her best pink track suit, face alight in anticipation of what was to come, Marie had no idea I was getting her ready to send her into hospital. Anna sat near us on the stool holding Marie's hairbrush and slides. Patrick kept watch out of the window for the ambulance which came from 8.30 onwards. Putting his hand conspiratorially to the side of his mouth as he watched Marie, he kept whispering to me that it hadn't arrived yet. He was so funny, and so sensible for a little boy. We had the records on as usual and I must have appeared a bit chattier than normal but it took all my efforts to hold myself together. I sighed dramatically as I faced Marie in the mirror.

'Oh Marie, you look so beautiful,' I told her as I released the curling tongs and her mousy hair fell in springy ringlets. She *was* beautiful too; everybody said so. Anna passed me the slide as her eyes rested adoringly on Marie.

'Will Marie be home tonight?' Anna enquired. I had been over it with them a hundred times but they were both too young to understand. I explained to her once again as best I could. Eyes growing like saucers she searched her little mind for something to say: 'What if she cries for us?'

Clearing my throat I sent her off to get some perfume to spray on Marie.

When the ambulance finally arrived we put on Marie's coat and took her out to the gate. Laughing and joking and being their usual cheerful selves, the ambulance men let the children have a ride up on the ramp with Marie. Giggling happily when they reached the top they were lifted down as Marie went and sat in the back. Standing the children on the garden wall so they could see, we waved to Marie through the windows as the vehicle slowly drove up the terrace. Beeping the horn when it reached the top, it turned the corner and she was gone.

# 18

~

THANK GOODNESS our lack of contact with the outside world in no way impaired Patrick's development. Though a little shy at first, when the time came for him to start nursery his feet hardly touched the floor as he ran across the playground. He was a very happy child with a great sense of fun. His appearance was almost comical with his big brown eyes and mop of dark curly hair. Sometimes I wondered if God had given me extra happy children to enable them to live with Marie.

Unlike Patrick who had everybody eating out of his hands, Anna liked to sit back and weigh people up. She was extremely observant for such a young child and seemed to know straight away whether or not people were sincere. Strangely enough Anna and Marie had the same colouring — lovely blue eyes and light brown hair.

'Can't you tell they're sisters?' I was often asked (much to my delight!) And of course, as far as the children were aware Marie *was* their big sister.

'Is Marie coming home today, Mummy?' That was the question I was greeted with each morning. Unaware of Marie's plight, the children thought she was having a wonderful time at the hospital but they missed her enormously and looked forward to her return on a Friday evening.

Already, by the end of the first week I'd had a row with the ward sister who had told me in no uncertain terms that Marie should not be on 'her' ward. She upset 'her' girls with her screaming and screeching and should be on the other ward — 'with patients of her own calibre' were the words she used. (A ward for the more profoundly handicapped person.)

I felt very hurt, not only at the way she spoke to me but also the callous way she spoke of Marie. I knew the psychiatrist had tried Marie on this ward as a favour to me. If the ward sister resented Marie that much her presence on the ward was counter-productive. I was alarmed at the thoughts of her speaking to other parents like that. I wrote to the Health Authority and complained about her attitude.

~

Each morning after we took Patrick to nursery, Anna and I went shopping. It was on one of these trips that her foot got trapped under the foot rest on her buggy and the poor little mite broke her leg and ended up with it in plaster. From then on Anna had to go out in Marie's wheelchair and just like Marie had done for Anna, she shoved over for Patrick enabling him to have a ride to school each morning.

When Fridays came around we made our great plans for Marie's homecoming.

'You won't forget the Maltesers, will you, Mummy?' Patrick enquired.

'And the crisps and rice pudding,' Anna would remind me.

The whole day was taken up waiting for Marie to arrive. Her twenty-mile journey could take up to two hours as the ambulance drove around the countryside dropping people off. However, there was always one of us looking out the window: we were all dying to see her. As soon as the ambulance was spotted reversing down the terrace the door was flung open and once again the children waited on the wall to welcome her home. The joy on their little faces made me almost eat my lips to avoid crying, especially the day I lifted Anna onto the wall and she had Marie's slippers in her hand.

Marie was obviously very happy to be home but she was always pale and tired looking. She was so badly behaved on the ward she almost exhausted herself and was usually starving because she'd hardly eaten.

The children adored her and did everything possible to make her comfortable. After Patrick had struggled to remove Marie's shoes, Anna put her granny slippers on (usually on the wrong feet). I didn't have the heart to tell her as she puffed and blew in an effort to do up the zips.

With everybody comfortable they'd sit on the settee either side of Marie and open the box of Maltesers for her. When everyone was munching away the fun would start.

'Mmmm. Mice!' Marie would remark when she offered Anna or Patrick a chocolate. Opening their mouths when it almost reached their lips she would change her mind and put it in her own. Of course they knew what she was up to; she'd done it to them so often, yet they always fell about laughing just as she had when I'd done it to her in the past.

~

Marie's diary was very helpful and a great source of communication between the hospital and home. Her behaviour varied from day to day depending on how bored she was and what kind of mood she was in. One day's comments went: 'Screamed for approximately half an hour this morning, pulling her own hair to make herself cry — stopped for a while then started again. Ripped her tights and pulled a button off her dress, was changed into trousers after lunch and spent the afternoon playing quite happily.'

Looking at her sitting with the children one would never have guessed she could be so badly behaved.

'Have you been carrying on for the nurses?' I would ask, pretending to be cross. Glancing over to me with her mouth full she didn't have a care in the world: 'Tut tut tut,' she'd say casually before turning to her two little companions and offering them another chocolate. 'Mmmm' was all she'd say for the next hour.

~

Constant reinforcement was the reason for Marie's good behaviour at home: two few nurses and too many patients was the reason for Marie's bad behaviour on the wards. Quite apart from anything else, I was worried about the infections she was bringing home. Dysentery was the biggest nightmare and it was not unusual for one ward or another to be in isolation because of it. Again we were swimming against the tide. It was obvious from Marie's disruptive behaviour on the wards that it wasn't doing her any good at all and if the children were to become ill because of some infection Marie had caught, then we would all go under.

On Mondays when Marie returned to the hospital we toddled off to school and got on with our lives as best we could. Each weekend she arrived in a worse state than the previous week. She was always very pale and tired and her mood swings were becoming more frequent, to such an extent that by the time she settled down with us it was time for her to return to the hospital again.

Things finally came to a head when she arrived home one weekend in the most appalling state. She had a very high temperature and a nasty scratch on her nose: accompanying her was a bottle of Valium with the following message:

'Due to Marie's behaviour, Doctor has prescribed 5mg Diazepam to be taken at 9 p.m. Some tablets enclosed for use at home.'

One side of Marie's face was like sandpaper it was so chapped, because she'd slept for so long sitting up in a chair soaked in dribble. She had diarrhoea which showed no sign of clearing up after two days. I was panic stricken, so scared of any infection spreading I wouldn't even use the washing machine and put the soiled linen and night clothes in a sealed bag in the bin. Our doctor was also concerned and said if there was no sign of it clearing by the next day we would have to take a swab to the lab.

I knew we'd come to the end of the road. A decision had to be made. We'd reached the stage where Marie either came home for good or she stayed at the hospital permanently. I knew deep down what we had to do. I think any mother would have done the same.

Only that weekend Patrick's term had ended and he'd collected his little school uniform in order to join the Kindergarten class upstairs in the private school after the Easter holidays. It was almost as if God had given me a certain amount of time to get myself organised and was now saying to me, 'Enough is enough'.

I wrote to the psychiatrist thanking him for his support and informing him that Marie would not be returning to the hospital.

During the Easter holidays Anna had her plaster removed, enabling Marie to go back into the wheelchair and the children to have a ride.

~

Pushing the children to school each morning I passed a lovely big old house for sale right opposite Patrick's school. With Marie now at home it seemed an ideal place to live. I could leave Marie sitting at the window where I could see her from the street and take the children over the road to school. The price was reasonable though there was a great deal of work to do on it. It seemed the answer to all of our problems: I kept my fingers crossed.

We were all thrilled at the prospects of moving. The house was the back half of a big old mansion. Not much of a garden but who cared, there was plenty of space indoors — large living room, kitchen and dining room, a cloak room and a small room large enough to make a little bedroom for Marie. She had always slept far enough away from the children not to frighten them if ever she woke up screaming from a nightmare or cramps in her leg. Upstairs there were three bedrooms and a large bathroom.

The owner, a little Irishman called Mr Cochran, still lived in the front of the house. He was a very trusting man. The house for sale had previously been let as two flats and was still fully furnished. I expected the house to be empty by the time the sale was completed. There was a few bob to be had for that second-hand furniture.

Most mornings when we went to school we looked across to the house with great excitement. John and I would find any excuse to collect the keys from the estate agents just to have 'another' look around.

I liked Patrick's school but there was never any information available for parents — no booklet, no news sheet, nothing. It could have been the reason the fees were so cheap but I would have preferred to pay the extra and be kept informed, instead of getting instructions by word of mouth from other parents. Often it was a nuisance but I turned a blind eye (thinking it was just me!). I shouldn't have.

On swimming day for example I arrived at Patrick's school only to be told by a helper in the nursery that the class met at the baths. The parents then stayed at the pool to help dress and undress the children. That was all very well but for me to have stayed at the pool with Patrick would have been impossible. Luckily John had driven us to school that day and we were able to go to the pool, but ordinarily I just couldn't do it. That's what we paid them for — that extra special attention.

As it turned out Patrick didn't enjoy the swimming session. It was too noisy and chaotic and besides, his Dad took him and Anna to the pool every Sunday, so that was the end of that.

The lady who ran the school also lived on the premises with her retired husband. She made no secret of the fact that they were getting divorced and the poor man, who looked like a zombie as he walked through the school, lived alone in the attic. His wife had been in her husband's shadow during his lifetime as Headmaster and had stepped into his shoes when he retired. With only three classrooms and so few children in the school one would have thought she'd have become familiar with the pupils and their parents but we hardly ever saw her. There was only herself and another full time teacher in the school. Patrick's teacher only worked four mornings a week and often the classes doubled up in the afternoons. Children who didn't want to go swimming went straight to school on the swimming day and sat in the nursery classroom downstairs until their own class returned.

For a while things went smoothly and then something awful happened. Anna was not very well one particular week so John arranged for Patrick to travel to school by taxi and I informed the Headmistress of this. We knew Henry, the taxi driver, very well. Often over the years he had taken Marie twenty miles to the hospital for us and continued to do so even after the following incident occurred: that's how much confidence we had in him.

Each morning when the taxi arrived, Patrick climbed into the car like a young prince, looking very smart in his little cap and blazer, a figure of the 'Incredible Hulk' clutched in his hand.

'Here's my driver, bye Mum!' he would shout as he marched down the path obviously feeling very important.

Arriving home with John on the last day I knew something was wrong when Patrick went and sat behind the couch. I don't think I'd ever seen him look miserable before. I was mystified. During lunch he picked at his food and just sat there looking very sad for most of the time.

Most afternoons the four of us usually sat around the big table colouring in. Usually it was difficult to get a word in edgeways as they chatted amongst themselves but Patrick remained very quiet and subdued. I playfully lifted him out of the chair and sat him on my knee.

My family had affectionately nicknamed him Pinocchio: ('I've got no strings to tie me down!') and here on my knee, head drooping and little legs dangling, he did indeed resemble a puppet — a sad one.

'What's the matter, Patrick?' I asked him gently.

'Nothing,' he replied sadly.

'I know!' I said cheerfully, 'let's play puppets!' I went to the toy box and brought out Sooty. He was definitely the favourite and had them all in stitches. Marie had them well trained as they'd imitated her over the years putting their tops back on the felt tips and putting their colouring books away. Returning to the table I was met with two bright faces full of anticipation as they waited for the show to begin. I cleared my throat.

'Hello!' I said in a stupid voice.

'Hello Sooty,' they replied.

'Did you have a nice time at school today, Patrick?' Patrick shook his head miserably: 'Oh no, Sooty,' he replied. 'There wasn't anybody there.' Alarms started to ring in my head.

'What do you mean? How can there be nobody at your school, Patrick?'

'Because, Sooty,' Patrick said earnestly, 'when my driver left me in the hall I hung up my cap and blazer and went upstairs and there was nobody there.'

'Oh my goodness!' Sooty said dramatically. 'What did you do then?' By this time the hairs were standing up on the back of my neck. Tears started to fill his big brown eyes.

'I ran out of school and across the road to find my way home but a van came along and nearly ran me over. He beeped at me and I was scared.' Searching my mind for something to say I lifted him back onto my knee and hugged him tightly.

For Marie to go away, for all we went through — for what? To end up with my little boy wandering around the street crying because the Headmistress had decided to have a swimming gala for the whole school and forgot to tell me the building would be empty. The taxi driver, noticing the school was quiet, had assumed the children were upstairs and left Patrick in the hall. I later found out one of the parents had found him ten minutes' walk from the school standing on the corner of a main road in the pouring rain, crying.

I could have dug a hole in the garden and quite happily have curled up in a ball and stayed there. It was too much for me to take in. I wasn't upset or angry — I was numb.

I rang the Headmistress who should have brought the matter to my attention and had obviously hoped I would not find out about it. She was so busy being defensive, telling me Patrick should have brought a letter home to me and she had just found it in his desk — very convenient! No matter how incompetent she was at running her school, at the end of the day it was I who had placed Patrick in such a vulnerable position, not her. It was I who had sent him to Kindergarten to enable Marie to live at home, not her....

He'd been through a very traumatic experience, the first time he'd been left in somebody else's care. I just did not know how to deal with it.

I felt like I'd been turned inside out. I was an emotional wreck as the days passed by and I thought of all the men who could have wound down their car windows and offered my little boy a lift. By the time Monday came around I was fit to be tied when John drove me to the school to confront the Headmistress. The woman was on another planet. She hadn't a care in the world, and even asked me how Patrick had got to school. I was absolutely livid with her and left her in no doubt what I thought about her school. I was so angry when I leaned over her she cowered from me because she thought I was going to give her a smack. (I wished I had done.)

Walking around in the pouring rain had left Patrick with a heavy cold. He spent the next few weeks closely at my side until he began to feel secure again and went off to play with Marie and Anna.

It took me quite a long time to recover from the shock. As usual I put on a front and pretended, but I was devastated. When someone you love very much is placed in such a dangerous and vulnerable position you can't help thinking of the awful things that might have happened. I seemed to go through three stages: at first, I was numb, then I was very distressed and angry and eventually (a stage I thought I would never reach) I understood and accepted and learned from it.

Surely, if I kept thinking of all the awful things that could have happened, then they might as well have. Nobody had picked Patrick up on the street: he had been found safe and sound. How could I feel such despair when I still had my happy, healthy little boy? God gave me a second chance — why couldn't I do the same for other people?

John and I had a long talk. I was not sure whether or not to go ahead with the sale of the house. We decided to thank our lucky stars things had turned out the way they had. We would put the past behind us and get on with our lives.

I wrote to the Headmistress sending her a cheque for Patrick's fees. I also told her that we didn't have any bad feelings towards the school and we would not damage her reputation. She replied by saying if we would like to return Patrick to her school the following term she would only charge half a term's tuition. I couldn't care if she charged me double, so long as she looked after him!

With that hurdle behind us we put in an offer for the house and hoped for the best.

# 19

~

THREE MONTHS later we collected the keys to our new home. What a difference it was going to make: no more treks to school with the three of them on the wheelchair.

I didn't know what to expect when I put the key in the door. With Marie holding onto one hand and Anna holding the other, we eagerly followed Patrick inside. I was overwhelmed at the sight that met my eyes. Our little Irish neighbour had left all the furniture for us. We had planned to move in after the builders had put the downstairs floors in. They weren't starting work for five days. My mind was working overtime. With all the furniture still in the house I had only to go home and get the cutlery and bedding (and the record player!)

I hardly saw the children that afternoon. Running away from Marie, they hid behind the doors. Sometimes it took her ages to find them as she plodded across the floor. Deathly silence was followed by screams of terror when Marie finally discovered where they were.

It must have been the only time in my life I enjoyed cleaning up. With a bucket of hot water and a cloth I set to washing down the doors and ledges, singing happily as I went from room to room. Standing in the middle of the sitting room I looked up to the ceiling as the loud thump, thump, thump, reached my ears. I could hear the three of them laughing and knew they were bouncing on the big double bed. I loved to hear them laugh: it was all that kept me sane.

~

John and I had been aware for some time that our marriage was over. With great difficulty we plodded on, for the sake of the children, until finally we decided to separate. At first, John had planned to work in Holland for a while with some of his workmates. Unfortunately, his friends returned after eight days because of the appalling conditions they were expected to work under, so John planned to stay in our other house for a while. Considering the pressures we had been under it was amazing we had lasted so long, but it was definitely over. I only wished we could have carried on pretending, for the children's sakes, but that was impossible. Most evenings John came to see the children from work and didn't leave until they had gone to bed so our situation made hardly any difference to them.

It made a great difference to me though — another failure. My response to this latest dilemma was to become a compulsive eater. From then on, when anything went wrong I ran to the cupboard for food.

~

I was still communicating with the Social Services on Marie's behalf and I was still waiting for day care. Anna was now in the nursery at Patrick's school for two mornings a week and Patrick had settled down in his class. I still had a niggling feeling about the safety aspect of the school. My heart was in my mouth when I saw a playground full of small children from age three upwards, usually unsupervised and with the playground gates wide open leaving the children to run into the road. Parents moaned and groaned but of course nobody spoke up. I was determined to keep quiet. It took me all my time fighting my own battles, never mind anybody else's. I just warned my children not to go near the school gates and to try to remember to put on their coats if it rained. On reflection I must have been mad. At the time it was all there was and I was under the misapprehension that children who didn't go to nursery or playground were deprived. Yes... I must have been mad!

One day during the school holidays a doctor called from Nottingham to assess Marie for the Attendance Allowance. This examination was carried out every five years in order to establish whether or not Marie still required the same degree of care to qualify for the Allowance. Most of the doctors who conduct these examinations are retired. Some of them are extremely nice — some are just cantankerous old men!

I had told the children I was expecting a doctor to visit Marie and they were to play quietly while he was here. We brought all their jigsaws downstairs and spent most of the morning piecing them together as they were spread across the kitchen floor.

I was quite nervous because the doctor was coming. I'd also had cramp in my stomach that morning and didn't feel too good.

On his arrival he walked through the kitchen and past the children without even having the manners to greet them. Following me into the sitting room he met Marie. I think he made the children feel very uneasy which was why they came to join us.

He got his notes out of his briefcase and the interview began.

'How old are you?' he asked Marie, to my astonishment. I went to tell him that Marie did not understand what he was saying when he put up his hand to silence me.

'Do you know your address?' he asked. A lump was rising in my throat. I felt incredible sadness when I looked over to Marie who was chattering back at the doctor, trying to imitate his conversation. I cleared my throat.

'She really does not understand what you're saying,' I told him firmly. Patrick, who was sitting on the little step near the hall door, started to giggle quietly at the idiotic way Marie was being spoken to. Anna, who never took her eyes off the doctor, climbed up on the sofa and sat next to Marie. Linking her protectively she continued to look in his direction. I sat there feeling a mixture of outrage and powerlessness. Taking off his glasses he looked at me as if I were some tiresome child: 'My dear,' he said pompously, 'the first thing I have to establish is that the young woman actually suffers from a mental handicap.' He was really pushing his luck! Tears were brewing in my eyes. My heart broke for Marie.

'How could she be classed as severely mentally handicapped for all these years if she wasn't?' I asked angrily.

'Just leave it to me, please?' he said, 'or I will have to interview her in a room on her own. Do you go to school?' he asked Marie. Anna, who'd sat quietly, decided to put him in the picture.

'She can't talk, can you Marie?' she said innocently. That was it, we'd definitely upset him. Taking off his glasses he shuffled his notes.

'I think I would prefer to interview her alone,' he stated. Unable to control myself any longer, the tears spilled out of my eyes and down my cheeks. The interview wasn't worth £100 a week never mind £25. I was not having Marie exploited by anybody. I stood up and opened the sitting room door.

'Get out!' I heard myself say to him. The man was obviously very shocked.

'I beg your pardon?'

'You heard me,' I said, this time raising my voice: 'Get out!'

Shuffling his papers back into his little case, he was obviously embarrassed. 'I can't be....'

I interrupted him. 'Out!' I screamed. I walked through to the hall door where he quickly followed me. Opening the front door angrily I stood there waiting for him to go through it.

'But I haven't done the interview,' he complained.

'Too bad,' I told him. 'Now will you please get out of my house.'

'Has something upset you?' he asked. 'I mean ... can you afford to lose all this money every week?'

'It's not worth what you have to go through to get it,' I snapped.

'But I've come all the way from Nottingham,' he groaned. My heart bled for him.

'What a shame,' I said sarcastically, 'but then you'll get paid for it, won't you?'

He shook his head. 'Not if I don't interview you,' he said. I suddenly felt very sorry for him.

'Look,' he said gently, 'I'm sorry we got off to a bad start. Why don't we just try again.'

'Okay,' I said, 'but you're not interviewing Marie on her own.'

~

The children were flabbergasted after he left. I rang my mother.

'I've just done the most awful thing,' I told her. I explained what had happened and how I'd spoken to the doctor.

'You were right to react the way you did and maybe he'll think twice when he goes into the next house,' she said, trying to reassure me. When I put down the phone I sat Anna and Patrick on my knee.

'I was really sorry I had to speak to that man the way I did,' I told them, 'but you see this is our home and when people visit us they should have some manners. He forgot his and he just needed reminding about them, that was all,' I said, wondering who it was I was trying to convince.

Since I'd been on my own with them things seemed to get me down more. I still played the happy mother and managed to hide most things from them but it took more and more effort just to get through the day.

I remember once when Patrick and Marie were not well and the doctor came out to see them. The following day I could feel my neck and throat becoming sore. Taking it as an early warning and knowing that I needed to muster all the energy I could to look after three children, I rang John at work and arranged for him to call in on his way home from work to look after the children so I could go to the doctor's. I then rang the doctor and spoke to the receptionist. Our conversation went like this:

'I'd like to make an appointment to see Dr Jacobs this evening, please?'

'I'm afraid the evening appointments are only for people who can't get in during the mornings because they're working. Do you work during the day?' she asked to my amazement.

Not knowing how to answer such a ridiculous question I hesitated. 'No,' I finally said, 'but just because I'm not in full-time employment doesn't mean my time isn't as committed as someone who is.'

'Huh!' she said, 'who do you think you are?'

'I'm a patient who would like an evening appointment to see her doctor.'

'I'll tell you what,' she said, 'why don't you put your duster down and let it gather a little dust and get yourself along here and leave the evening visits for those who really need them.'

I didn't have the energy to argue with her. 'Can I have your name please?' I asked.

'No you can't,' she said incredulously. The next thing I knew the phone was banged down on the desk and she was telling the other receptionists about my 'cheek'. Standing in the hall with the phone to my ear the tears ran down my face when I heard them all giggling. The phone was picked up again.

'Hello, can I help you?' a different voice asked. Trying to keep my voice steady I asked for the name of the receptionist who had taken my call. She refused to tell me. I wouldn't let it drop and asked her again. Realising I was not going to be fobbed off she said she would put me back on to that receptionist. When she came back on the phone she refused to give me her name.

'Look,' she said irritably, 'do you want an evening appointment or not?'

I was so upset I could hardly speak: 'It doesn't matter,' I whispered and hung up. I was so fed up, I didn't know how much longer I could go on.

I gave myself a few days to put things into perspective so as not to be too hasty. Then I wrote a letter to my doctor and told him what had happened. I knew that writing that letter could have left a big black mark against my personality on the doctor's file but it was worth it for all those poor sods who for one reason or another were bullied by receptionists and didn't have the nerve to speak up. A few days later, my doctor called to visit me, very upset about the incident.

~

With Christmas almost upon us and the children in school Marie and I used to go window shopping in town. Catching sight of myself in shop windows I could not believe my size. Still eating when I felt anxious, the pounds were creeping on. I didn't know myself any more. I had disappeared.

The final blow for that year came two days before the end of Patrick's school term. Taking him back to school after lunch one day I found there was no teacher in his classroom. The children, from age three up, were jumping over desks and throwing things around the room. An eleven-year-old girl had been left in charge while the Head-mistress gave private piano lessons. I'd learnt to follow my instincts.

Looking around the room I knew I couldn't leave him.

'I don't really like to leave Patrick without a teacher,' I said to the young girl. 'I'll take him home because he's got lots of Christmas cards to write and he can bring them in with him in the morning.' I was very pleased with such a sensible excuse to go home. I planned to have a word with the Headmistress when the opportunity arose.

Patrick spent all afternoon writing out his cards and the next morning when he was ready for school he took them in, with his little present for his teacher.

When lunch time came Anna and I strolled over to collect Patrick. Standing in the brightly decorated hall the parents were collecting their Christmas cards which were spread across one of the dinner tables. Someone handed me mine. I gave it to Anna to open. She smiled from ear to ear as her little fingers pulled out the card. A letter dropped onto the floor so I picked it up curiously. Someone burst a balloon. Looking at the sad little boy who wailed miserably I exchanged a few words of sympathy with his mother as he held out the little piece of blue rubber for her to make better. Anna gripped my hand very tightly, having been unnerved by the loud bang. I lifted her up and casually opened the letter in my hand. I could feel the lump in my throat and my eyes filling with tears. I was devastated.

It read:

'Dear Mrs Daly,

'Following the incident of today regarding your removal of Patrick because, and I quote, "No teacher was left in the Kg classroom," I feel it would be in both our interests if you removed Patrick and Anna at the end of this term.'

~

I, who cried in front of nobody, stood in the middle of the school hall with tears rolling down my face. Hoping nobody would notice I collected Patrick's cap and blazer from the peg. I took them both by the hand and they skipped out of school unaware that they would not be returning.

There was great excitement in the school and Patrick told us how he'd posted his Christmas cards in the big Santa box which was to be opened the following day. I cleared my throat.

'Hey, Patrick,' I said as I gently squeezed his hand, 'I'm such a silly Mummy, I forgot to tell you you were leaving today.' It was the best I could do. Besides, I'd much rather my children thought they had a crazy scatter-brained mother than let them know they lived in such a rotten world.

'But what about my cards?' Patrick said as we crossed the road. 'I have to go to school tomorrow to collect the cards from all my friends.' Every time I went to speak my voice faltered.

'Don't worry,' I managed to say cheerfully, 'someone will probably drop them off for you.' That seemed to satisfy him for the time being.

Going indoors and being greeted by Marie's smiling face was too much for me. I ran upstairs to the bathroom and locked the door. Sliding down the wall to the floor I drew my knees up to my chin, hugging my legs. I truly thought it was the end for me. I couldn't bear my children being punished again because of differences with me. I felt like a noose around their necks. I hated myself ... I wished I was dead.

I don't know how long I stayed on the floor in that little corner with my face turned to the wall, I seemed to have lost all sense of time. Hearing footsteps on the stairs, I knew it would be one of the children coming to find me. Dragging myself up off the floor I swilled my face at the sink. Someone tapped on the door.

'Mummy, are you in there?' Anna whispered. I pretended to cough and blew my nose before I answered her.

'Oh Anna, I've caught the most awful cold,' I lied. 'I'll be down in a minute, love.'

I looked at the bloated red-eyed face in the mirror. I was a burnt-out wreck. Sapped of all my energy and hope I wanted to curl up and die. Three and a half years and still no day care. I wondered what was to become of us all. Tears spilled down my face as the sound of children's laughter reached me from the playground. I just couldn't take any more.

~

When I awoke the following morning my eyes were so swollen I could hardly open them. As the morning went on the street became alive with cars as the parents came to see the school play.

Most of my time was spent distracting the children from the window which overlooked the school. My face was like a pumpkin and I dared not venture out with them for a walk. We spent the morning blowing up balloons and wrapping the last of our presents. They didn't mind not going to school. Fortunately, because the house was so large and was heated twenty-four hours a day, there was so much for them to do they were never bored.

At lunch time the doorbell rang. With the children on my trail I went to see who it was. There on the step stood Patrick's teacher. She smiled at me sadly and said hello. Declining my invitation to come in she gave me a knowing look and said she was just calling on her way home to give Patrick his Christmas cards.... I could have kissed her. His face was a picture when he took the little pile from her.

I later learned she'd known nothing about the incident the previous day and when she had found out she had waited for the Headmistress to go out before she came over to see us. She left the school at the end of that term. When I closed the door that day, she had restored my faith in humanity. Patrick, as proud as punch, was sitting by the Christmas tree with Anna busy opening his cards. I sat on the couch next to Marie and smiled over at them.

'My goodness, you're a lucky boy,' I marvelled. 'My teachers couldn't wait to see the back of me and yours are knocking on the door to say goodbye!' They both giggled happily. I looked up to heaven and thanked God....

# 20

'LADIES AND GENTLEMEN, we will be approaching Dublin shortly. Please ensure your seat belts are fastened and any baggage is tucked safely away.'

Travelling on an Aer Lingus flight above the Irish Sea, my brother, Peter, and I were off to Ireland for a few days holiday. With the excitement of a child I clasped my hands together and stretched my neck across Peter's handsome face in an attempt to get a glimpse of this great city which, as yet, I had only travelled through. Peter's eyes danced as he straightened up dramatically allowing me a better view through a tiny window.

It was my second visit to Ireland that year. Only a few months before, driven by a longing to discover more of my grandmother's past, I had spent two weeks in Co. Mayo, on the west coast of Ireland.

I smiled at Peter as the plane started to descend. Despite being ten years older than him, we were very close. At the age of twenty-six he was the last of the brood at home. The rest of us had flown the nest and travelled our different paths. Cathy, the eldest, was teaching in Spain. Maureen, who like myself had left school at fifteen, had worked as an auxiliary night nurse when her children were young before going on to become an SRN and later specialising with cancer sufferers as a Macmillan nurse. Trish, Liz and John all worked with the Civil Service.

Only three months before, we had all met up for my father's funeral. I pictured my mother once more as she stood at the family grave where her mother and her first-born, Michael, had been laid to rest so many years before. Surrounded by her grown up children on that hot July morning, the gentle summer breeze dancing around her black crepe skirt, the sadness in her face as she watched the coffin being lowered gave no indication of the hard and lonely life she had led as she stuck by my difficult and domineering father to the end. Time alone should have ravaged her good looks but at the age of sixty-two, standing there at the graveside I thought she was beautiful.

Two grave diggers sat no more than ten feet away. Resting on their spades, bored with the routine events of the mourners, they smoked indifferently, occasionally glancing at their watches as they waited for this meaningless daily event to end.

With the service almost over, I followed the others to the edge of the grave. Taking a handful of soil from the old margarine tub the priest held out to me, I scattered it gently onto my father's coffin. 'My mother's funeral will not be like this,' I swore to myself as I strolled out of the cemetery. When her time came, red roses would fall onto her like raindrops. But there ... I was being morbid.

I knew Peter's loss was greater than mine could ever be. My father had mellowed a little in his old age and was very close to Peter. He would miss him dreadfully.

A few days after the funeral, just before I returned to Lincolnshire, Peter and I arranged to go to Ireland later on in the year.

I squeezed his arm affectionately as the plane hit the runway. At last, our plans had materialised. Yet things had happened in my life since my father's death which made my visit to this country a far more serious venture. In my bag was an Irish property guide. Throwing caution to the winds, I was determined not to return to England until I had found a new home in Co. Mayo for myself and the three children — though at the age of twenty-four, Marie could hardly be described as a child. John planned to stay in England and come over in the holidays to see the children.

~

The most important thing to remember when one is fighting for a cause is that one doesn't lose sight of what one is fighting for. I eventually recovered from the shock of the kids being kicked out of school and tried to get on with our lives as best I could. A year had passed in our new home during which time I had very reluctantly gone to the local Press, who had immediately taken up Marie's case. Weeks went by before any comment could be squeezed out of the Social Services, who finally promised the *Lincolnshire Echo* that when the new ATC opened in six months time at Lincoln, it was possible they could offer Marie a place.

'Handicapped Marie's New Year Gift,' the caption read but they were empty words. When the ATC was due to open I waited in vain for the post every day. I then wrote and reminded them of Marie. No reply. I rang them. I was met with both surprise and astonishment that I could even contemplate Marie attending that particular day centre as her needs were far too great for the type of care they were offering.

Nothing shocked me any more. I expected nothing from anybody and whether it was a healthy sign or not, I seemed incapable of being hurt. Never again would I buckle under as I did after the incident with the school. Concerned about the safety of the other children in the school I had eventually contacted the NSPCC. Angry that the Head-mistress was a law unto herself and left little children unsupervised, but angrier still that she had the audacity to put it in writing to me, they contacted the Department of Education and Science, who sent one of their inspectors to see her.

~

I had been wondering for some time about the possibility of approaching another county for help. I knew I had a moral obligation to see Marie's plight through to the end. The Social Services were wrong to reject her and I was the only voice she had. In the meantime I would grab at anything for her to have some kind of life outside the home and for me to have a bit of freedom in the day. One afternoon I rang the Social Services in the next county and explained my *desperate* position. I told them that if I didn't get any help soon Marie would have to go away. I felt like a long-playing record. I had recounted our story so many times. How often had I been about to have Marie admitted to hospital and been saved on the eleventh hour.

The gentleman who spoke to me listened patiently, occasionally interrupting with a question. Finally he said: 'If you can get Lincoln-shire Social Services to pay your daughter's fees then we'll be only too happy to look at your application.'

I could have sworn the earth moved when he said that! For a long time after our conversation had ended I sat in the chair, motionless. I could not believe there was someone out there who cared.

Later that same afternoon I took Marie out in her wheelchair to post our application. I had done all the donkey work for them; surely they would find it in their hearts to sign the stupid cheque. Just how long we were going to have to pay for *my* sins I did not know — forever, it seemed.

Months went by with no news. Tired of waiting and angry at being ignored *again*, I brought the matter to the attention of the Press. And once again they had to chase and badger before anybody would actually confirm that Marie's fees would be paid and that the application for day care could go ahead.

The Press were very angry and very fairly pointed out that though this decision had been made three months ago, nobody had had the decency to tell me. I had learnt the good news through their newspaper. No moves had been made to implement this decision. It seemed that nobody would deal with me. The director apologised to me through the newspaper, stating that he wanted an inquiry as to why I had not been informed of this decision long ago. I thought they were all a load of hypocrites. While they were all passing the buck and cutting each other's throats I was busy making plans for my daughter's debut into the world once again.

~

After four years at home, Marie did a forty-mile round trip in a taxi provided by the Social Services every day for the next two years — two hundred miles a week, in all weathers.

~

After Patrick left the private school, when the time came six months later I sent him to the local state school. This was highly recommended by the parents in the area. It was the old, old story — they had gone there and now their children were following in their footsteps. What I hadn't realised then was that they accepted everything and questioned nothing. They had to say the school was wonderful because if it wasn't they would owe it to their children to do something about it.

The first thing that struck me was the overcrowded playground. Lonely children stood miserably in corners with nobody to play with. Harassed teachers who were too busy to notice them. All of this came under the description of education. By dumping our children in overcrowded schools every day we were preparing them for life — weren't we?

Already I had been in to see Patrick's teacher because he had been scared half out of his mind when on the second day of his new term, his class of four-year-olds had had to sit in with a class of eleven-year-olds who were being given a lesson in Greek mythology. I found this out after he'd been crying all night and shouting for me to move the bag with the head in it from under his bed. The following morning at breakfast he was trying to explain about the lady with the snake hair who turned people to stone. Her head was chopped off and thrown away — hence the dream that it was in the bag under his bed. The lady, of course, was Medusa.

Patrick's teacher, a lovely woman, was obviously very embarrassed when I had a word with her and promised to speak to the teacher concerned.

Two weeks later when it was raining and all the children were stuck in the hall at playtime, two boys from the top class started fighting and running mad when the teacher went out of the hall for a moment. Running past Patrick one of them knocked the feet from under him and he fell, banging his face very badly on the bench. When I collected him that evening I could have cried. One side of his face had almost doubled in size, pulling the corner of his mouth up. His poor teacher was white. As I stooped down to face Patrick, the fear in his eyes almost made my heart ache. His teacher explained what happened.

'I would have called you only I knew you were due any minute. It's just getting bigger and bigger,' she said anxiously. 'I think you'll have to take him to hospital.'

Sitting in the out-patients at the local hospital my heart bled at the thoughts of him returning to that overcrowded crisis centre they called a school.

After Patrick had been examined by the doctor and no broken bones had been discovered, John drove us home.

'If this is school for you then I'd do a better bloody job myself,' I said to him. My main fear was that Patrick would end up with such little faith when he was left in other people's care that he would be afraid to leave me.

Returning him to school a week later with his face still slightly swollen, I felt a wretch leaving him there. Though he put on a brave face it was obvious he was very nervous as he chewed his lip and frowned.

I no longer understood the logic of sending a child to school. However for the time being I put that thought in the back of my mind. Two days later, armed with a list of schools from the Education Department, I set about trying to find a decent school for Patrick. The first one I approached was full. I had walked the three miles to the little village school on the outskirts of the town one sunny April afternoon. I was not sure it would be the right place anyway as I walked through the overpopulated village past the boring executive houses. I imagined it to be very cliquey and middle class. It was.

The second school was seven miles away but with only thirty-two pupils and two teachers, I felt I had to go and see it. It was there that I met Pat Haddrell, the most amazing lady who had run the school for twenty-five years. I told her all about Patrick's school experience.

'He really needs to know he's safe when he's in other people's care,' I told her. I could tell she cared. Had I not met this marvellous woman at that particular time I don't know how Patrick would have ended up. I didn't know how long he'd be going to this little school, but for the time being it was worth travelling seven miles a day just to experience the warmth and exuberance this amazing lady generated.

~

I started taking driving lessons!

'You can do anything if you put your mind to it.' That was what my mother had drummed into me all my life, but in all honesty I never

ever thought I would be able to drive. When I finally passed my test she was the first to hear the good news. Of course, she was delighted — so was I. For days afterwards I kept pinching myself. I couldn't believe it.

Taking the children out in the car would have seemed quite comical to an observer. Having stressed the need for quiet in order for me to concentrate on my driving they hardly breathed as they sat in the back seat. Driving along, making sure I didn't get too near the kerb, gripping the wheel as though I was flying an aeroplane, a little voice would say quietly from the back seat: 'Is it all right to speak now, Mum?'

When I became more confident we had a stereo installed. Then it was the children's turn as the Beatles blasted out.

'Can you turn it down, please Mum?' they'd keep reminding me as I drove along without a care in the world. Often I created more noise than they did.

With standards dropping in the town schools, more and more discontented parents sent their children to the little village school. The numbers of pupils started creeping up.

Travelling from so many different areas often denied the parents the opportunity of getting to know each other. It seemed such a shame, especially when the two teachers were so friendly.

One day I approached the Headmistress about the possibility of starting a parents' magazine. This would enable us to welcome new children and their families to the school, have features from parents, articles for sale, a birthday page and school work submitted by the children.

All for progress, she jumped at the idea and very kindly gave me the use of the photocopier. During the year I was Editor I had great fun. Most of the parents made contributions of some kind. Their articles made very interesting and varied reading. Some parents looked the other way when they saw me coming, feeling they had nothing to contribute, but I usually managed to wangle something out of them (usually of great interest).

It was during this time I took myself off to stay with Cathy in Spain for two weeks. Leaving the children with John, I didn't feel too bad about going alone. It was a healthy break for all of us, and besides it was school holidays and I knew the kids would have lots of fun.

Sitting on the London Underground on my way to Heathrow, I felt as though I'd been stuck in a convent for twenty years as I watched the various people travelling along the busy route. I could have gone up and down on that line all day.

When the plane took off I sat back to drink in the experience — I had never flown before.

~

As time went on the school became more and more popular and the classrooms became more and more crowded. Almost doubling the number of pupils, the little school had finally outgrown itself and lost that special quality which had attracted so many people to it.

Armed with facts and information for when the education officials came to read me the riot act, I decided to de-register Anna and Patrick and educate them at home. But I shall never forget that little school and the marvellous lady who ran it.

The children love being taught at home. I am lucky because they both love to read and write and are always occupying themselves in some way. Visited regularly by the inspector from the Education Department to ensure they are thriving and happy, I was very pleased with the steps we took.

# 21

I N 1989, shortly before the local hospital for the mentally handicapped was to close, one of the nurses opened a home in our area
for some fourteen profoundly mentally handicapped people who
were then living on the ward. Imagine my utter astonishment when I
learnt these people were all being found places at the local ATC. People
with handicaps and behaviour problems as severe as Marie's — not
one, but fourteen! I certainly did not begrudge these people their places
but there was a principle involved regarding Marie. She was still
banished from the county and still travelling forty miles a day: no —
it wasn't on. I wrote to the Social Services asking for confirmation of
this. As usual the issue was dodged and the buck was passed until
finally when it could no longer be avoided a statement was given to
the Press. Yes, room had been made for fourteen people but they
wanted to assure me that Marie had not been forgotten about and they
would have a fresh look at her case. That night when I said my prayers
I asked God if he would give them some souls.

'If those people start at the Day Centre and there is no word about
Marie going there then I shall just take her there every day and leave
her,' I told John angrily. I was kidding myself. Many, many times over
the years I had threatened to do the same thing, but how can anybody
leave her daughter in a place where she isn't wanted? Yet I knew this
was the final straw and drastic steps would have to be taken. And then
the letter I had waited nearly six years for finally arrived, one morning
a month later. I almost giggled when I read the first two paragraphs:
their sense of urgency was touching.

'Dear Mrs Daly,
   The Director of Social Services has asked me to contact you regarding your recent comments relating to Marie's difficulties in obtaining
a place at Gainsborough Enterprises. Having reconsidered the position
I would like to move speedily to agreeing satisfactory day care provi-
sion for Marie.'

It was ironic that the meeting was arranged when we would be away on holiday in Ireland. I wrote to cancel it. The next meeting, a month later, was the day of my father's funeral. The third meeting eventually took place in September.

I was very nervous. I was also very frightened of my reaction to meeting these people. How could I even be civil to them? These people had caused such heartache and destruction, had sentenced Marie to four years at home and had almost deprived my little children of a normal life. What beast would emerge from my being if I looked into their empty eyes? Shivers ran through me as I imagined being locked in a room full of dead bodies — that was how they seemed to me.

Yet at the end of the day they were still the ones who held all the cards. I was still that same person they had met and disliked six years ago. I still had strong views on people's rights and individuality. I would still not be dictated to and bullied. Could they now accept my views or would the meeting break down?

Unable to face them alone, I asked my friend, Jo, if she would accompany me. Jo worked as a counsellor for both 'Rape Crisis' and 'Mind'. She was very good with people and very observant. She was also my witness.

~

Thanks to the open-mindedness of Colin Pitman, the senior social worker who chaired the meeting, it went very well indeed. There were times we could have locked horns but we compromised and most importantly we heard each other out.

After much discussion it was suggested that Marie be introduced slowly into the Unit because they didn't want to cause her any upset. That was a logical attitude; the illogical one was that she continue in her old Training Centre for one half of the week and go to them for the other half. There was no way I wanted her to attend two different places with two different sets of people with different ideas and I told them so. Then the Manager, who had hardly looked my way, took the opportunity to enlighten me.

'We find if our trainees start straight away on a full-time basis it can cause them great upset. You really have to introduce them into a new environment very slowly.'

'I wouldn't expect Marie to start full-time straight away. Maybe at first I could bring her up to you for a few hours in the mornings and collect her at lunch time: then perhaps another week she could come in the afternoons.'

'That's a good idea,' Colin Pitman said cheerfully. 'If Marie comes in the afternoons she could travel home with the others on the bus. Save you from having to pick her up.'

The Manager did not answer me. Her face remained cold and expressionless. She still did not like parents to have ideas. Thank goodness total decision making was no longer in her hands. What was noted as being difficult and awkward six years ago was now accepted as a relevant point of view.

Sitting around the table discussing Marie's day care in such a rational way seemed almost unreal to me. I had thought I'd have to be dragged out of the meeting screaming obscenities at them all, yet I was sitting there as if it had all happened to someone else.... I was playing their game.

'What about the contract?' the Manager asked Colin Pitman. He suggested she give me her copy to take home and read, telling me I would receive an official one through the post along with confirmation of Marie's placement. Not really taking much notice of it I stuck it in my bag. I should have queried it! The meeting ended and we left.

Jo linked me affectionately as we hastily left the building and walked out into the blazing sun. It was all over. At long last we could get on with our lives. At that minute I wanted to go and see Marie. I wanted to put my arms around her and give her a big hug.

Feeling a bit drained I had hardly spoken since we left the meeting but Jo had a spring in her step and jollied me along.

'You were bloody marvellous,' she said giving me a nudge, 'but what on earth did you ever do to that poor woman, Michelle?' she asked dramatically. I laughed knowing she meant the Manager. She hadn't been clever enough to hide her personal feelings about me and quite frankly, I felt she'd hung herself with her own rope.

'Well, Jo,' I said in mock remorse, 'I wouldn't let her pull my strings because as you well know, I like to pull my own.' Sticking her tongue in her cheek, she looked up to heaven.

'Oh God,' she said sarcastically, 'wouldn't you think somebody would have warned her?' I stuck my elbow into her ribs as we made our way to the car park.

# 22

I HATED BEING on the motorway. I was such a dreadful back seat driver. Being sandwiched between two lorries almost made my heart stop as they sped along boldly, flashing their lights to send messages to each other.

Having arranged an extended holiday for Marie from the ATC, I was going with the three children to stay in our new cottage for a few months. The furniture had gone on ahead and would be waiting for us when we arrived. Flying to Ireland from Manchester airport was a great day for us, not only because we had found an alternative lifestyle but also because it was the first time Marie had ever flown.

Sitting in the back seat with the children, unaware of what was happening, Marie looked a picture. I had heard the care in the west of Ireland for the mentally handicapped was very good. I hoped this would be the beginning of a new life for her: she deserved the best and somehow I felt I'd find it for her in Ireland.

I knew I had reached the end of the road when I had eventually read over the Contract of Attendance I was supposed to sign before Marie could return to the ATC. No wonder they hadn't discussed it with me at the meeting. No wonder the Manager had made sure I had a copy. Designed to protect the staff and not the students (or trainees) or their parents, many rules and stipulations were laid down. I was very angry when I read it.

I wrote to the Manager stating that while I wished to co-operate with the staff in any way possible I felt that the Contract of Attendance was a very narrow way to discuss a policy for future care for Marie. I didn't agree to her being suspended for bad behaviour and said that in view of Marie's physical and mental handicap I regarded the Contract of Attendance as void whether a signature was on it or not. A suspension was a punishment and a punishment was futile if the recipient had no comprehension of warnings leading up to and including suspension. I refused to sign it.

Though there were many changes for the better since Marie had first attended six years previously, they had introduced certain policies which, I felt, took us back thirty years as far as attitudes towards the mentally handicapped were concerned.

I was filled with sadness when I saw that all the staff wore uniforms. Dressed in navy blue skirts and cardigans with a white shirt, they resembled prison wardens. As nice as the staff were, having such a custodian image could only be damaging to the mentally handicapped people the staff took out into the community. Having always taken such care over Marie's appearance I deeply resented her being 'led' about by people in such drab attire. It was a great insult.

If Marie had remained at the ATC, these were issues I would have fought to change. But wouldn't there always be something to fight about? No... I decided, it was time to move on and have some peace in our lives.

~

Arriving at the airport in plenty of time, John parked the car while the children ran off to get the luggage trolleys. Laden with carrier bags, shoulder bags, four suitcases and Marie, I waited at the busy drop-off for them to return. Laying one of the suitcases flat on the trolley I sat Marie on top of it and we followed Anna and Patrick into the check-in area to wait for John. Strolling over to the Ryanair information desk I enquired about the 1 p.m. flight to Knock, in the west of Ireland. Keeping one eye on Marie I spoke to the lady behind the desk. She smiled mechanically.

'Did you say you're on the 1 p.m. flight to Knock?' the young man standing next to her asked. I nodded. He came around the front of the desk to me.

'I'm sorry to have to tell you,' he said, 'but we changed our flights to summer schedule and we forgot to inform you. Your plane left at 11.30 this morning.' Raising my eyebrows in disbelief I wondered if he was for real! There wasn't another flight for two days.

'There is an Aer Lingus flight to Dublin due to leave shortly. We could put you on that and then pay for a taxi to take you to your destination at the other end.' The more he tried to help the worse he made it. Oh God... the thought of a four-hour drive across Ireland with a car full of luggage, two kids and a young mentally handicapped woman — and a strange driver... Choosing my words very carefully I explained how travelling in a car across Ireland was impossible because of Marie and though I was sure he meant well, I wouldn't dream of it. John arrived. I filled him in.

'I'll tell you what, if we let your husband go with you he can drive the car at the other end.' At least that was feasible but, after negotiating, the car hire firm needed John's driving licence and he didn't have it on him. By this time the children were looking really fed up. Marie was starting to screw her face up, making great efforts to force herself to cry. Frequently looking at his watch, the man was obviously pushed for time.

'How about if we lay a coach on for you from Dublin to Knock?' Now he was talking. At least there'd be plenty of space!

'That would be fantastic,' I told him. I've never seen anybody move so fast.

'Right then,' he said, 'you're going to have to dash. You've only got four minutes.' Shouting to the Ryanair staff that we would be boarding the Dublin flight, there was a mad panic as they ran to the Aer Lingus desk to get our tickets. With no time to check the cases, the stewardess told us to run as she grabbed one of the trolleys to push.

Poor Marie. I knew I should have brought her wheelchair but at the last minute I'd sent it with the removal men, not really thinking she'd need it at the airport. She wasn't able to walk for long, let alone run. Forcing her to run when she wasn't able, I knew, could bring on an epileptic fit. That was all we needed.

Arriving at Customs we still had to go through all the usual procedures. John walked Marie on ahead slowly while I put all the cases through the barrier. One of them set off the alarm...

'Can you open this case, please?' I was asked. As disorganised as ever, I had gone around the house at the last minute throwing in all the things I had room for so I didn't really know what was in the case: it could have been anything! Searching frantically for my keys I suddenly remembered John had them in his pocket. Chasing him down the passage I retrieved them but not without a few choice words for the Customs men. Returning to the barrier I was shaking so much I could hardly turn the key. One of the ornaments who'd been standing gorping at me suddenly came to life and unlocked the case. Rummaging through my belongings he suddenly picked out my metal stapler and deciding that had been the culprit held it in the air for the others to see. Such a clever boy!

Locking the case I quickly threw it back on the trolley and ran like mad with Anna and Patrick at my side. Catching up with John as he crossed the departure lounge, we swapped luggage and I took Marie by the hand and got her to run.

'You're going to miss this flight if you don't hurry,' the steward warned. She was really pushing her luck. On reaching gate number two we ran down the stairs as fast as we could, all things considered, only to be told when we reached the bottom that the doors had been locked and the flight was taking off. Sure enough as we looked through the glass doors the plane was reversing. My eyes returned to the officials with their walkie talkies before resting on two sad little faces looking wistfully out of the window. 'Now Michelle,' I thought, 'get out of this one.'

'Don't worry,' I said and just as I was about to promise them the earth the doors opened. The signal man was waving to the pilot and they'd stopped the plane and were bringing the steps back for us to climb aboard. Picking up our bags we ran out to the plane.

Stepping inside the doorway to an aircraft full of curious people, relieved but exhausted, we almost fell into our seats. With hands that still shook I strapped Marie into the seat beside me as the engines once again roared and the plane cruised towards the runway. The happiness in Marie's face showed the unexpected pleasure as the plane gathered speed and soared into the sky.

# 23
~

CONNAUGHT AIRPORT is situated midway between Kilkelly and Charlestown and was officially opened on May 30th, 1986. Building the airport at Knock must have made a tremendous difference to the people of Mayo. I, for one, would certainly have had second thoughts about living in Ireland had I not been able to fly back to England in an emergency.

The route from the airport to Ballyhaunis is very picturesque. Green sloping fields are scattered with cattle and sheep, with men in the distance busy working on the land. Every so often we see a tractor crawling along the road, almost stopping as we near to let us pass. What is so surprising, apart from the scenery, is the friendliness of the people. Drivers put up their hands to greet us as they go by. Driving through the busy market town of Ballyhaunis there are numerous shops and pubs, banks and a railway station (with a main line from Dublin to Westport!) but what impressed me most of all was the cinema!

Living only one mile from the town meant we were able to benefit from all the local amenities it offered and still enjoy the peacefulness of village life. We had a lot to look forward to!

~

Pulling up at the gate I smiled appreciatively at the puffs of smoke which burst from the little white chimney pots. Gus, our next door neighbour from whom we'd bought the house, had lit the fires in preparation for our arrival!

Bikes, scooters, skates, filing cabinets, photocopier, computer, word processor, desks, TV and video recorder, deep freeze, fridge and many other items were all waiting to be unpacked when we arrived. Moving so far away from home and still being amongst their familiar possessions enabled the children to settle down fairly quickly.

In England we'd had no garden and with the streets no longer safe for children to play alone in, they spent most of their time indoors. Here in Ireland they could play outside all day and in all weathers.

The move to Ireland had been a gamble and a big financial outlay. With the house in England remortgaged to pay for the cottage, then having a toilet and hot water tank installed along with various other jobs, it was now either sink or swim: there was no going back. John had arranged to drive the car over in the summer when he came to visit the children.

I was looking forward to seeing more of Ireland and perhaps finding out what kind of services were available for Marie.

~

Our little home, cosy as it was, lacked many of the mod cons we'd been used to in England. The move had been worth the sacrifice — but what I would have given for a bath or shower to dip Marie and the children into every evening after a fun-filled day outdoors!

Normally when people move into a new house they are all fighting over who is having what bedroom. We didn't have that problem. With only one bedroom between us, Marie, Patrick and Anna all had to share! In all honesty I was not too happy with this arrangement. Marie had always slept far enough away from the children so as not to disturb them if she became distressed in the night. I just had to put her to bed when all was quiet and they were asleep and hope for the best.

I slept on the sofa in the living room. In those first few weeks I'd have slept standing up. Pushing the wheelchair to town every day, sometimes twice, with the children taking it in turns to have a ride when they grew tired, made me more than ready for bed in the evenings. I was wiped out. Curled up on the little two seater sofa, for the first time in years I slept like a baby.

When I awoke in the mornings the first thing I did was rake out the two fires. Our living room had a lovely old-fashioned fire crane where the hooks still hung down for the pots and pans. When the grates were done, if all was still quiet in the bedroom I would take out the ash bucket and leaving it at the side of the shed, I'd stroll around the garden for a while on my own and drink in the peace and quiet.

The pace was so much slower here. Time almost stood still. Listening to my neighbour's cattle lowing in the field and the birds chirping in the trees, it often seemed like I was dreaming. My life had altered so dramatically. I prayed I had done the right thing.

On the way in from the garden I'd gather bits of old wood out of the shed, and then light the fires. The rooms were usually lovely and warm when the children got up, unless it had rained heavily during the night, making the chimney smoke into the room.

They were always awake early, often reading for an hour in bed before they decided to get dressed. If Marie was in a good mood she would get up and go and sit on the end of Anna's bottom bunk with an open book and pretend to read to them both. Looking very serious with both hands holding the book in the air Marie would proceed with her story.

'One day!' she'd say in an authoritative tone as she turned each page respectfully, trying desperately not to giggle. She could be so funny sometimes. It wasn't long before she had Patrick and Anna choking with laughter, and the louder they laughed, the more she performed.

Listening to the three of them together I would be filled with sadness, wondering how on earth I could prepare the children for when Marie left home. Patrick was almost nine and Anna was two years younger. Marie had always been there for them. They had never known anything else.

~

The highlight of our day was the walk into town. Rain or sunshine, we went in every day.

As the weeks went by, we became a familiar sight around the shops and people would stop to greet us or wave from the other side of the road.

The shop assistants were always pleasant. Nothing was too much trouble to them. I'd go to buy one of the children a pair of shoes and the staff would have half the boxes out from the back of the store.

Buying the groceries brought back many childhood memories from when I'd had to walk from one shop to another to buy the cheapest food for my mum. With seven children to feed and my sailor father hardly ever sending any money when he'd docked in the various ports around the world, she'd had to scrimp and scrape for most of her life. Here in Ireland I found the food to be so expensive, for the first time in a long, long time, I had to watch the pennies.

~

The neighbours were very obliging, advising me where to shop, when to get the turf and where the doctor's was, though they were naturally curious about 'the Englishwoman', a lapsed Catholic, coming all the way from England and leaving her husband behind. I did not tell them John and I were separated: I would deal with that later. For the time being I just wanted to settle down with as little fuss as possible.

Throughout the years with Marie I have always introduced her as my daughter, for that was how I looked upon her. It was only when I came to Ireland, and people asked her age that things became complicated. Even though I am no spring chicken, had Marie been born to me

I'd have been a mother at twelve years old! Feeling embarrassed and wondering if they'd think I was being deceitful I'd explain that although I was Marie's mum she had not been born to me.

Living in such a small community, word soon got around about Marie's past and people seemed to warm to her and to the children all the more because of it.

~

'And how are you keeping, Michelle?' Tom Caulfield, my next door neighbour, would shout over the dividing fence. His garden which he tended daily was like a picture postcard showing off his big green two storey house which stood proudly at the top of the hill. Tom had spent many years in England before returning to the village and buying the house he had only been able to admire from a distance as a young boy. Everybody raved about Lil, Tom's wife, whom he'd lost through cancer only two years before. I couldn't help but admire this obviously contented man who while offering his hand in friendship still managed to retain his privacy.

'Who's that singing in the garden, Mum?' the children asked when we first came here. It was of course, Tom.

'Do you know, Tom?' I shouted over one day, 'you've got such a lovely voice!' Chuckling to himself he waved his arm modestly.

'Aye,' he joked, 'I sing like a bird — but it's a pity it's a crow!'

~

Kitty Healy lived in the next house to Tom's. Born seven miles away in a little place called Tooreen, she came to the village a widow with two little children in 1946. She then married a widower, also with two young children and together they had another son and two daughters. When John Steven, Kitty's youngest son, married, he remained with Kitty where he still lives today with his wife and four children.

Pushing Marie's wheelchair down her path, we'd wave to Kitty through her kitchen window where she was usually standing baking her brown bread and treacle cake.

Opening the kitchen door when we reached the house she'd welcome the children with open arms. Marie couldn't get out of her wheelchair quick enough. Sometimes in her struggle to leave it she would fall back in the seat, bringing loud protests before she'd give anybody a chance to help her. Well used to her impatience and mood swings, Anna and Patrick would giggle playfully as they went to her rescue and tried to drag her out by both arms.

'Come on in out of the cold, loveens, and have a mug of tea,' Kitty would say softly. In those first few weeks that warm invitation was music to my ears. Marie's unpredictable and manipulative behaviour still limited our social life, making it easier to stay at home or just go for walks. In Kitty's house I felt comfortable enough and confident enough to be assertive with Marie when she started to misbehave. I think Kitty realised how little Marie understood and that without my gentle reminders and constant reinforcement she got out of control so she took no notice when I disciplined her, enabling us to enjoy our visits.

We never left Kitty's empty handed. Treacle cake, soda bread, an apple or orange, English newspapers — she was always pushing something into our hands or pockets.

'Oh hey, Kitty!' I'd protest on the way out, 'you're too kind and you've got enough to feed!'

'Arra, will you stop!' she'd scold, 'and we'll see you tomorrow, with the help of God!'

~

For me, despite the geographical distance from Liverpool, being in Ireland felt closer to home than any other place where I'd lived. Surrounding myself with such friendly, gregarious people, I knew, would help cushion the blow when Marie finally went away.

In the mornings when I was doing the washing I loved listening to Gerry Ryan on the radio. He seemed a caring and articulate human being. One minute he could be quite outrageous and the next I would find myself in the middle of the floor, having been stopped in my tracks as I listened intently to one of his interviews.

I remember one day when I was shopping, his voice was blasting out from a stereo in the corner of the store. We all giggled in disbelief as he rang the Vatican and asked to speak to the Pope!

Through Gerry's broadcasts I learnt a lot about life and about attitudes in Dublin and in the rest of Ireland — the women's refuge, alcoholism, incest, the Rape Crisis Centre, education, surrogate mothers and many other informative topics.

Being up so early in the mornings meant the days were very long. Some nights the library was open until eight in the evening so we'd go down there and have a cup of tea with Anne, the librarian. She was the same age as me, and we found we had many things in common. She soon became a wonderful friend. Anne was a busy housewife with four school age children, and had made the daily seventeen-mile journey from her home in Ballyglass for the past seven years and was spoken of with great affection by many of the townspeople. The first time I took the children into the library, we sat in a little room at a long table with Marie close by in her wheelchair. We all nearly jumped out of our skins when a fire alarm rang out through the building — I hadn't realised that the Fire Station was next door! I laughed until I almost cried.

Anne, on seeing our surprise, attempted to explain, until, infected by our hysterical laughter, she finally gave up. The fire engine came charging out and parked outside the building causing us further fascination as men ran from all directions to form a fire fighting team.

'Hey, look, there's Michael, the taxi driver!' Patrick shouted as we stood by the glass doors to get a better view of the drama. Sure enough, there was Michael, helmet and all, abandoning his taxi as he clambered up into the big engine, followed by the man from the local superstore, still clad in his white coat.

The library turned out to be our second home. When things became too much for me, that's the place I would head for, especially in those early days. It was a distraction from my thoughts, and Anne and I had regular chats, exchanging news of our friends and family.

~

Mary Durr was another favourite of mine. In her seventies, she was still living in the village on the land where her grandfather had been born and bred, along with her twelve hens, four cats, two dogs and twelve cows!

Mary was the first person I met when I came to Drimbane. Driving down from Sligo with John we'd managed to find Ballyhaunis and as much as we'd followed the directions the townspeople had given us we could *not* find the little cottage that was advertised in our property brochure. Up and down, up and down we drove along the Irishtown road and still we could not see a sign for the village of Drimbane. Up ahead there was a little old lady walking along the road wearing a blue headscarf and accompanied by two dogs. We pulled up alongside her and on seeing the English car I guess she realised we were lost.

'Can I help you?' she asked, sticking her head in my window. I smiled at this tiny, plump, rosy-cheeked Irishwoman, the strands of white hair peeping from under her scarf.

'Oh, I hope so!' I said passing the property brochure through the window. For a moment I thought she couldn't see it. I leaned over to point the house out to her before I realised, with some amusement, curiosity getting the better of her, she was standing on the roadside scanning the information below the picture, obviously looking for the price!

She knew the house well, it was only about three hundred yards down the little lane where we'd stopped.

After that day I always had a soft spot for Mary. From the day I first came to the village her door was always open to me. We talked about anything and everything. I liked her especially because she didn't gossip — and only went to church when she felt like it!

~

Not long after I first came to Ireland my mum came over for a holiday. Not only was it her first visit to this country, it was the first time she had ever flown. Driving out of the village on that beautiful May morning we could see Mary resting against the hedge at the side of her lane. On seeing us approach she pulled herself up with the support of her long cattle stick and together with Arnie, her dog, she came onto the road as I stopped and wound down the window.

'Hiya Mary,' I said as she leaned on the car door. 'And how are you today?' Mary typically answered a question with a question.

'Is your Mammy coming?' she asked me eagerly. I nodded.

'We're just going to fetch her, Mary,' I replied.

'Ahhh,' she whispered. Her blue eyes filled with tears as her face began to glow with joy. 'Well I'm happy for you!'

I loved Mary. She was such a genuine woman, not always saying what people wanted to hear but at least they knew where they stood with her. 'You'll have to come over for your tea, Mary,' I told her. Her face broke into another smile.

'Aye, I'd be very happy to,' she answered as she slowly made her way across the road towards home. 'And good luck to you,' she shouted as I started the engine and began to wind up the window. Suddenly Arnie left Mary's side and ran in front of my car. With her stick waving madly in the air Mary called to her dog: 'Come here you little cunt!'

From the back of the car the children giggled quietly. Unfortunately, I lacked their diplomacy and burst out laughing. Arnie immediately obeyed and was soon back at Mary's side heading towards her little house.

'See you, Mary,' I shouted as we moved off.

'Aye,' she answered, 'with the help of God.'

I laughed all the way to the airport. She was such a colourful character. I couldn't wait for my mum to meet her.

~

Arriving in plenty of time, I took Marie's hand and slowly followed the children upstairs to the viewing lounge. The atmosphere was charged with excitement as people anxiously awaited the arrival of their friends and relatives, frequently glancing at their watches, smoking one cigarette after another.

My heart started to pound when the plane came into view and slowly nosed its way to the landing area below.

It was only ten months since my father had died. I knew my mum was only coming because she was worried about me moving so far away on my own with the children. She was staying for six days. I desperately wanted her to enjoy it.

We continued to wait patiently at the window as the aircraft came to a halt and the passengers started to descend. Patrick and Anna sat on the high stools either side of us, stretching their necks in all directions as they eagerly awaited a glimpse of their nanny. Minutes passed before she was spotted.

'There she is, mum!' Anna yelled and sure enough, almost the last to leave the plane, my mum came down the steps.

'Look Marie,' Patrick said as he gently tried to turn Marie's head in the direction of the plane, 'here's your nanny!'

Marie was busy pulling tongues at her reflection in the glass and did not pay any attention.

Standing at the window shouting and waving frantically, I was afraid we'd never catch my mother's attention. Just as she was about to enter the check-in area she spotted us and threw her arms in the air with excitement. Almost the last to leave the departure lounge, the children took Marie's hand and led her downstairs to arrivals.

'Oh buddy ell!' she shouted incredulously. Pleased as punch, the penny had dropped — she had finally spotted her nanny!

~

My mum was thrilled with the cottage. She scrubbed and cleaned from when she got up in the morning until she went to bed (on the couch) at night. The windows gleamed, showing off the new cream nets she had brought us. The tiny toilet and hallway were transformed from a dirty yellow to a brilliant white. Standing in the living room doorway I watched her put the final touches of paint around the back door.

The beautiful weather enabled us to spend lots of time outside in the garden. The grass was knee high and waiting for some kind neighbour to cut it for silage.

My two noisy children spent most of their time up in their den swinging on the long rope which hung from the tree.

Strolling through the garden, Marie giggled happily as the long strands of grass tickled her legs. The cattle in the back field frequently poked their noses over the barbed wire fence to see what all the commotion was about. Marie loved to see the cows. Pulling us by the hand she'd drag us past the side of the house to have a closer look.

~

The day my mum arrived Kitty sent over an invitation for the five of us to go to her grand-daughter's Communion dinner at the local hotel the following day. My mum was very impressed. So was I! Her kind gesture wiped away any doubts my mum might have harboured about me being isolated so far away from home. Marie could not go, of course, so I suggested to my mum that she go with the children. She wouldn't hear of it and insisted that I go.

'Oh, you'd really enjoy it, Mum!' I said persuasively.

'I came here to be of use,' she stated, 'and it's about time you started getting out and having some kind of social life.'

'But you're supposed to be on holiday. I don't want to go off and leave you on your own.'

'Will you listen to this one?' she joked with the children, 'always has to have the last word. She'd argue with Our Lord, you know.'

And there the matter rested. From since I can remember she has said those words to me. I laughed and went into the bedroom to find something to wear.

The more my mother saw, the more impressed she became. When Patrick's friend came to play one day, his mother, Mary dropped him off. It was hard to believe Mary was the mother of five children. I had a lot of admiration for most of the mums I'd met. Apart from the enormous cost of school books and uniforms, I was amazed at the amount of time parents were expected to spend after school each evening supervising their children's lessons. Without their time and co-operation children would not get through the stack of text books parents have to buy. Introducing Mary to my mother, she shook her hand as if she were a long-lost friend. It was then that I realised what that quality was that I liked so much about the Irish: their warmth and physical contact made everybody they met feel special.

Having my mum around had been a welcome distraction but those few days flew by so quickly, and before I knew it, it was nearly time to say goodbye. In that short time I was ashamed to admit that as much as I made the effort, I was often depressed. Painfully aware of the difficulties Marie's handicap presented, I was trying to come to terms with sending her away. My mum was very supportive and constantly reminded me of the wonderful life Marie had been able to live through being at home, but she was also aware of the heartache her departure would bring.

Neighbours popped in and out during my mother's stay. Patsy, Michael's wife, came over with their daughter Rachel, and as promised, Mary came over for her tea.

Because Marie hated crowds we didn't venture too far but we did manage a trip to Knock shrine before my mum went home.

~

I have always made it clear to the children that Marie would one day be leaving home, letting them know it was out of the question that they would ever be allowed to take over her care in their adult life. Marie was my responsibility, not theirs. But I noticed that the older they got the more they questioned it, raising very logical points. 'Ah yes, but what if?' was constantly put to me: 'What if she cries for us?' 'What if nobody understands what she's saying?' It was like walking on eggs. Sometimes Anne and I would discuss this in front of them when we were at the library. There were waiting lists for day care in Ballyhaunis but I had heard that a new residential centre had opened in Swinford and it seemed ideal. Trying to sound as laid back as possible I'd tell the children how when most people grew up they liked to leave home and be more independent and how Marie would probably benefit from the social interaction life in a hostel would bring. It helped, but still they weren't convinced. I knew there was only one thing to do and I had to get on and do it! I decided to ring Paddy Greally.

I first met Paddy, a social worker with the Brothers of Charity in Galway, when he had called to the village one day to visit his two brothers, Michael and Gus. At the time both brothers, with the use of a digger, were laying pipes in my garden and Paddy, on hearing I had a handicapped child, came over to introduce himself. I was immediately impressed with this kind, unassuming man who was obviously very experienced in the field of mental handicap. What impressed me most was the respect and understanding he had for the parents of the handicapped. He'd seemed so approachable. If I could ask anybody for advice, I considered, I could ask this man. But how much would I have to tell him? How desperate did I need to feel before I took such a drastic step and requested residential care for my twenty-six-year-old daughter?

Emotionally isolated, I was my own worst enemy. So used to shutting myself away and dealing with my own problems it was very difficult for me to open up to anybody and ask for help. Feeling sick with anxiety I picked up the phone with my clammy hand and dialled his number. From somewhere, I had to find the courage to see this through.

When Paddy answered the phone, without going into too much detail I explained the situation. He listened patiently, asking a question now and then. He was familiar with the new centre at Swinford and promised to make enquiries on Marie's behalf and call me back. I didn't expect to hear from him for weeks. He must have called back within twenty minutes, having spoken to the director of the centre and established the best procedure for me to follow in order to obtain day care with a view to a residential placement. I listened nervously as he relayed the conversation. Paddy suggested I send in a formal application to Finbarr Kilgannon, the Director of Services, explaining the position. With a mixture of gratitude and relief, I thanked him and placed the phone back on the receiver. So that was that: between us we had set the ball rolling.

# 24

~

ETURNING FROM holiday in England (compliments of Ryanair after the inconvenience caused on our previous trip) I did not bother to unpack Marie's suitcase. With only a few more weeks at home, it seemed less painful. Up it went on top of the wardrobe while awaiting its final journey to Áras Attracta.

Travelling to Swinford on a daily basis for two weeks had enabled Marie and the staff to get to know each other. With the use of her diary (which had been met with enthusiasm by the staff) there was frequent communication between home and work which not only avoided misunderstandings through lack of contact, but also gave Marie the best possible start because of her own lack of speech.

'Poor Marie!' Patrick chuckled that first morning, 'she can't get away with anything, can she? Everything she does is written in her snitch book.' I loved his sense of humour! Taking it in turns to jump off the rock at the side of Kitty's house, he and Anna kept Marie busily distracted as she waited for the minibus to collect her.

'Deady! .. deady! ... DO!' she chanted happily.

I could not believe things had gone so well. With Marie about to step into her new world, we were all facing the future with optimism.

~

In 1983, Paddy O'Toole, the then minister for the Gaeltacht, announced on behalf of the Department of Health that financial approval had been given to the Western Health Board to build a much-needed residential centre for the mentally handicapped in Swinford, Co. Mayo.

The centre was planned to form part of the overall services for the mentally handicapped in the Western Health Board area, and to co-ordinate with all other services for the mentally handicapped, both statutory and voluntary, and provide services to the catchment area of Co. Mayo and North Roscommon.

Services for the mentally handicapped had for a number of years been provided by voluntary organisations — the Western Care Association, Brothers of Charity in Galway, Sisters of Charity, Galway

Association for Mentally Handicapped Children and Co. Roscommon Association for Mentally Handicapped. The only places offered by statutory bodies were either beds in psychiatric hospitals, or with other Health Boards, sending people miles away from their families. In 1974, staff from the Western Health Board carried out a survey to establish the needs which were not being met and it became apparent that long-term residential facilities needed to be provided by a statutory body with continuing interest and support from the voluntary organisations. The Health Board accepted the need to provide these services and the Department of Health approved the Board's proposal resulting in a project team being set up to establish how best to meet these needs.

One of the advantages of the services being developed so late was that planners were able to sit on the fence and learn from the mistakes other European countries had made.

The village complex took two years to build on a twenty-acre site, providing residential care for some of the moderate, severe and profoundly handicapped people in the community. Offering 140 beds, it was the biggest building project undertaken by the Western Health Board at the time. The centre was so impressive that it went on to win an international award for architecture.

The accommodation comprises sixteen bungalows, enabling the residents to live in small family groups under the care of mental handicap nurses, a thirty-bed unit for the multiply handicapped and an eighteen-bed unit for the older retirement group. There are also four short-term beds available, offering both clients and their families a welcome break, which can vary from an overnight stay to as much as a week.

The Day Centre offers varied activities with a pool of professional services at hand — physiotherapy department, central assessment clinic, workshop, vocational training unit and day centre workshop. Adjoining these facilities is the Recreation Centre with a swimming pool, gymnasium and weight training room.

The bonus, to me, was that Marie would be under the care of people who were highly trained to look after her. I am very aware that in this day and age the title of 'nurse' sets off alarm bells, implying that handicapped people are sick and need nursing care. In my own experience as a parent, I believe the three years training, covering many aspects of the world of the handicapped, more than equips them for the job. It's the title that needs doing away with, not the nurses.

For me, it was a dream come true. To set up home only twenty miles from the most modern centre in Ireland without even knowing of its existence was quite astonishing. And what was even more astonishing was that after they looked at Marie's application, she was offered a bed there.

~

The following introductory letter was written for the Áras Attracta brochure by Eamonn Hannan of the Western Health Board.

'Each client is the most important person in this complex.

'Clients are not dependent on the staff. The staff are dependent on them.

'A client's need is not an interruption of our work, it is the purpose of it.

'We are not doing a favour by serving them, they are, in fact, doing us a favour by giving us the opportunity to do so.

'It is sufficient to say that quality is the result of commitment and so quality and commitment are the hallmark of the service provided at Áras Attracta, Swinford.'

~

Leaving the children at Kitty's, I drove over to Swinford as requested to finalise the details for Marie's admission in twelve days' time. Arriving at Áras Attracta, I left Marie in the unit while I went over to the office. Unfortunately an obstacle had arisen. A big one! I was told that Marie could not be admitted to the Unit unless I had her mother's permission. It was also necessary to establish who was responsible for Marie in case of an emergency — myself or her mother. I was stunned. I know I should have foreseen this hiccup and been prepared. Of course I should have! I had barely given Marie's mother a second thought. I hadn't been in touch with her for twelve years and did not expect her to be still residing at the same address. I had no doubt at all that she would consent to Marie's admission. She had always co-operated on important issues: the problem was finding her.

But what if Marie's mother was never found? Would I have to return to England and start all over again? Questions, questions, questions, spinning around my head like a roller coaster. It had taken so long for the children to come to terms with Marie's departure. What was I going to tell them?

'We'll write to the area Social Services in England,' they said optimistically, 'and ask them to obtain permission from her mother.' I was a cynic. I had very little faith in the Social Services in England and doubted if they would put themselves out. Also it was only two days away from the August bank holiday weekend which meant that apart from the skeleton staff, the Social Services would probably be closed down for a week to ten days. I was numb with disappointment.

I must have spent all the next day on the phone to England. I had Marie's grandmother's address though I didn't have much hope of her

197

being alive. Yet she would know her daughter's whereabouts. I had to give her a try. I *had* to get permission in writing. I had only eleven days left.

I decided the best course of action was to ring the Catholic church in their area: the priest would be able to tell me if she had died. First of all I rang my sister, Liz, in Blackpool, explaining why I desperately wanted to contact Marie's mum. She obtained the relevant information for me through the directory and rang me back.

'Good luck!' she said. 'Let me know how you get on.'

Unfortunately, the priest was away on holiday for the next fortnight. I didn't know whether to laugh or cry. I did neither. I explained the situation to his housekeeper and pleaded with her to look up the deaths for the last twelve years to see if Marie's grandmother had died. She didn't mind in the least and asked me to call her back late that afternoon.

'I'm hungry, Mum,' came little reminders that I still had to run a home and be a mother to three famished children.

I cooked lunch with great haste as I imagined all kinds of exciting discoveries taking place at that little Catholic church. However when I did ring back later that day I spoke to a very apologetic housekeeper who had been unable to find Marie's grandmother listed in the deaths. Did that mean that she was still alive or had she just been buried somewhere else?

~

'Only ten days to go,' I thought when I awoke the next morning. 'What am I going to do?' My body must have raked the fires and cleaned out the ashes but I do not remember doing it. So preoccupied was I with my thoughts that I once again had to be reminded to feed my children. Had it all been too good to be true? I wondered miserably.

Try as I might, I could not shake off my sense of doom. For some strange reason I truly believed that if Marie was not admitted on the arranged date then she would not be admitted at all.

It was Friday, the beginning of the holiday weekend. With the afternoon drawing to a close I knew I was running out of time. I was almost crawling the walls with frustration. I didn't have a clue what to do next.

And then it came to me like a bolt out of the blue. Only God knows why I hadn't thought about it sooner. Why not send a telegram? In fact two telegrams could be sent, one to Sonia, Marie's mum, the other to Marie's grandmother.

Unsure of the time it took an overseas telegram to arrive, I rang John in England and asked him to send them for me.

The telegrams asked quite simply if they could ring me regarding Marie. The phone number given was John's so that whoever phoned him could give their number. He would immediately ring me in Ireland and I would call them back. It was a long shot. I didn't expect much to come from it but a little hope was better than none at all. If there was no response, I would have to assume they no longer lived at those addresses: then the long search would begin!

~

'Only nine days to go!' I told myself the next morning when I awoke. Filling the kettle at the sink, I wondered what the day was going to bring. The phone rang constantly as different members of my family called up to see if I was still sane! When it rang at 1 p.m., it was John.

'Hi Mish,' he said quietly, 'Marie's mum has just been on the phone. Can you believe, she'd moved from her old address but her daughter lived next door and took the telegram over to her.'

That day I promised God I would never moan about anything again.

~

The children were filled with a sense of awe about Marie's mother and could not believe I had spoken to her on the phone. I found the whole experience very moving. After exchanging news of each other and our families I stumbled over the words as I explained about Marie leaving home. Sonia promised to write immediately giving her consent to the admission. And then she asked me something that almost wrenched my heart out.

'What does she look like now, Michelle, is she still pretty?'

Not only had I my own two healthy children, I had been privileged to bring up someone else's. Painfully aware of this woman's loss, I could feel the tears welling in my eyes. For a moment I couldn't speak.

'Oh yes!' I said lightheartedly, 'she's gorgeous. And she knows it too!' A gentle laugh came down the phone, but my heart broke for this mother who had bravely entrusted her daughter into my care all those years ago.

~

By the middle of the following week, with only four days to go, I had a phone call from Áras Attracta confirming that the placement could go ahead. I should have known Marie's mother wouldn't let me down!

On September 3, 1990, Marie went to start her new life in Swinford.

~

Many, many times in the weeks after Marie left home I would be sitting at my typewriter with great determination as I struggled to put our past into words. Sometimes it was too painful to face. It was at times like these I would take myself off to the library. Not wanting to burden Anne with my troubles I would casually mention my despair of ever completing my task. She would have none of it.

'But what're you saying? You've got to do it!' I was told. Five minutes later we'd be sipping cups of tea and having a good laugh about something or other and then off I could go with my batteries recharged, ready to carry on.

When November came the village seemed to fall asleep. Birds had flown away, the trees were bare and the cows went into the sheds for the winter. Sometimes the nights were long and lonely.

Not only did Anne take us home with her for odd weekends, she also took me to meet her parents who lived in the next village. I loved seeing Anne's mum, Winnie, who always made a fuss of me. Tall and slim, she was always smartly dressed in layers of cardigans and jumpers, with a thick tweed skirt to protect her from the cold she so fiercely felt. Sitting at the side of her range she'd pull up a chair for me, and get Anne to make me a 'hot one'. At first (in my ignorance of Irish customs) I had thought she meant a cup of tea. I'd watched Anne curiously as she'd put a teaspoon into the glass before half filling it with boiling water. She then added some whiskey until it was about three quarters full, dropped in a spoonful of sugar and some cloves.

Winnie always made me feel good about myself. She'd laugh and joke and pretend to envy my single status. She loved to hear news of Marie — how she was settling in and if she was happy: did I like the home and were the staff nice? It was painful to admit that I did not visit Marie as often as I felt I should, but Winnie would have none of it and said Marie needed to be left to settle down.

She had settled down very well and seemed extremely happy but the children were terribly upset when they left her after each visit. Apart from the emotional upset, we didn't have much money so by the time I put petrol in the car, bought fuel for the fire and our bits of groceries, there was nothing left to take them to a café or buy them a little treat, though I didn't tell Winnie this.

Sitting by Winnie's range, sipping hot whiskey, watching the cloves dance about on the top, I felt like one of the family.

'And how are things beyond?' she would ask if I had recently returned from England. Winnie was one of sixteen children with brothers and sisters scattered all over the world. Head teachers, priests, doctors, they followed many different professions. That fascinated me about Irish people: if they haven't travelled themselves, they're bound to have one relative or another overseas, especially in America.

~

Those weekends at Anne's did us the world of good. Arriving home late Sunday afternoon, our little house would be freezing so I'd hurriedly light the fires and sometimes we'd go over to Mary's for a cuppa while the place warmed up a bit. Going through her back door into the kitchen we'd sometimes find her dozing in the chair by the heat, having recently come in from seeing to the cattle.

'Come in out of the cold... And don't let that little whelp out!' she'd say as the dog came over to the kitchen door to greet us.

Trying to squeeze through the door without letting the dog out was not only difficult — it was bloody hilarious. I'd be laughing my head off before I had even sat down in the chair.

'And how are you, children? Come on! Come on!' she'd say brusquely as she cleared the old newspapers off the chair for them to sit down: 'Come and get a warm!' They were both a little shy of Mary at first and didn't know how to take her.

'Put on the kettle,' she would cheerfully instruct, 'and get some biscuits out of the press for the children.'

'And how have you been, Mary?' I'd enquire, filling the kettle at the sink.

'Arra, not too bad,' she'd say quietly, 'as long as that wind stays away I'll be all right.'

Mary looked forward to late Spring when the village seemed to come back to life and the cattle went out to the fields once again. Although she lived alone there were plenty of people ready to help from around the village. Gus's brother, Michael, was the most frequent visitor, calling to see her every evening after work and spending the best part of Saturdays and Sundays helping with the cattle and mending the fences they frequently tried to break through.

Mary loved Michael. Seeing her face light up when he walked into her little kitchen, I often thought he was like the son she never had. Mary and I were friends but she did not depend on me because I was limited in what I could do for her. I was at the other end of a phone if she needed a loaf or maybe a lift into town and once she even asked me to stand at the head of her lane while she moved around the cattle, but that was only during the day when Michael wasn't around.

'And how's your friend?' she would ask, busying herself at the table to make room for the cups. Mary loved to hear news from Ballyglass. I had often spoken to Mary of Anne and Winnie, just as I had spoken of her to them.

~

One day, almost a year after Marie had left home, I had to go to a meeting in Dublin. In order for me to catch the early morning train, Anne and Kevin offered to have the two children overnight. By this time Anne had left the local library and was working in the new library at Castlebar. Arriving at Ballyglass on the Sunday afternoon I was met by a very pale looking Kevin. Winnie had died that morning and Anne was still over at the house. Confused and not wanting to intrude I'd wanted to return home but Kevin wouldn't hear of it as he sat us down at the table for lunch. The house was strangely quiet. Sitting on the kitchen chair near the window I looked out at the dull grey sky.

Only four months before, my friend Maureen Caulfield had died suddenly from a brain haemorrhage. I was devastated. Forty-four years of age and leaving behind three lovely children, her death sent the whole town into mourning. Strangely enough it was Anne who had introduced me to Maureen one day at the library.

A month after Maureen died, Mary was found dead one evening at the side of her field. She'd had a heart attack on the way home from checking the cattle and as the priest so aptly put it in his sermon, 'She'd died as she lived, under the fullness of nature.' I shall never forget Mary — kind, strong, forthright, opinionated: she'd even helped to change the course of history the previous year.

Apart from Marie leaving home, three major events had taken place in Ireland in 1990. The pound coin had been introduced, Ireland made it to the World Cup and the Presidential elections were held. Unfortunately I had not been in the country long enough to be on the electoral register and therefore could not vote, but I hoped with all my heart that Mary Robinson would be elected as the new President of Ireland.

It is a sad but inevitable fact that politicians have to sell themselves in order to win public votes. When they fall foul is when they start attacking each other to justify their own campaigns. Mary Robinson did not need to do this. Watching her on TV I had grown to admire her many qualities. I remember watching the leaders of all the parties on the Gay Byrne show and cringing with embarrassment as I'd listened to Brian Lenihan shoot himself in the foot. 'Behave yourself, Mary!' he'd said arrogantly in response to a remark she'd made, demonstrating to the viewers of Ireland how women were still being patronised and not taken seriously.

~

A few days before the elections I gave Mary a lift home from town.

'Are you going to vote, Mary?' I enquired cautiously. I was aware that asking someone about their political persuasion can sometimes seem as personal as asking what's in their bank account, but Mary knew me well enough to tell me to mind my own business and I knew her well enough not to take offence. She looked at me like I had three heads: 'And why wouldn't I?' she asked me indignantly. She didn't seem in a very good mood and I wondered if I should leave her alone. Turning right under the railway bridge we passed the school and graveyard as we headed towards home.

'I wish I could,' I said miserably, 'but my name isn't on the register yet.'

'And what'll you be missing?' she asked me irritably. 'Isn't one as bad as the other?' It was often difficult to be serious when I was with Mary. She'd only been in the car half a minute and she had me laughing. I slowed down as we approached the brewery to make room for an oncoming lorry full of beer.

'I don't know about that, Mary,' I replied, 'I'd like to see Mary Robinson having a go, but it's going to be a hard slog for her for the simple reason that she isn't a man.'

Mary sighed impatiently. 'I'm telling you, they're all the bloody same!' she said as we drove on past Maura and Paddy the postman's house and up over the hill. 'And ... maybe ... it's a job for a man!'

I tutted in mock disgust. 'I'm surprised at you making a statement like that, Mary. Couldn't you do the job as well as any man, if not better?'

That brought a smile to her face. 'Aye, I could at that!' she chuckled.

We drove the last few yards in silence — a comfortable rather than an awkward silence. Turning left into Mary's lane I stopped outside her house and went and opened the car door for her.

Her face was radiant as she stepped out.

'And did you know,' she beamed, 'that she's a woman from the west like myself?'

'Well, it just goes to show you then, doesn't it, Mary?' I said in admiration as I handed her her shopping.

I saw her again a few days later.

'Well, I've done my voting,' she said in her no-nonsense way, 'and ... I thought ... I'd give the woman a chance!'

Only five feet in height, I think that day Mary towered over the world.

'Good on you, Mary,' I said affectionately, 'You're a credit to the women of Ireland!'

~

When Anne returned home, looking tired and drained, she took us back over to her mother's with her. By the time we arrived it was dusk and the children were playing in the garden. I bit my lip nervously as I followed Anne into the house.

Winnie's coffin lay in the comfortably furnished front room where neighbours and family sat on the surrounding chairs to pay their last respects. People spoke in hushed respectful tones as they exchanged warm, often funny, and sometimes moving stories of their long association with Winnie.

'Ah but doesn't she look grand!' somebody said softly.

Unable as yet to look Winnie's way, my eyes slowly travelled towards the coffin and rested reluctantly on this great character who was going to be missed by so many people. 'And by God,' I thought sadly, 'doesn't she just!'

Cups and saucers clattered in the kitchen where the family were preparing food and drink. Anne sat me down near the window and put a glass of whiskey in my hand.

'Look, they're getting the grave ready,' Anne's sister said sadly. 'I suppose they have to do it today while the weather is fine.'

Picking up the tea towel she dried the cups mechanically, occasionally turning to greet people as they came to offer their condolences.

The graveyard was indeed visible through the large kitchen window. Glancing out discreetly I could see two men digging in the distance. I felt very humbled to be amongst these people at such a sad time: despite their grief, they went out of their way to make me welcome.

~

That evening I headed off towards Ballyhaunis. Despite my protests Anne and Kevin had insisted I left the children who were still playing in Winnie's garden with the rest of her grandchildren.

Driving off into the distance I could see through the mirror the house still lit up behind me.

'Who would believe me,' I thought incredulously as I drove past the graveyard... And where else in the world could I have left my children on a day like this?'

# Epilogue

I T WAS APRIL and my visit to Liverpool coincided with the Grand National. Driving through the busy traffic on that hot, sunny afternoon, with my brother-in-law Tommy, I approached the Picton Clock in Wavertree. I looked around me nostalgically. The road to the left led to where my grandmother, Annie had first lived when she came across to Liverpool from Co. Mayo.

Across the road to the right was the 'big hospital'. I knew we shouldn't drive past it. 'Shall we go in and have a peep?' I asked Tommy impulsively as we neared those high walls that shut out the world. Always ready to oblige he turned down the side road towards the gates. I sat back apprehensively. I didn't know why I kept punishing myself and returning to this gloomy place. When we approached the entrance. I was shocked at the sight that met my eyes — it had all been pulled to the ground!

'If stones could speak, what stories they'd tell,' I thought sadly.

I looked across to the crumpled remains of what was once the hospital lodge. I could almost hear the stifled giggles from Liz, John and Peter when, so many years before, they had marched behind me through those hospital gates with their collection of old toys tucked under their arms, passing the porter on the lodge, noses in the air as if they knew where they were going. They had followed my trail into the wards for our first tour of inspection!

And months later, having satisfied myself with the conditions, Liz and I had pushed Marie through those same hospital gates in Sara's squeaky old red pram. Feeling like a lamb going to the slaughter I had gone to meet Dr Rogerson for the first time.

Looking over to where the ward once stood, I remembered the day of Sophie's case conference a few years later when the 'professionals' had almost fought each other to have their ideas put into practice, even at the risk of the little blind girl's welfare. Shivers ran through me as I once again pictured the knitting nurse wheeling a frail child through the hospital grounds in the snow when she had only been dressed for a summer's day. My heart felt heavy. Memories, memories ... so many memories. But now it was gone forever: just a piece of history.

~

As I stood there, the years seemed to roll back like a film. It seemed remarkable that I should return to the homeland of my grandmother almost as if I'd been beckoned: to find people who really cared for Marie, to be able to let her go almost without a backward glance — such was the faith I had in the staff at the centre. Coming to Ireland was the best thing I ever did. I love going to England to see my family but I can't wait to get 'home' again.

The strangest thing of all was that the month Marie went to live in Swinford my Aunty Terry died. Throughout the years so many people helped and encouraged me, but without a doubt my Aunty Terry was my backbone. It doesn't seem that long since she met me off the train in the freezing cold that Christmas when I first brought Marie up north from Taunton. Like a second mother she had always been there when I'd needed her. She was one in a million and I still miss her today.

I believe it was God who gave me the strength to look after Marie. When people pulled the feet from under me it was he who offered me his hand and stood me back on the ground again. And just as each of us is chosen to do a certain task, I am glad I was given the job of looking after Marie. I'm sure when God brought us together he must have had a twinkle in his eye — and certainly a sense of humour to put two such strong-willed characters side by side.

I never saw Sister Michael after the convent closed down, yet I will always be grateful for the day she came onto our nursery floor like a breath of fresh air and gave Marie the freedom she so desperately needed. Then there was Matron at Taunton who offered me a job, and Sister Green who, despite her 'difficult' reputation showed me nothing but kindness: Dr Prentice, who took the time to help me have Marie transferred, and Dr Rogerson who took a chance and trusted me by accepting Marie in a hospital hundreds of miles from her home. Marie's mother, Sonia, took the brave step of entrusting her daughter into my care and Dr Kidd was always there to recharge my batteries whenever they started to go flat.

But I remember, as though it was yesterday, the day almost twenty-two years ago when Marie first pulled me to the floor by my hair: she must have seen me coming! I can still feel her grip on my hand as she dragged her little feet across the polished floors in an effort to walk. Looking back now, it makes me wonder — had I really taken Marie's hand all those years ago, or had she taken mine?

Great Reading From
## WOLFHOUND PRESS

### On Borrowed Ground
*Hugh Fitzgerald Ryan*
'Beautifully written, subtle, uplifting, a novel of an Irish writer
come of age.' Benedict Kiely
ISBN 0 86327 295 9 paperback £4.99

### The Kybe
*Hugh Fitzgerald Ryan*
'The first thing that strikes the reader about this remarkable
first novel, is the agreeable clarity with which it is written.' *Irish
Independent*
ISBN 0 86327 012 2 paperback £3.50

### The Voyage of Mael Duin
*Patricia Aakhus McDowell*
'A scholarly yet exciting and vivid rendition of the voyage of
Mael Duin, one that has never before been accessible to those
without fluent Old Irish. It rings true, and that's what becomes
a legend most.' *New York Times*
ISBN 0 86327 309 2 hardback £11.95

### Thy Neighbour's Wife
*Liam O'Flaherty*
O'Flaherty's famous first novel. A powerful and passionate
story of an island priest's conflict between religion and love.
ISBN 0 86327 328 9 paperback £5.99

**WOLFHOUND PRESS**
68 Mountjoy Square
Dublin 1
Tel. 01 740354

*Write or call for our catalogue.*